Can't Buy
Me Love

Can't Buy Me Love

How Martha Billes
Made Canadian Tire Hers

ROD McQUEEN

Published in 2001 by
Stoddart Publishing Co. Limited
895 Don Mills Road, 400-2 Park Centre, Toronto, Canada M3C 1W3

www.stoddartpub.com

To order Stoddart books please contact General Distribution Services
Tel. (416) 213-1919   Fax (416) 213-1917
Email cservice@genpub.com

10 9 8 7 6 5 4 3 2 1

National Library of Canada Cataloguing in Publication Data

McQueen, Rod, 1944–
Can't buy me love: how Martha Billes made Canadian Tire hers
ISBN 0-7737-3322-1
1. Billes, Martha 2. Canadian Tire Corporation — History.
3. Businesspeople — Canada — Biography. I. Title.
HD9745.C32B54

Jacket Design: Angel Guerra
Text Design: Tannice Goddard

THE CANADA COUNCIL | LE CONSEIL DES ARTS
FOR THE ARTS | DU CANADA
SINCE 1957 | DEPUIS 1957

*We acknowledge for their financial support of our
publishing program the Canada Council, the Ontario Arts
Council, and the Government of Canada through the
Book Publishing Industry Development Program (BPIDP).*

Printed and bound in Canada

CONTENTS

	INTRODUCTION	I
ONE	The Growing Years	5
TWO	A Private Planet	28
THREE	The Lady Is for Turning	49
FOUR	The Dogs of War	66
FIVE	The Power of One	87
SIX	The Little Red-haired Devil	108
SEVEN	The Waiting Game	129
EIGHT	Good Money after Bad	154
NINE	Hope against Hope	178
TEN	Tire 'n' Me	202
ELEVEN	Adventures as a Capitalist	227
TWELVE	The Reigning Queen	248
	INDEX	271

INTRODUCTION

I was twenty minutes early for my scheduled interview in December 2000 with Martha Billes, the controlling shareholder of Canadian Tire Corporation Ltd. Martha's assistant, Marie Gram, soon appeared and headed into one of the several meeting rooms off the reception area at the company's Toronto headquarters. At precisely three o'clock, Gram re-emerged and directed me into a room where Martha was already ensconced at a boardroom table. If a person can reign, even in a place where she had been alone, that's what Martha was doing. Her icy blue eyes suggested a wary woman who trusted no one at first, and only a few people over time. At five foot eleven she was taller than average and serious of manner, as if being Martha Billes wasn't easy.

Martha first hove into public view in 1980 as one of the rare female corporate directors of that era. In 1986 she briefly became notorious when she and her brothers, Fred and David, feuded over a takeover attempt at Canadian Tire, the family business. She was summoned to appear before the Ontario Securities Commission, castigated for greedy behaviour, then promptly withdrew from sight. The red hair of those days became long blonde tresses and was now a silvery page-boy cut. Her translucent skin, lightly peppered with freckles, remained her most transfixing feature. Many a man wrongly believed her skin was transparent and thought he could see inside to her very soul. In fact, Martha had in the past revealed so little of herself and her motives that she might as well be masked.

Arrayed before her on the table was a treasure trove of corporate material and personal memorabilia. She looked like the leading lady in her own life's story. There were two bound volumes, each about three inches thick, which recorded deals with Fred and David. The first, signed on October 30, 1989, set the terms for their shared ownership of Canadian Tire. The second, dated August 1, 1997, marked the moment when she bought out her brothers, became Canadian Tire's controlling shareholder, and bid them both goodbye. There was also a copy of *Our Store*, the corporate history published in 1997, a flurry of birth and marriage certificates for several generations back, a large three-ring binder of family and business photographs, and some colour copies of advertisements for *Napoleon*, the musical she backed financially. Smiling down approvingly from the wall were framed portraits of Canadian Tire's founders: her father, Alfred Jackson Billes, and his brother John William Billes.

Getting this far had been a tough ticket. My curiosity about Martha had first been piqued in September 1999 when I interviewed her for a *National Post* feature article about the fifty most powerful women in Canada. Martha was ranked third, after Suzanne Labarge, vice-chair and chief risk officer at the Royal Bank of Canada, and Barbara Stymiest, president of the Toronto Stock Exchange. Martha struck me as one of the most complex people I'd ever encountered during my twenty-five years in business journalism. Beneath the self-assured shell there was a strangely shy demeanour and the promise of many mysterious layers. I wanted to find out more.

Some facts are self-evident. Canadian Tire is the country's best-shopped retailer. Ninety per cent of Canadians live within a fifteen-minute drive of a Canadian Tire store, 60 per cent of all adults buy at least one of the company's 100,000 items each month, and the catalogue is delivered to 10 million households a year. As controlling shareholder, Martha Billes owns 61.4 per cent of the voting shares of Canadian Tire, with its 441 stores, 206 service stations, 38,000 employees, and $5.2 billion in annual revenue. Her holdings in the company are worth about $100 million and she likely has a further $25 million in private investments, making her one of the ten wealthiest women in Canada.

At sixty-one, she belongs to a generation of women who were not supposed to work. They were meant to attend school, find a man, get married, and settle down to raise a family. In times past the only way a woman could assume control of a business was through the death of a husband. In 1939 Muriel Richardson stepped in at Winnipeg-based James Richardson & Sons Ltd. after her husband died. Richardson ran the company for twenty-seven years, overseeing expansion in the securities business, grain elevators, and pipelines. Wendy McDonald ran B.C. Bearings Group of Burnaby, BC, following her husband's death in 1952. McDonald outlived two more husbands and brought five children into the business, before retiring in 2000. Jeannine Guillevin became head of her late husband's Montreal electrical distribution company in 1965. She sold the business thirty years later, having achieved annual sales of $500 million.

Since Martha bought out her brothers in 1997, daughters have begun to inherit businesses from their fathers. Ron Southern anointed Nancy at ATCO Ltd. of Edmonton, Frank Stronach gave way to Belinda at Magna International Inc. in Aurora, Ont., and Linda Hasenfratz is succeeding her father, also called Frank, at Linamar

Corp. in Guelph, Ont. In one case the daughter beat out a brother, but none of these women fought their brothers as fiercely as Martha did to win the prize. Moreover, Martha's father was dead when she took over; he had neither groomed her for the role nor passed the mantle along to her while he was still alive. In comparison with the other two groups, widows and daughters, Martha is unique.

Martha differs from senior businesswomen in another important dimension. An increasing number of female executives have been able to achieve success because they have supportive husbands. Linda Cook's spouse gave up his job as a gas trader to stay home with their three children so she could become chief executive officer of Shell Oil and Gas. Bobbie Gaunt climbed the corporate ladder at Ford Motor Co. by commuting each week to increasingly responsible jobs in a series of cities in the U.S. northeast while her husband worked in Michigan and kept the home fires burning. Twenty years ago, when Carly Fiorina met her husband-to-be, Frank, he said, "You're going to run a big company some day, and I'm going to help you get there." Fiorina became president and chief executive officer of Hewlett-Packard in 1998.

Martha had no such constant support. As a result, she had to fight her way to the top against all odds, doing battle with her father, her brothers, two ex-husbands, a business partner and lover, a posse of regulators, and a sexist society.

Intrigued after that first meeting in 1999, I began researching Martha and her company. A five-week trial in Calgary in March and April 2000 laid bare salacious aspects of her personal life. Feeling wounded and vulnerable, Martha was not interested in being interviewed. Months passed before I found myself face to face with her again for the first of three interviews for this book. The ascendancy of Martha Billes to the throne as Queen of Tire may have been a triumph of the head, but, for her heart, there was only tribulation all along the way.

ONE

THE
GROWING YEARS

*"I certainly knew what a monkey wrench was
because they always told me I put the monkey into everything."*
— MARTHA BILLES

$\mathcal{M}$artha Gertrude Billes was born in Toronto on Saturday September 7, 1940, at the private patients' pavilion of Toronto Western Hospital. "To Mr. and Mrs. A.J. Billes, a sister for Fred and Davey," proclaimed the five-line newspaper announcement published the following Monday. The proud parents were so happy that the notice ran not just once, but twice, and not in just one newspaper, but two, the *Toronto Daily Star* and the *Evening Telegram*.

It was a brave time to be born. The Second World War dominated life and delivered death. Adolf Hitler's Luftwaffe had changed tactics that day. Rather than target military bases, the bombers struck at London for the first time, killing 450 civilians. In Toronto the day was fair and the skies were clear of clouds and free of enemy aircraft. The thermometer reached seventy degrees and there was a slight southerly breeze on this last day of the Canadian National Exhibition.

Officially called Citizens' Day, it was also known as Children's Day because the midway rides were specially priced at five cents each. That reduction, along with motorcycle races at the grandstand, the death-defying leap of a parachutist on the Lake Ontario waterfront, and the closing fireworks display, were enough to push Saturday's attendance to 168,000, bringing the two-week total to 1,642,000, slightly ahead of the 1,626,000 visitors in 1939.

Goods were more plentiful in Canada than in war-torn Britain. The pastoral scene on the cover of the 1940 spring/summer Canadian Tire catalogue, current at the time of Martha's birth, depicted a man who had stopped his car at his rural mailbox while a dog bounded happily in his direction. The ninety-eight pages offered sparkplugs at 39 cents each, fancy hood ornaments for $1.15, a chrome-plated replacement bumper for $5.98, and first-line tires starting at $12.75 apiece. Items for the home or outdoors included light bulbs at 14 cents, a fifty-foot rubber garden hose for $2.98, a Coleman stove at $7.65, fishing rod-and-reel combinations for under $10, and a five-tube table model radio for $29.95.

Women were just beginning to make the transition from motherhood to the modern era, but the momentum towards equality was perilously slow. While the newspapers of the day were full of the Miss Canada beauty pageant, there were also stories about the Canadian Women's Service Force. The members of the land army, as the group was called, had hoped to be motor mechanics or ambulance drivers, but their first duties hardly made them essential workers in the war effort. The women were sent to farms, where they harvested crops and picked apples as replacements for the male field hands who had enlisted.

A short story entitled "Business Woman," published in the women's section of the *Telegram*, promised a better future for females, at least in fictional form. The central character was a woman named Betty, who had bet her fiancé, Lee, that she could buy a car at a specific price. If she did, he was never again to denigrate her business skills. If she failed, she agreed to turn over all her financial affairs to him. Betty negotiated the auto deal and showed Lee the bill of sale as proof of her prowess. At first he was dumbfounded, then he swept Betty into his arms and said: "Let's get married next week. I need a good head like yours in my business." For Martha Billes, neither the love of a good man nor doing business in a man's world would ever come quite as easily as that.

THE SURNAME BILLES (rhymes with Phyllis) likely had roots in Huguenot France. Martha's grandfather, Henry Billes, was born in 1859 in Lambeth, England, the second youngest child in the second marriage of his soap-maker father, Joseph Henry Billes. When Henry was in his early twenties he emigrated to Toronto, where he met and married Julia Constable, the daughter of a Toronto innkeeper.

Henry worked as a butcher in the Cabbagetown area of Toronto and later ran the shipping department of a wholesale meat company in the nearby Riverdale neighbourhood. The couple's seven children, four girls and three boys, learned the work ethic from their father. Bill had a *Toronto Star* newspaper route, the largest in the city. Alf, his younger brother, would pull the wagon while Bill folded and delivered the papers. When it came time to share the earnings, Bill would occupy the second-floor bathroom in the family home at 23 Sackville Street. Alf would present himself at what Bill called his office to get paid. And so was established the deferential relationship that would dog Alf all his days and cause bitter rivalries in the next generation. As the daughter of Alf, Martha would grow up feeling the need to avenge the past and overcome that second-tier status in the name of her father.

At first, however, Bill offered an excellent role model for a younger sibling. He studied accounting in high school and, when he had reached third form (later called grade eleven), he had accumulated $1,000 — a stupendous sum for a young student, the equivalent of $15,000 in today's dollars. Bill sold seeds but didn't waste time selling packets of pansies to individuals for pennies; he took bulk orders from the school board for redistribution to all the classrooms.

Such success meant that Bill left school at sixteen in 1912 and was soon named sales manager of Hamilton Tire and Garage, a one-bay Ford service garage that had opened in 1909 at the corner of Gerrard and Hamilton streets in Riverdale. He bought surplus tires at reduced prices from manufacturers in the winter, when roads were impassable and demand was low, and sold them with hefty markups in the summer when plenty of cars were buzzing about.

But Bill was headstrong and not yet ready for the responsible life, so he quit work in 1913 and headed west. Word reached him in Banff, Alberta, that his father had died of a heart attack while trying to break up a street brawl. Duty to his widowed mother and six siblings called; Bill returned home and went back to work. That unexpected death also caused life changes for Alf. Forced to leave school at fourteen, he gave up his boyhood dream of becoming a missionary. He worked for a god of a different sort, Mammon. For four years he ran errands, cleaned pens, and swept out the vault at the Dominion Bank.

Martha's mother, Muriel Moore, sprang from equally hard-working stock of Irish and Welsh extraction. Her great-grandfather, George Orr, married Martha Owen, after whom Martha Billes was named. George and Martha in turn had a daughter Bertha, who married Delford Moore, a well-to-do builder and developer who worked in Detroit and lived in Woodstock, Ont. There Muriel, Martha's mother, was born. It was said of Delford, who later became a used-car dealer in Toronto, that he could swear for ten minutes straight without using the same word twice.

IN 1922 THE OWNERS of Hamilton Tire and Garage offered J.W., as Bill by then preferred to be called, the chance to buy the business for $1,800, so he invited his brother to join him. J.W. was twenty-six; Alf, who also came to be known by his initials, A.J., was twenty. The brothers opened for business on September 15 under the name Hamilton Tire and Rubber Co. and almost immediately suffered a set-back. The two-storey brick garage sat on the easterly end of a bridge over the Don River. On October 2 the bridge was closed for repairs and remained closed all winter. Traffic they had counted on to carry customers past their door dried up. In the months that followed, they sold a few auto parts, but most of the income came from parking fees. Doctors, dentists, and lawyers who worked in the neighbourhood needed a heated garage because automobiles in that era were hard to start on cold days. The brothers remained on the premises at night and took turns staying awake, one tending the fire while the other slept, to keep a watch for burglars.

Over the next three years they tried five locations before finally settling on the northeast corner of Yonge and Isabella streets in 1925, where they stayed for more than ten years. Signs on the store promoted tires at factory prices. No middleman would take a piece of the action and no wholesale markup would be passed on, a retail concept commonplace today but novel for the time. The mansard-style three-storey building on Yonge Street (now the House of Lords hair salon) also featured another sign bearing the slogan "The longest run for your money. We make your dollars go farther." The words were accompanied by a smiling cartoon tire on the run, holding the hand of a silver dollar that was happily keeping pace. Tire prices were low because the Billes boys bought in bulk from Dunlop and sold them under their own label, Super-Lastic. "We didn't have staff to shop around and see what the competition was charging. We just took our cost and added what we thought was a reasonable markup," said A.J. "For years we were known as the cut-rate boys."[1]

In 1913 there were 23,700 cars in Canada, but by 1922 the number had grown to 210,333, of which 40,000 were in Toronto. In 1920 the entire country boasted only 1,000 miles of paved road. By 1930 there were 80,000 miles of road and the number of drivers had reached one million. The car meant new-found freedom. The nation was brimming with self-confidence and the individual was becoming supreme. Jobs abounded, money was plentiful, and a car was an obvious sign of personal prosperity. "The automobile was the quin-tessential expression of individualism: the driver was in control of a machine that magnified human speed and power to a degree that no one before had ever experienced," wrote Heather Robertson in *Driving Force: The McLaughlin Family and the Age of the Car*. "Walking, by comparison, was tedious and laborious; even cycling was too much work."[2]

For the brothers, tires were their stock in trade, so on December 1, 1927, they named their company Canadian Tire Corporation Ltd. It made them sound bigger than they actually were, as if outlets already existed from coast to coast. J.W. was president and A.J. was secretary, then vice-president, relegated to his familiar role of second banana.

The business was impervious to bad times. The stock market crash of 1929 ended careers and plunged Canada into the Great Depression. Personal income fell by 50 per cent and unemployment reached 20 per cent. New car sales evaporated, but Canadian Tire flourished in the face of economic disaster. People might not be able to afford a new car, but they maintained the flivver they already owned by buying parts and doing their own repairs.

In the 1930s the products available at Canadian Tire expanded to include motor and chassis parts, radio batteries, and camping

---

1   *Reader's Digest*, July 1977, 69.
2   Heather Robertson, *Driving Force: The McLaughlin Family and the Age of the Car* (Toronto: McClelland & Stewart, 1995), 140.

equipment. Even the weather cooperated. After two successive winters in Toronto with no snow, one desperate supplier dumped his entire stock of tire chains. "We bought tons and tons of chains at a ridiculous price," said A.J. "The day they started to haul those chains to our shop it started to snow, and it snowed for three days. We made a small fortune."[3]

For entrepreneurs such as J.W. and A.J., there was only one way to expand the business — through owner-managers. The brothers couldn't oversee every outlet personally, so they wanted someone on site who would not just wait for payday but would see his hard work rewarded with personal wealth. A similar form of mutual ownership had been pursued at the American department store J.C. Penney, but it was not common in Canada. "Make a man a branch manager and he'll do only what he has to do to keep his job and salary," said J.W. "Make him an owner, one whose fortunes are tied to his own commitment and effort, and his energy will know no bounds."[4]

In 1934 Walker Anderson became Canadian Tire's first associate dealer. He paid $3,000 for his inventory at the King Street store in Hamilton, Ont. As the number of outlets increased, if a new dealer didn't have enough money to buy the inventory he needed, the Billes boys would lend it to him. There was no legal contract, just a handshake. (By 1988 the contract ran to fifteen pages, with eleven pages of schedules.)[5] No franchise fee was required up front, nor was there any royalty payment. Instead, Canadian Tire acted like a wholesaler, shipping goods to the dealer, who added a markup. The dealer paid for the cost of the goods, overhead, and salaries, and pocketed the rest. By 1940 there were 105 locations in Ontario and eastern Canada.

Mayne Plowman, who joined in 1931 as employee number eleven,

---

3 *Reader's Digest*, July 1977, 69.
4 Commendation, Canadian Business Hall of Fame, April 3, 1990.
5 University of Western Ontario, Canadian Tire Archives, J.J. Talman Regional Collection, box CTP0872.

recalls J.W. and A.J. as two very different men. J.W. was in charge of purchasing and administration. A.J. oversaw mail order, sales, and service. Where J.W. was stern and distant, A.J. was willing to swab floors or install tires. "If you put a windbreaker on J.W., or a pair of skis, then he was normal, but he became reserved in his office. He was afraid to talk to you. He'd slap the side of his leg just from self-consciousness," said Plowman. "Alf was very verbose. I had many a toe-to-toe with him and, ten minutes later the phone would ring and he'd say, 'Where are we going to have supper tonight?' He'd say, 'Don't ever agree with me. I don't need you if you agree with me.'"

A.J. was the dreamer who wanted a bigger business. If J.W. had had his way, Canadian Tire wouldn't have expanded at all. "I wish the thing would stop growing," J.W. said more than once. "I just want a little sporting goods store." By the mid-1930s Canadian Tire had forty employees, sales of $1.2 million a year, and profits of $92,000. The business had grown so much that there was traffic chaos around Yonge and Isabella, so the Billes brothers shifted locations again. A new two-storey food market had opened farther north at 837 Yonge Street, but it closed within a year. J.W. and A.J. were undaunted by that failure. Bread had nothing on the real staff of life: car parts. In 1936 they bought the building at the northeast corner of Yonge Street and Davenport Road with its terrazzo flooring, arched facade, and 45,000 square feet of space. "We grew like Topsy," said A.J. "We never did anything until we had to do it. We were always understaffed and underbuilt."[6]

And misunderstood, according to the inside front cover of the 1937 catalogue. The headline read: "Who are we?" Underneath was a photograph of fifty Canadian Tire employees and these words: "While the vast majority of motorists know our firm through many years of business contact, others have been incorrectly informed as to

---

6   *Reader's Digest*, July 1977, 69.

our personnel. Every day some new customer tells us that he had been informed that we were Yankees or a subsidiary of an American firm, others are told that we are Jewish, still others that we are Germans, Italians and almost every nationality under the sun. ALL OF THESE STORIES ARE WRONG. The Canadian Tire Corporation ownership, management, and staff are Canadians of Anglo-Saxon descent and the vast majority are natives of the city. While nationality or creed should not, in our opinion, enter into business matters, we are proud of the fact that we are an out-and-out Canadian organization and feel that our customers should have any false impressions corrected once and for all."

In those days, clerks waited on customers from behind curved counters. There was no self-service; every item sold had to be retrieved from storage out back. Because clerks were on commission, they complained about the time the return trip took and demanded more compensation. "I had to resist that," said the always parsimonious A.J. "And the answer was roller skates. They would travel this great distance with about one-third the effort they had previously. Now they were making more money than ever before." Clerks had no trouble learning to skate on the four fiber wheels strapped onto their shoes. Said A.J.: "It's surprising how quickly you learn when there's a buck there."[7] (Skates were used in the store until the 1950s, and in the warehouse into the 1960s.)

Once the Second World War was over, Canadian Tire rode the ensuing economic boom: disposable income exploded and a growing population built new houses and bought new cars. By the end of the 1950s there were 190 stores. Most of the growth came in Ontario, but the first French-language catalogue was published in 1957 and the number of stores in Quebec grew from four to sixteen during that decade.

---

7 "The Secret of My Success," interview with Pierre Berton, 1988.

Throughout the expansion, the Billes brothers took on no corporate debt. The business was a veritable money machine. In 1944 payday arrived for the young entrepreneurs when they took their company public by selling shares with the help of Alex Barron of Fry & Co., a Bay Street brokerage firm. J.W. owned 60,000 shares and A.J. 40,000 shares, an indication of their relative power. Canadian Tire became a public company when each of them sold 7,500 shares at $10 per share to investors. In 1946 they sold a further 10,000 shares each at $39.50 per share, for total proceeds of $940,000. J.W. and A.J. retained 65,000 shares between them, worth more than $2.5 million. They were multi-millionaires in an era when a million dollars meant something — all from an investment of $1,800 just two decades earlier. The capacity to sell shares to the public while retaining control of the corporation proved to be a cash cow for the Billes family in the decades ahead.

By 1952 annual profits had reached $908,000, a sixfold increase since going public eight years earlier. That year, shareholders received a special payout of one preferred share for every common share held. Most of this manna from heaven went to the Billes brothers because, with the stroke of a pen, it increased their wealth by a further $2 million. "It was," wrote Michael Bliss in *Northern Enterprise: Five Centuries of Canadian Business*, "a classic story of low-cost, price-cutting chain development."[8]

WHEN MARTHA WAS BORN in 1940, Canadian Tire was well launched and there were two older brothers already at home. The eldest, Fred, had arrived in 1935; David, the middle child, in 1938. Martha's earliest recollections involve the beauty of cars and the pleasure they brought her. "During my childhood the family car was a source of thrills and

---

8 Michael Bliss, *Northern Enterprise: Five Centuries of Canadian Business* (Toronto: McClelland & Stewart 1987), 437.

fascination for me. I remember the first family outing in Mom's beautiful new Dodge sedan, I was three years of age. The car's sleek body was blue, like shimmering water, and the interior perfumed by new paint and oiled leather. I can remember the sumptuous joy of our first ride!"

The importance of cars to Martha was established early. "[Canadian] Tire and all the bits and pieces that serve our automobile-oriented society have been a dominant part of my life," she said. "The car is both our society's slave and its master. For some folks among us a fancy automobile is a symbol of success. For others it is a tool without which we cannot live our daily lives. For me the smell of tires and cars is in my blood." But cars also created a divisive yearning in her young life. Fred and David were allowed delights that were denied to Martha. "Oh how I craved for a ride in the 'Rumble seat' of dad's shiny black Buick coupe," she remembers still, "but alas that was a thrill reserved only for the boys and denied this four-year-old daughter. Inside wasn't so bad, perched there on mom's knee, feeling quite the little princess."[9]

When A.J. and Muriel were first married, they vacationed with her parents at Big Bay Point on Lake Simcoe, sixty miles north of Toronto. In the mid-1930s A.J. and Muriel built their own cottage at Shanty Bay on the north side of Kempenfelt Bay on the same lake. As soon as school was out, the family would drive to the cottage — "going north" the trek was called — with its 900 feet of shoreline and twenty-four acres of land. Martha, her brothers, and her mother would stay all summer. A.J. would motor up on the weekends and one afternoon during the week. The five-acre garden contained a dozen fruit trees: apples, peaches, and pears. The rest of the plot produced strawberries, raspberries, black currants, carrots, beets, potatoes, and lettuce. Martha and her brothers helped with the harvest and watched the changes at

---

9 Shirley Kachur, *Auto Talk for Women* (Calgary: Horse & Musket Ltd. 2000), foreword.

Canadian Tire. "Different products were added to the business," said Martha. "I saw the milking machines come and go at Canadian Tire. The radio department grew and grew but farm tires died out completely. Hardware, saws, hammers — all those things were always of interest to me — they were always being used. I certainly knew what a monkey wrench was because they always told me I put the monkey into everything."

Martha was not close to her cousins, the three children of J.W. and Gladys. The age span didn't help. Gwen, John, and Dick were born between 1925 and 1929. Fred, David, and Martha were born between 1935 and 1940, so there was fifteen years' difference between Gwen and Martha. Moreover, away from the office, J.W. and A.J. didn't socialize. Where A.J. was a cottager, J.W. loved boating. J.W. would sometimes stop with his family for a brief visit at A.J.'s cottage, but for the most part J.W. took day trips on Lake Simcoe or he'd spend a week negotiating the locks of the Trent-Severn waterway. J.W. owned a series of three boats all called *Jogwendi*, a compilation of the kids' names. The *Jogwendi II* was the biggest, a fifty-five-foot Ditchburn made in Gravenhurst, Ont., with a double-planked mahogany hull and two six-cylinder 650-cubic-inch gasoline engines. The boat slept eight and later belonged to Toronto financier and boat collector Nelson Davis. It's now owned by Gordon Russell of Toronto, who still operates it on Lake Ontario as *Windswept III*.

Amid such family wealth, Martha enjoyed the privileged life of a rich heiress. In 1949, aged nine, she moved from Chaplin Crescent in Toronto to 24 Old Forest Hill Road, a twenty-seven-room mansion of limestone and leaded glass in the city's best residential area. Her wealthy neighbours in Forest Hill included mining magnates and bank executives. The previous occupant was John Northway, owner of the upscale ladies' department store in Toronto that carried his name.

The family's only earlier link to great wealth had come in the 1920s, when Martha's Aunt Elsie, sister to A.J. and J.W., married Melville Gooderham, son of Sir Albert and Lady Gooderham, the family that owned the Gooderham and Worts distillery. To make the point that the Billeses could be just as grand, A.J. installed panelling from Lady Gooderham's estate. Soon Martha's new home was sumptuous enough to make Gladys envious because it was so much bigger than her own house in Lawrence Park. In an attempt to remind Muriel of her place, Gladys once referred to her as an "employee" because, as far as she was concerned, J.W. had started the business and then brought his younger brother in to work for him. "There was tension there all the time. I witnessed it even before I joined the company," said Arch Brown, who started at Canadian Tire in 1958 and later became a dealer in Barrie, Ont. "The Billeses are not a unified family. It really bothered me to see the conflict between the A.J. family and the J.W. family."

For Martha the family business was ever present. "A.J. and Muriel made a real fine pair," said Martha. "They had their highs and their lows. The fun things in business were the real highs in our family, when something was completed. When there was a new venture, a new product, we were often there to see what it was. We'd often spend Sundays rummaging around in the back part of 837–839 Yonge, which was the head office when we were growing up. Father would just have to go in for a couple of hours and we'd just roll around getting into the display department and getting into the back of the business. She'd be there, keeping an eye on us, and working with him." To the employees, Muriel looked like the Queen Mother on a walkabout. Mayne Plowman would be working away, when, suddenly, Muriel would be at his elbow, watching what he was doing. "She went to see, not be seen," he said. By contrast, Gladys rarely stopped by.

For the most part, Martha was reared by her mother. "My mom grew up between the wars, had young kids during the Second World

War, wasn't involved in the business world, but she was very, very interested in the business," said Martha. "She was a very strong individual that my father turned to for counsel. She had a neat perception of the retail customer. She just seemed to be a natural. We were raised in a household where *Leave it to Beaver* hadn't really come along yet, but she wanted a lot of perfection from her family and her kids."

At the age of six, Fred was sent to a boarding school, Appleby College, in Oakville, Ont. There, as many as twenty-five students in grades one through eight were dumped into a single classroom under the disorganized supervision of one teacher. Some practices were almost murderous. The older students tossed coins onto a grassy hill and sent the younger fellows looking for the treasure while they fired bullets at targets on the other side of the slope. "The older kids were hoping we'd get shot," said Fred. After three years at Appleby, Fred switched to De La Salle College, a Catholic school in Toronto, where he flourished as a Protestant under the Christian Brothers' tutelage.

Neither Martha nor David received the same preferential treatment. They both attended the Forest Hill Village school system with its separate prep school, then the junior high two blocks from their house for grades seven through nine, followed by Forest Hill Collegiate Institute on nearby Eglinton Avenue for grades ten through thirteen.

Muriel was very ill for several years following Martha's birth, according to Martha, but she would not elaborate on the nature of the illness. It was for this reason, she said, that the rambunctious Fred was dispatched to Appleby, while Martha and David were looked after by nannies. This emotional separation from her mother during these crucial early years must have been difficult for Martha. Psychologists believe that children in such situations can, as adults, suffer from insecurity, low self-esteem, and an inability to trust others. After giving birth, some women suffer postpartum depression, but Fred denied that his mother's health problem in any way involved her emotional state. "She wasn't crazy. She wasn't ill. There was nothing wrong with her. She was always sharp as a tack. She had no operation that had to be done. She never went to a boo-boo hatch. As far as I know, she never went to a psychiatrist," he said.

Fred saw himself as the whipping boy, always blamed by his mother for everything bad that happened around the house. Martha did her best to stoke that fire by making sure that Fred was always seen in the worst possible light. "Martha was a heller from day one to the present time," said Fred. "She's just a heller, simple as that. She makes up stories. She gets the other kids in trouble as much as possible. She breaks things and blames the other kids."

When Martha was five or six she had a baby carriage in which she pushed her dolls. She relentlessly banged the carriage against the wall of the house and bumped it up and down the outside steps until, finally, a wheel fell off. Martha ran to her mother and blamed Fred. Muriel believed Martha and ordered Fred to fix the damaged toy. Fred muttered, "You little bitch," and plotted revenge. He told Martha that restoring mobility was simple. All she had to do was place the wheel on the axle and spin the wheel to secure it. Of course, the cotter pin that held the wheel in place had been lost, so no amount of spinning made any difference. The wheel fell off as soon as she tried to push the carriage again. Fred eventually carried out the repairs, but, he gloated, "she had to turn that wheel for a couple of days."

Martha was constantly being led astray by Fred. When he was sixteen or seventeen, he set out one sultry summer day to rebuild the engine in his 1946 Chev sedan. Muriel had some errands to do and Martha wanted to stay home, so Fred was told to keep an eye on her. "His pesky pre-teen sister whose nose was always getting into everything now was thrust into the midst of his hobby," recalled Martha. She had promised her mother she'd keep out of the way, so at first Martha stood silently by as Fred dismantled the engine, washed each part, and laid them all out on the floor of the garage. Martha worried that Fred wasn't going to be able to put the pieces back together again. "I dared not utter any such blasphemy in big brother's presence. Oh, how I was afraid for him! Yet I was absolutely wrapped up in the procedure. I can still remember my heart pounding with excitement."

Mesmerized by what Fred was doing, Martha dreamed about the day when she would be equally dexterous. Finally, she could contain herself no longer and began asking questions about specific parts and their function. Fred was helpful to a point, but then became fed up and told her a tale about something he called the carbonator. "For the last time, Martha, it takes the gasoline, mixes it with air and makes carbon," said Fred. "Thus the car goes and the part is called the carbonator! And that is the last question I'm going to answer."

The carbonator. Martha carefully filed that lesson away, but Fred's misinformation was a mischievous time bomb. When Martha was in grade nine, her homeroom teacher took it upon himself to explain the mysteries of a car engine. He drove his vehicle onto the school playing field and gathered his students around the open hood. "I could feel my fellow students watching me," recalled Martha. "They must have been thinking that cars were something that I would know about. I was the daughter of the Canadian Tire family." Martha did not want to disappoint, so she told them everything she knew about the carbonator. "And oh I remember well the intensity of the red flush which overcame me as I heard my kindly grade nine teacher query, 'Carbonator? What is that, Martha?' And so naively I had fallen prey to Fred's brotherly little carburetor joke in front of all my peers."[10]

For Fred, such victories were few and far between. He grew up feeling that his parents cared more for Martha or David than they did for him. Rather than being special because he was the first born, Fred

---

10 Kachur, foreword.

felt picked on. At the cottage Fred sat at one end of the long table to eat while Muriel sat at the other end, with the toaster beside her. If a piece of toast burned, she'd always blame Fred, no matter who had put the bread in.

The situation changed little with the passage of time. After Fred graduated from university, A.J. took him aside and said that he'd figured out how much money he'd saved by not having Fred around the house for four years, then handed him $58. "I didn't think it was very funny. It was a stupid thing to do," said Fred. Still, he took the cash. "David was much better looked after than the first born, but not as well looked after as the third born," said Fred. "The first child has to break all the ice. Whatever the first child does is wrong because the other children weren't doing it. All they had to do is be nice and there would have been no problem. But if they wanted to try and control me, forget it."

Martha was even less likely to be submissive. If character is destiny, she was always headed for trouble. She was a wilful child, a trait made worse by her placement in the birth order as the youngest in the family. She would rebel or use her status as the "baby" to get her way. "She's a very abrasive person. The boys used to call her Aunt Mae," said Mayne Plowman. "Aunt Mae was Alf's sister and she was a bitch if she wanted to be. I drove her to and from work and we got along, but every once in a while we'd have a blowup. Martha was like this. But you don't hold Martha down, no damn way. If the boys walked past her, she'd stick her foot out and trip them."

For Martha, this devilish demeanour was deliberately used to claim the recognition she felt she deserved, to make her feel worthy. "Striving always to do better was always one of father's credos," said Martha. "For me, [it was] striving always to do every bit as well as they did, or better if I could. I was always into everything, the young one always trying to catch up." Catching up and getting ahead for

Martha meant fighting constantly, with Fred in particular. Whenever the family travelled by car, David was strategically placed in the middle of the three siblings in the back seat. "That was to separate my brother and my sister," said David. "My mother told me I was a diplomat, and that's what I had to be. My brother and sister clashed their whole lives. If one is black, the other's white. If one is red, the other's green," said David. Martha has a different recollection. "I remember being in the middle more than David being in the middle," she said. "We all had fiery tempers, good Irish-type people, but that doesn't mean we didn't have good relationships."

A.J. and Muriel, though devoted to each other, were equally prone to having heated arguments. They quarrelled so much and so often that Fred and David finally told their parents they should seek marital counselling. As a result, Martha did not grow up in the warm arms of a close-knit family, bound by loyalties where each one defended the other against the outside world. The family was deeply dysfunctional in ways that produced three very different individuals: Fred was rough and ready, David meek and mild, and Martha embittered and embattled. "The tone of our family was different from the tone of the wage-earning family," said Fred. "You're not dealing with a family that was anything like the accepted norm anywhere." The lack of a close relationship with either of her brothers meant that Martha might as well have been an only child.

As for her father, A.J. was not a demonstrative, loving parent who tried to make peace among the battling siblings. "He was like a mentor, an instructor, someone that you tried to please. You appreciated your effort being appreciated," said David. Martha did, over time, learn from A.J. some of the skills normally associated with male members of a family. "My father loved his handiwork," she said. "I learned to do handiwork. He wasn't so good with electrical wiring and he wasn't so great with carpentry, but he was a darned good plumber. I was, I suppose, a frustrated engineer, revamping things for the business, warehousing, distribution. Children copy their role models. I had two older brothers, and I copied brothers who copied Father, and I copied Father. I've always been involved in doing those things. I am a handy person to have around."

Martha's paternal grandmother, Julia Billes, was bedridden and in poor health, so Martha's contact was limited to brief visits with her and her pet budgie. The impact of Martha's maternal grandmother, Bertha Moore, who died when Martha was thirteen, was more profound. Grandmother Moore often baby-sat Martha and her brothers and would share her favourite recipes with them. She encouraged Martha's voracious reading habit. In junior high Martha read everything in the school library, so her grandmother loaned her books that she owned herself and obtained titles for her from the public library. Martha's reading selection was unusual for a young girl. A favourite was *Mutiny on the Bounty*, the swaggering tale of love and life at sea in the South Pacific. She also enjoyed the works of Rudyard Kipling, a storyteller popular with generations of children.

Grandmother Moore also taught Martha how to use a sewing machine before she began home economics in grades seven and eight. The curriculum involved hand sewing, something that Martha couldn't master until she turned to her grandmother for help.

"Try your left hand," suggested her grandmother.

"I'm not allowed to use my left hand," said Martha.

"I was a seamstress in my youth. You try your left hand," insisted her grandmother.

"That's when I learned I was quite ambidextrous. It began to dawn on me how I'd been forced to use my right hand in school. She was a strong mentor for me."

Unlike some children who grow up with no idea of what their father does for a living, Martha was well aware of A.J.'s place in the working world. In addition to time at the cottage, summer holidays included trips when the family would all get into the car with the dog, a West Highland White, and head for Ottawa or Montreal, visiting Canadian Tire stores along the way. While A.J. talked to the local dealer, Fred and David were free to wander around the store. Muriel and Martha were often left stranded, waiting outside in the car. As a result, Martha grew up in the knowledge that the most important member of the family was the business itself. That's where the wealth came from, where attention was paid. She could also see that men could participate, but women were not welcome. Sons mattered; daughters were second class. "Tire goes back my whole life," she said. "Everything that we ever did or had revolved around Tire. The Billes brothers went into a business, turned the business into their hobby, and the hobby then pervaded the family. Canadian Tire was a sibling. It really and truly was. It was a living part of our family. Father was there always, every night except one, and Saturday mornings. I learned all the fibres that make Canadian Tire happen at home." As a result, Martha wasn't competing just against Fred and David; Tire was her rival as well. Controlling Tire would prove more difficult than keeping the boys at bay.

TIRE, MARTHA CALLED IT. Sometimes Canadian Tire, but never *the* Tire, and, more often than not, just Tire. While Tire was a member of the family and a family business, it was a business of families, too. A.J., ever the missionary with a cause, sought to reward his employees. Originally he used a bonus system, a catch-as-catch-can affair based on fear and favour, but in 1946 it was replaced by a profit-sharing arrangement. As a result of this scheme, 10 per cent of each employee's salary was withheld, invested in the company, and then paid back, with interest, after ten years. Employees were no longer just workers in the organization; they were owners. A.J. posted a memo that said, "The man who bargains for immediate wages . . . [is missing] the long-term equity that in yesteryears belonged only to the wealthy classes."[11] A.J. saw himself as the lord of the manor, one who set his serfs free by giving them a way of sharing in the bounty and prospering from the sweat of their brows.

The boy who had wanted to be a missionary had become a man with an evangelical fervour of a different sort. Rather than wait for joy in the hereafter, A.J. promised heaven on earth by providing a way for employees to achieve wealth and independence. When A.J. preached on the topic, his cadences were biblical, the message uplifting. "Like man himself, a Company's virility may be gauged by its mental and physical mobility," A.J. said in the 1962 annual report. "A company's employee incentive plan must be as young as tomorrow. For Canadian Tire, the challenge of each day, each month, and each year will motivate and guide us." Employees could become wealthy. Starting in 1956, employees could invest their portion of the profit-sharing in company shares. One share worth $8.50 in 1956 grew in value by 1987 to the equivalent of $4,900, an annual growth rate in excess of 22 per cent. By 1970 a typical employee with ten years' service who had optimized profit-sharing opportunities owned $150,000 worth of Tire shares.[12] One long-time switchboard operator was so well off when she retired that the local police mistakenly charged her with embezzlement, so unlikely was her wealth.

If employees did well, dealers fared even better. Store openings in small cities and towns were major celebrations. The fall 1953 grand opening of Vic Muncaster's new store in Sault Ste. Marie, Ont., featured prizes that included "a shotgun, sun visor, electric kettle, polishing kit, auto robe, seat covers, tire or battery, combination spot lamp, two gallons of paint and a tricycle," wrote Sandy MacDonald, a dealer in North Bay, Ont., in an edition of *Mouthpiece*, the company newsletter. There was a particularly spirited competition for the roses given to the first seventy-five ladies. Among the winners was Laird,

---

12 *Globe and Mail*, January 17, 1987.
13 *Traction*, September 1970 issue.

the owner's brother, who came dressed as a woman. Wrote MacDonald: "Laird got his rose even if his cheeks got a little pink in doing it."[13] Being a dealer was an opportunity to build real wealth. "From our $2,800 stock [of merchandise] that started us in the business, we now have approximately $50,000," said MacDonald in 1952, ten years after his own store first opened. "We don't live over the store any more, we own a house. We have a car and a half-ton truck. All through our association with C.T.C."[15]

In 1953, when Elizabeth II was crowned queen, Canadian Tire celebrated the event with a papier mâché replica of her crown above the front door of the Yonge Street store. Measuring eight feet high and twenty-five feet around, the crown was flanked by two full-size Grenadier Guards and contained 316 lights to represent the jewels. Christmas always featured a huge Santa in the same spot. At thirty-two feet, he was the equivalent of three storeys tall, boasted a size seventy-six hat and size eighty-four boot, and had to be hoisted into place by crane. Tire had become an integral part of its many communities, celebrating public events along with its customers.

Between 1945 and 1953 only six new stores were opened, but during the next three years the number grew by thirty-two, all owned by Canadian Tire and with the dealer paying rent to the corporation. By 1952 fifty-seven tons of goods were shipped daily to the dealers, first from a temporary five-storey warehouse behind the Yonge and Davenport store, then from the former Canada Bread factory, an 86,000-square-foot facility a few blocks away. Continued growth required a new warehouse, so a forty-five acre site was acquired on Sheppard Avenue in north Toronto. J.W. was scheduled to turn the first sod on November 13, 1956, signalling the start of construction on the 225,000 square foot depot.

---

13 Hugh McBride, *Our Store: 75 Years of Canadians and Canadian Tire* (Toronto: Madison Press Books, 1997), 60.

14 McBride, 60.

A chain-smoker, J.W. always seemed to be battling throat problems, and in September he'd come down with yet another throat infection. His doctor prescribed chloromycetin, a heavy-duty antibiotic in widespread use at the time. J.W. returned to work, but by November he'd fallen ill again and was unable to attend the sod-turning. Gladys stood in for her husband, and she and A.J. carried out the ceremonial honours with a gold-plated spade. Three days later J.W. was dead at fifty-nine. "Chloromycetin causes a pernicious anemia which is not unlike AIDS in its results. You have no immune system left," said his son Dick. "I think he died of some simple thing because he had nothing to fight it." The life-long partnership between J.W. and A.J. was abruptly ended. The family business would never be the same again.

TWO

A PRIVATE
PLANET

"She was not easy to get to know as a young woman.
She was careful, she was guarded. With that
came just a little bit of a shell around her."
— ROGER PERKINS, MARTHA'S CLASSMATE

When Martha entered grade ten at Forest Hill Collegiate in 1955, the competitive scholastic environment meant she was confronted by new rivals and the potential for more isolation. Three-quarters of the high school's student body was Jewish, many of them the sons and daughters of immigrants. "They were eager for us to become part of Canadian society through education," said Martin Sable, a classmate. "They pounded it into us that that was the way to succeed. When you're with competitive people, you either compete or you fall by the wayside."

Of the 137 graduates in Martha's class of '59, more than 96 per cent went on to postsecondary study. Two-thirds of that group enrolled in the University of Toronto, many of them in honours arts, medicine, or dentistry. Others were admitted to prestigious American institutions such as Radcliffe, Smith, and UCLA. Among Martha's high-achieving classmates were Irving Abella, who later taught history at York University and was president of the Canadian Jewish Congress; Anne Richmond Golden, president and CEO of the Conference Board of Canada; Sandy Goodman Chapnick, who became an Ontario high court judge; and Myra Miller Sable, an entrepreneur who co-founded the Sable & Rosenfeld line of gourmet foods.

In addition to the highly competitive atmosphere, the preponderance of Jewish students created two solitudes, Jew and Gentile. "You felt the difference," said Roger Perkins, the only male Gentile student in Martha's class during their four years together at Forest Hill. "When I think about Martha, I think, 'Oh yes, she was one of the Gentile girls.'" Martha's relationship with Joan Kagan, now a Toronto potter, typified the chasm. Kagan has few specific recollections of Martha, an unusual amnesia given that the two were classmates for ten years. They were seated beside each other at the back of the room in grade four because, even then, both of them were tall for their age. In their grade eleven class photograph, Kagan and Martha stood beside each other. Both had reached their full adult height, a head taller than most of the other female students, and slightly taller than many of their male contemporaries. That shared physical similarity and their years together in the classroom should have created a bond between them, but religion and culture conspired to keep them apart.

As a result, Martha mixed and mingled with her contemporaries far less than she would have at almost any other high school in Toronto. The Jewish students tended to form cliques, participated in temple youth groups during the school year, and went to summer camp together. The school did not close for High Holidays, so Gentiles were expected to attend, but teachers presented no new course material. As a Gentile in such surroundings, "you'd probably feel a little marginalized," said Martin Sable, who practised law and later taught at Forest Hill. "She seemed benign and shy. One wouldn't have thought she'd become a mover and shaker in the business world."

Martha tried to cope as best she could. "Popularity at Forest Hill was a bit of a difficult thing," she said. "As for helping other kids and that type of situation, I was on a call list for a number of kids to get help with science or math homework. I made some good friends. We did things together."

Martha was involved in trying to start a branch of a sorority that had chapters at other Toronto high schools. Among the students she approached to join was Sylvia Sutherland, now serving her fourth term as mayor of Peterborough, Ont. "Even then I was politically enough aware that I didn't think at a high school that was largely Jewish it made a lot of sense to join a Gentile sorority," said Sutherland, who had come to Forest Hill Collegiate from Midland, Ont. "I was a kid from the sticks. She was certainly welcoming to me." The sorority never got off the ground.

Martha once invited Roger Perkins to Shanty Bay for an afternoon visit. After he drove through the gate and began heading down a long laneway, he worried that he was lost. A man wearing work pants and an undershirt was toiling in the field beside the road, so Perkins called out, asking if the small structure ahead belonged to the Billes family. That's just the guesthouse, Perkins was told, keep on going. Perkins was astonished to arrive at what he described as "a French provincial mansion with terraces everywhere." Perkins, Martha, and Muriel sat outside, chatted, and drank gin and tonic. At one point the man in the undershirt appeared. "It was A.J.," said Perkins. "Was I ever glad I hadn't said something like, 'Thank you, my man.'"

Martha was a good student, though she won no academic awards. She played intramural volleyball and was a member of Tri-Y, a service club co-sponsored by the school and the YWCA. She chose the music option and played violin in the school orchestra, a demanding activity that meant three practices a week. Because she had begun violin lessons at the age of ten, Martha was better than most of the other student violinists, so she served as concertmistress throughout her four years at Forest Hill. She did not, however, play well enough for the dog, who hid whenever she practised. Martha wore the orchestra uniform, a white blouse and a plaid skirt, and sat in the prestigious chair to the conductor's left when the orchestra played during school assemblies or serenaded parents at the Parade of Talent, an annual student show that featured dancing, singing, and skits. "This year, the noted improvement of the musical groups and the talented black-face actors combined to produce a show which led the audience from awe to laughter to nostalgia and back again," said the *Forester*, the school yearbook, about the 1957 show. The following year's review was less laudatory. "Too much work, not enough result," it lamented, although the writer of the unsigned item found some aspects to praise. "The music of this year's P.O.T. was better than ever. Because of early training and the guidance of the music staff, we are no longer hearing 'screechy' violins but some very good musical compositions."

THE YEAR MARTHA STARTED at Forest Hill Collegiate, Fred left home to study business at the University of Western Ontario in London, Ont. After a year, he transferred to Bryant, in Providence, Rhode Island. His departure from home did not reduce the tension. Instead, a new rival appeared. While in London he had met Barbara Kitchen, a kindergarten and primary school specialist who followed him to Rhode Island, where she taught. When Fred graduated in 1958, they were married. It seemed to Barbara that Martha viewed her as someone else who would vie for familial attention. "She was number three and she resented the fact that she wasn't number one," Barbara recalled.

At school, Martha seemed to shrink from social contact and resisted friendly advances. "She was not easy to get to know as a young woman," said Perkins, who played oboe in the school orchestra and is now a pianist and conductor in the Ontario theatre towns of Stratford and Niagara-on-the-Lake. "She was careful, she was guarded. She had that kind of streak of independence and wanted to be recognized for her brain, for her abilities. Martha saw herself as a person first, rather than just as a woman. I don't think Martha saw herself as a flirt or as somebody who went to great pains to make herself especially attractive to boys. She didn't identify with girls whose main interest was boys. With that came just a little bit of a shell around her. She wouldn't have been popular, I think that's fair to say."

As a loner, Martha established her brand of personal identity by holding strong views that she was not afraid to voice. After all, she had little to lose by being outspoken. She could be no more ostracized at school or at home than she already was. "I remember her for her independent mind," said Perkins. "She had convictions of her own and stood up for herself. In class, I remember her being able to voice her opinions. She wasn't shy about speaking up."

Martha's sense of self-esteem was not enhanced by her summer jobs at Canadian Tire. Her brothers were given rewarding roles where there was big money to be made. Fred and David were pickers, filling orders, and could earn commissions of up to $80 a week, a huge sum of money for a student and enough for a working man to raise a family. Martha made much less because she was relegated to the steno pool or the switchboard. She could be a cashier at the gas bar, but she could not operate the pumps. For a woman in a man's world at Canadian Tire, little had changed since the 1930s when Martha's aunt, Mae Tuckman, worked in the office.

At home, at school, and at Tire, Martha was learning to be self-reliant. Even her graduation photo set her apart from the other students in the Forest Hill Collegiate class of '59. All the other head-and-shoulders shots appear to have been taken by the same assembly-line photographer. By comparison, Martha's likeness was glamorous and must have been done by a professional studio. The image was tightly focused on her face and showed just a hint of her sweater, with a butterfly brooch at the neck. Her wavy hair was worn collar-length, her teeth were strong, and her smile full. The eyebrows were gracefully arched over dancing eyes that looked happily at a spot somewhere over the photographer's right shoulder. There were artful shadows on her face that did not appear in any other student's photo.

The words that accompanied Martha's photo added to the sense of her "otherness," her driving desire to be different. The tongue-in-cheek theme of the yearbook that spring compared school life to jail terms. The students were described as "prisoners of Row 13, the Life or Death Row." Extracurricular activities were called "previous offences," and a student's intended destination was termed "post parole."

The last section under each grad's photo was a mock courtroom "plea" for the future. Many comments were meant to be zany. "A zoo in Forest Hill, we have the people for it," said one. "I want to be healthy, wealthy and wise, but most of all Zsa-Zsa," joshed another. Some pleas were hopeful: "To get what I need, when I want it." Others were thoughtful: "To have parents stop talking about the modern generation as if they had nothing to do with it." By comparison, Martha's plea was as pretentious as it was telling: "A private planet on which Newton, Descartes, Dalton, Avagadro [sic], Shakespeare and Hemon have never been mentioned." Her fellow students would have recognized the names of William Shakespeare or Louis Hémon, author of *Maria Chapdelaine*, the novel about Quebec peasant life that they'd read in French Authors. Some might even have heard about Sir Isaac Newton, the man who discovered gravity, or philosopher René ("I think, therefore I am") Descartes. But how well known was the English chemist John Dalton or the Italian physicist Amadeo Avogadro?

The point, however, was not the depth of Martha's knowledge about the great thinkers. She was not merely showing off her intelligence or asking for relief from textbooks and homework. What she wanted was a private planet where she could escape. A private planet. Difficulties with personal relationships would follow her all the days of her life.

AS THE 1960S ARRIVED, women were just beginning to break into previously male-dominated bastions such as engineering, law, and accounting. Even so, there would be only one or two female students among the many men in universities who were heading towards a profession.

Martha was given no opportunity to prepare herself for her career of choice, as had her brothers, Fred into business and David into engineering, at the University of Toronto. As with many female high school graduates of that era, she wasn't even allowed to follow her preferred educational interest. She'd enjoyed chemistry and physics at school, so she wanted to attend Ryerson, a Toronto polytechnic institute, then become a lab technician. Her parents disapproved. In their view, home economics was a more appropriate place to prepare for the role they expected Martha to fulfill: wife and mother. A.J. may have preached independence for his sons, but the message to Martha was totally different. Where he was proactive with Fred and David, he was protective of Martha. Be sweet, said A.J., obedient and passive.

Martha acquiesced and enrolled at the Macdonald Institute in Guelph, Ont., an hour west of Toronto. It was a fitting place for such a girl to go. The school had been founded in 1903 on the campus of the Ontario Agricultural College (OAC) with the encouragement of Adelaide Hunter Hoodless, a reformer who did not support suffragette causes because she believed that women belonged in the home. In 1964, the year after Martha graduated, Mac — as the students called it — was amalgamated with the OAC and the Ontario Veterinary College (OVC) to become the University of Guelph. While Martha was there, however, the three institutions were, in effect, wards of the province of Ontario. All members of faculty were civil servants. So, despite attending classes at Mac in Guelph, Martha's Bachelor of Science degree was awarded by the University of Toronto.

Guelph did not, however, have U of T's reputation. It was disparagingly dubbed Cow College or Hog U because many of the students hailed from small towns or farms. There were few women at either OVC or OAC (where the students were called Aggies), but women made up the total enrolment at Mac, with forty-four students in Martha's year. In the first two years, everyone studied the same curriculum; then, in the final two years, each student focused on one of three options: food and nutrition, clothing and textiles, or home management. Martha was not interested in a career in food sciences. Nor did textiles appeal because she was short-sighted and had worn glasses all through high school. By elimination, that left home management. At least that stream included courses in sociology and a continuation of the physical sciences she had previously enjoyed. Students in home management also cooked in a classroom kitchen, learned the proper use of home appliances, and were involved in running an on-campus nursery school program.

All the women at Mac were trapped by the same pinched circumstances. "There weren't that many things for women to do in those days: nursing, teaching, or something like home economics. In the late fifties and early sixties, women were still doing pretty much what their parents thought was wise," said Nancy Kerr, Martha's roommate for three of the four years at Mac. "She was in home management, where she would have courses most to her liking. That was more the business end of managing a home. She was a very good student, one of the top students, worked very hard, and was very efficient."

Martha's high marks seemed to come easily. "I still remember biochemistry where I thought I'd aced the exam and Martha got a better mark than I did," said Rita Crow, who later obtained her doctorate and became a research scientist with the Department of

National Defence. "I always admire excellence and the fact that she had first-class honours all the way through. I don't think she had to work that hard at it."

In first, second, and fourth years Martha lived in residence, Macdonald Hall, where the house rules meant that any gentleman caller waited respectfully in the ground-floor reception rooms. First-year students were subject to an eleven o'clock curfew, after which the doors were locked. In second and third years a resident could obtain four "keys" during the year — four occasions when the curfew was relaxed. Fourth-year students were given their own individual keys so they could come and go as they pleased. All students on campus ate in Creelman Hall, a cafeteria with long trestle tables, where a dress code meant no slacks for women. On Sundays, men wore jackets and ties. Compared with the other co-eds, Martha cut quite a swath. "She would just float in with her fur coat and her hair flying. She was very glamorous, very worldly looking, compared to the rest of us," said Marjorie O'Neill Dennis, who grew up in the small Ontario city of St. Thomas. "Martha just had an air about her that said she was different." Among some of the male students Martha was known as "Miss Canadian Tire," a title that managed to contain a smatter of ridicule along with a grudging respect.

For any young adult, one of the benefits of leaving home to attend school should be increased independence and new-found freedom. "Roots and wings," said those parents who did it well. Attending college in Guelph held potential for Martha, but she did not seem to fully seize the opportunity presented. "She didn't have a lot of friends. She was pretty well a loner. She had a vehicle so she could escape when she wanted to," said classmate Aileen Selves Burgin, who now runs a bed and breakfast in Kirkton, Ont. With Fred away at school and David busy with his own studies, Martha could have her mother all to herself. Moreover, she had fallen in love with Roger Henry, an engineering student at the University of Toronto. As a result, rare was the weekend Martha spent on campus. Most Fridays she'd head for Toronto in her car, first a Biscayne, later a Corvair, both bedecked with every ornament and gadget available at Canadian Tire because the vehicles had previously been used as floor displays in the store. She'd live at home, see Roger, and return to Mac on Monday morning in time for class.

That schedule suited Nancy Kerr just fine. Martha's absence meant Kerr had the room to herself three nights out of seven each week. In first year they were assigned a room that was one of the smallest in the residence. There was barely enough space for two desks and a set of bunk beds. Martha slept in the bottom bunk — quite a change from her more sumptuous bedroom with its own aquarium in Forest Hill. "I don't think living in Guelph was much to her liking. She hated the food in the dining hall. I think there was much more for her at home," said Kerr, who took her doctorate at North Carolina State and is now a professor of textiles at the University of Alberta in Edmonton.

As the daughter of an air vice marshal, Kerr grew up in Ottawa and Trenton, Ont. While at Mac, she enrolled in the University Reserve Training Plan. Martha decided to do the same, but the airforce program was full, so she signed up for the equivalent army program, the Canadian Officers Training Corps. In addition to on-campus training, Martha spent two summers at Camp Borden, near Meaford, Ont., and attained the rank of second lieutenant. "We were all surprised," said Kerr. "She was from a well-to-do family, had all the privileges, a wonderful summer home north of Toronto, so why would she be out there polishing shoes and marching?"

The likely answer is that Martha was rebelling. She badly wanted to be involved in Canadian Tire, but only on her terms. From the rumble seat through relegated roles at the store, she was constantly being shown that she was not as good as her brothers. Martha found particularly galling the cafeteria job that A.J. wanted her to take one summer. She did work in food services at the Bell Telephone offices on University Avenue in Toronto, but she refused to accept A.J.'s offer to work in the Tire cafeteria. "She considered that an affront," said David. "I always assumed that the reason to go to university for what she was going through was to end up doing dietary work. You had to have some practical experience. She thought she was going to wash pots and dole out mashed potatoes, but there obviously had to be planning. Whoever's running the cafeteria had to buy ahead, estimate how many tons of potatoes they're going to sell, how many pork chops, and, if they have two entrees, how much of each, the correct balance, and not have a whole bunch left over."

As far as Martha was concerned, the Tire cafeteria was no place to eat, let alone work. "It wasn't a cafeteria at Canadian Tire. It was three below grade, it was next to the boiler room. It was not a similar offer [to Bell]. I was in a dietetic internship training plan to satisfy my parents' desire and, when that one year was over, that was the end of it," she recalled.

That difference of opinion between Martha and her parents demonstrated the divide that was growing between the girl Martha was allowed to be and the woman she wanted to become. If she couldn't get sufficient status in the business, she'd rather wait than accept second best. That perseverance may be admirable, but the inability to reach a compromise meant that Martha was building a barrier between herself and others. "Martha was invisible. Fred grew up believing *he* was the heir apparent; Martha became the frustrated aspirant," said Sherrill MacLaren in *Invisible Power: The Women Who Run Canada.* "She seemed to be the child who really cared about the quality of the business, and her illimitable drive both for ownership and recognition by her father would become manifest in a competitive nature equal to that of any male who had ever stalked a controlling share. Canadian Tire was her father's first child and it was Martha's identity denied."

"They seemed to think that I should run the cafeteria or [at best] become an expert on the new Kevlor radials," she told MacLaren. Along the way Martha learned how to handle her brothers. "I am able to compartmentalize," said Martha.[1] In fact, said MacLaren, the capacity to go within, to muster strength and wait for the right moment, all the while appearing imperturbable, is a talent that's transferable to other elements of life. "That strategic calm is a skill of self-defence learned by many little girls mounting counterattacks against older brothers."[2]

At Mac, social relationships with her fellow students seemed to come to Martha no more easily than in high school. Just as there had been two camps at Forest Hill, so at Mac the majority of students were farm girls. Among the handful of big city girls, Martha had by far the most money. She joined a group of third-year students on a one-week school bus trip to New York to visit the Metropolitan and Guggenheim museums and to see *Camelot*, the Broadway play starring Richard Burton, Julie Andrews, and Robert Goulet. The trip was expensive, a big stretch for most student budgets, but Martha was also able to shop for sweaters, a self-indulgence that the other participants could not afford.

Another year, when a busload of her classmates took a field trip to the Royal Ontario Museum in Toronto, Martha invited them all to afternoon tea at her home in Forest Hill. "Most of us were rural, but she certainly wasn't," said Burgin. "Her lifestyle was a fairy tale for those of us who were used to living in farm houses out in the country and cleaning out stables, milking cows, and doing whatever was necessary. It was a taste of a lifestyle that we still — well, I don't dream about it any more."

The day was wet, so the guests were told to leave their shoes at the front door to avoid staining the oriental rugs. Inside, despite the elegant surroundings that included a grand piano, a plant-filled conservatory, and a uniformed maid, the mood was more high-strung

1   Sherrill MacLaren, *Invisible Power: The Women Who Run Canada* (Toronto: Seal Books, 1991), 164.
2   MacLaren, 162.

than hospitable. "It was the cook's day off and somebody had forgotten to impart some information, so it was rather unpleasant when we arrived because a maid was doing things she wasn't accustomed to or didn't prefer to do," said Burgin. "You could feel a tension that I was not accustomed to feeling in a family, especially when you were entertaining. You knew enough to maintain at least a pleasant facade, if nothing else. It never dawned on me that there would be discord in a household where there should be ample organization and finances. There was just an aura there that was frigid."

A similar coolness marked Martha's ongoing relations with her classmates. To them, she appeared standoffish and vigilant. Martha seemed fearful that people might take advantage of her wealth, so there were occasions when she came across as downright stingy. When she was asked to supply decorations from Canadian Tire for the class Christmas tree, no baubles were forthcoming. "Because of the money she was different from the rest of us," said Rita Crow. "I felt sorry for her because I think she always wanted to be part of the group and she really wasn't."

Martha could not seem to share what she had. Anyone who wanted a ride with her to or from Toronto on the weekend was asked to pay. Martha knew the bus fare between the two cities and would charge passengers slightly less. "Lots of people would say, 'I'm going anyway, not a problem.' That's a different personality," said Kerr. "Because of her position she was used to having people wanting things from her, wanting freebies, something special. She didn't want to have people take advantage of her. If people were willing to pay to go to Toronto with her, then she'd know that she wasn't being taken advantage of — they really did want to go."

On one occasion when Martha made an attempt to share, her efforts went for naught. The class of '63 planned a dance with a Hawaiian theme. Martha had holidayed in the islands and learned the hula, so she offered to teach the hip-swaying moves to her classmates and their dates. On the night of the dance, when the hired band took a break, a grass-skirted Martha cranked up her recorded Hawaiian music and took her place in the centre of the dance floor. Some Aggies had got wind of her plan and were lying in wait outside. As Martha's demonstration was about to begin, the pranksters opened the windows and released a flock of pigeons into the room. "The whole party deteriorated into chaos. We all had to catch pigeons. I still remember feeling sorry for Martha," said Crow.

In Martha's third year, the only year she did not stay in residence, she lived with Astrid Bush, now Astrid Schulte-Nordholt, a music teacher in Combermere, Ont. Schulte-Nordholt had attended U of T in her first year and then switched to Mac. Because they both came from Toronto, she and Martha were drawn to each other and became friends. They decided to share a two-bedroom apartment in a building that was ten minutes' walk from Mac down the hill on Gordon Street, the main thoroughfare between the university and downtown Guelph. Living together snuffed out the incipient flame of their friendship. Schulte-Nordholt soon realized that Martha's character was far different from her own. "We started off the year being fairly good friends and, at the end of the year, we weren't," she said. "It was quite frosty." Relations deteriorated to such an extent that they argued over who owned what food in the refrigerator. "I was always brought up to be generous and to look out for the other person, and she wasn't. I may not have come across that way to her, but that's certainly the way she came across to me," said Schulte-Nordholt.

In fourth year all Mac students were required to live in residence, so Martha again roomed with Nancy Kerr. "I was probably the only one that was willing to live with her," said Kerr. Despite three years as her roommate, Kerr never really warmed to Martha. "We used to take turns cleaning the room. I never cleaned the room to her satisfaction. We weren't soul mates. I had other friends at Guelph that I was much closer to. She meant well and she probably didn't understand why she didn't have more buddies."

In May 1963 Martha graduated summa cum laude. "Home economics students have a special role to fill," Dr. Margaret McCready, dean of Macdonald Institute, told the grads in her message in *Libranni*, the school yearbook. "More than many other students they have an opportunity to PREVENT mishap and breakdown in our homes, through a unique concern with the values and goals we seek." Martha would not follow that wise admonition.

With the education her parents had insisted on completed, she took the next traditional step for a woman of that era and married Roger Pearson Henry, her long-time beau, later that same month. Martha wore a full-length gown of French white satin with lace appliqué and carried a bouquet of pink roses, orchids, and stephanotis. Her attendants were Deanna Copeland, a friend from Toronto, Cathie Graydon, a cousin, and Nancy Kerr. The wedding party also included David, but not Fred. All three Toronto newspapers published reports of the grand society occasion held at Forest Hill's Grace Church-on-the-Hill. The *Telegram* carried a photo of the bride; the *Star* ran a picture of the couple. The reception following the wedding was held at the family home on Old Forest Hill Road. Wedding presents were displayed in such abundance that guests must have thought they were browsing in a gift shop. For her going-away outfit Martha wore a blue designer suit with matching hat and white kid accessories. The honeymoon included stops in Jamaica, Puerto Rico, Barbados, and Trinidad.

Martha and her new husband had little apparent personal chemistry. "I think she was very fond of him," said Kerr. "I think she loved him, but there wasn't a lot of outward huggy-kissy warmth kind of stuff that you might see in lots of young couples." Martha was repeating her family pattern by marrying a man who was not demonstratively affectionate.

❦

AFTER J.W.'S DEATH, A.J.'s role had expanded from tires and batteries to include distribution, inventory, administration, and marketing. "That was the turning point when the hobby wasn't so much of a hobby anymore," said Martha. "It really became a very, very difficult job for him. His father's untimely death forced Dad to withdraw from school. He went to night school for a few more years, but he didn't have any formal education. He certainly traded well on his relationships with people and his desire to get in and change and fix, change and fix. [He'd say], 'Let's just try this. Let's just try that.'"

That character trait caused problems for others. "Nothing was straightforward with A.J. He never did anything and left it alone. He never stopped tinkering," said Richard Hobbs, who was a dealer in two Ontario centres, Orangeville and Hamilton, in the early 1960s. "You'd get two or three directives a week from A.J. on changing the tire program. He just never stopped. Maybe that's the way to do it, but it was tough on the organization." Some ideas were wacky, like the car wash he built at Yonge and Davenport that was far too mechanized. "We spent more damn money on that thing. A.J. tried to fix it, and it never worked. That money all went down the drain, but that was his way," said Hobbs.

J.W.'s last will and testament was an even more cumbersome contraption. His estate was worth $6.2 million, but the Canadian Tire shares that made up the bulk of that value were neither passed on to J.W.'s children nor made available for A.J. to buy. Gladys and the three children, Gwen, John, and Dick, were given annuities. But the shares themselves and the rest of the annual income that flowed from those shares were left to twenty-three charities and educational organizations, including the University of Toronto, the Canadian Red Cross Society, the Salvation Army, and the Toronto Humane Society. The gift was so large and so unusual that the *Telegram* featured the bequest in a front-page headline using typeface of a size normally reserved for mining disasters: "$6 million left to kin, charity."

J.W. left his own family in the lurch. Not only was the money tied up but the next generation had no ownership position in the company. "It bothered me that he didn't look after his own wife," said John, J.W.'s elder son. "The cost of living was accelerating tremendously after my father's death. The amount that she got, she never could have lived on. This is where my dad's foresight went down the tube, I guess. I'm not trying to look a gift horse in the mouth, but he certainly didn't look after his family. He had to come up by hard knocks, and he felt his family should be the same way."

In one last controlling manoeuvre, J.W. had prevented A.J. from taking charge. "That was a real shock to my father," said Martha. "It just ripped the heart out of him. He'd been his brother's partner. It also ripped the heart and soul out of Dick in that his dad did that to their family." "It's a classic bad will," said Dick, who, along with his mother and a representative from National Trust, was executor. "I think they even use it in universities to say this is what you shouldn't do."

Even in death the discord between the two families continued. Muriel wanted a large public funeral, despite J.W.'s stated wish for a private family service. "Muriel phoned to get my OK on it. I said, 'It's right there in the will,'" recalled John. "'That's the way it's going to be.' I was on her bad black list from then on." Muriel never again spoke to John.

John had worked at Tire since graduating from Northern Vocational in 1945. His first job was rebuilding generators, then he moved into automotive parts, followed by an office role in accounting. With his father's death, John realized that the way ahead was blocked for his side of the family. "John got caught in the middle of it," said his wife, Betty. "Finally, he couldn't take it any longer and he said, 'The heck with it, let them run the darn company. I'm out of there.'" So John retired. "We're not social climbers," he explained. "My brother, that's a different story." In return, Dick had a similarly testy view. "He didn't want to do the mundane things to learn how the business worked," Dick said of John. "He's not exactly the proudest moment in my life. I did everything in the business that I could do and he wasn't prepared to do what I was prepared to do."

But Dick and Martha had another competitor for A.J.'s attention: Dean Muncaster. After all, there was family and then there was *family*. Dean's father, Walter, had opened a Canadian Tire outlet in Sudbury in 1945, one of five among the seven Muncaster brothers who became dealers. Two were partners in Sault Ste. Marie, one in Fort William, and another in Kirkland Lake. In those days, picking a dealer was a hit-and-miss proposition, a combination of instinct and nepotism. If your brother was a good dealer, there was an expectation that you would be too. Among the Muncasters, there were more misses than hits. Four of the five later left the company to become automotive dealers, leaving only Walter.

Walter was one of those natural-born retailers who was willing to take a risk. He was the first dealer to institute self-service in the store by ending the old way of merchandising with clerks behind counters filling orders. Costs fell, customers flocked in, and in 1956 his outlet was the first Tire store in Canada to reach $1 million in annual sales. Dean Muncaster was born in 1933 and started work in his father's store at the age of twelve for $15 a week. By the time Dean was eighteen, Walter had sufficient confidence in his son to take a month-long summer holiday, leaving Dean in charge of forty employees. After obtaining his undergraduate degree in business at Western, Dean Muncaster did his master's in business administration at Northwestern University in Chicago. He did not plan to have a career at Canadian Tire; like many young men of the time, he wanted to be a brand manager at Procter & Gamble. But while he was at Western he'd done a research paper on Tire that so impressed A.J. that he offered Muncaster a job at $100 a week.

In 1957, nabbing a man with an MBA was a big step for Tire. "They had never hired anybody off a university campus," said Muncaster. "I think A.J. had come to the realization that the time was coming when he better start hiring some younger people. He was a very intuitive guy. If things felt right to A.J., that's the action he would pursue."

A.J. was not, however, much good at giving direction. "What is it you expect me to do here?" asked Muncaster. "I don't know," replied A.J. As a result, Muncaster's earliest roles were project oriented, assignments to solve specific problems such as transporting battery acid. As time passed there were more complex tasks. He showed dealers that they should be measuring their success by financial yardsticks beyond just sales and profits. He taught them modern merchandising methods using inventory turns, sales per square foot, and sales per employee.

Working in such close quarters with A.J., Muncaster learned better than Martha ever could how to handle him. "The word was to get up early in the morning and get close to the front of the line going into A.J.'s office, so you got a hearing, rather than waiting the whole day to see him," said Muncaster. A.J. thrived on confrontation. "He was one of those people that believed that conflict was a good thing. He'd send different people off on the same task, then see what resulted. There was always friction."

Muncaster soon concluded that Tire was the wrong place for his own upward progress. Although it was a family business, it wasn't A.J.'s offspring that Muncaster feared — certainly not Fred, who by rights should have been first in line. Fred was rebellious, disrespectful, and would swear at A.J. "He used to have disagreements with his father and walk off in a huff. It was pretty regular," said Fred Sasaki, who was treasurer. "It was terrible, but A.J. would just ignore it. Freddy didn't know he was swearing, but to an outsider it was a shock. To Freddy it was a common thing. All of a sudden he'd flare up."

Fred's manner put people off. "Fred was boorish as hell, but he wasn't a dummy," said Mayne Plowman. "He had a lot of the practical abilities that Alf had. Fred's mouth turned into a garbage can, the swearing would come out. Alf was not a swearing man. Fred didn't give a darn who it was, the garbage just tumbled out of his mouth. Even in normal conversation you had your fingers crossed that he wouldn't say the wrong thing."

With Fred an unlikely successor to A.J., David showing no interest, and Martha given no consideration, Muncaster assumed that J.W.'s son, Dick, was the most likely heir apparent. Muncaster liked Dick, but not well enough to work for him. In 1960 Muncaster found a convenient solution. He returned to Sudbury to help run the store for his father, who was ill. A.J. appointed Muncaster a director, so he could keep a close eye on him in the Toronto boardroom.

Dick had his own problems with A.J. He had attended a business college before joining Tire in 1950. His father assigned him to Fred Sasaki in accounting, then told Sasaki that Dick would spend six months with him before moving on to other departments as part of his grooming. "Unfortunately it didn't happen that way," said Sasaki. "He stayed with me all the time until his father died. Dick was quite stubborn. I found him quite difficult, but it was the boss's son. J.W. noticed that and I guess he didn't want to disrupt A.J.'s area. He didn't carry out his original plan." Relations between A.J. and Dick deteriorated further with the death of J.W. The day after J.W.'s funeral, Dick moved into his father's empty office, and A.J. never forgave Dick for his presumptuous behaviour.

An incident in December 1961 gave A.J. the excuse he needed to get rid of Dick. A.J. and Muriel had taken a Caribbean vacation, leaving Dick in charge. The dealers wanted to close the stores on Boxing Day, and Dick agreed. When A.J. returned home, he was livid. He took out full-page newspaper advertisements announcing that all Tire stores would be open on Boxing Day. "There was a power struggle," said Sasaki. "They had their outs."

Dick fled within days. At the annual meeting on June 22, 1962, A.J.'s victory was complete: Dick was the only member of the board of directors who was not reappointed. He worked for Shell, then Imperial Oil, advising them about the tire, battery, and accessories businesses both were trying to launch in conjunction with their service stations. He would later try for a comeback, but the J.W. branch of the Billes family would never again regain power. A.J., Martha, and her brothers would see to that.

THREE

THE LADY IS FOR TURNING

*"It was a regrettable part of my life. It's history for me,
and I don't want to go back over any of it anymore."*
— ROGER HENRY, MARTHA'S FIRST HUSBAND

*N*othing more accurately captured the macho culture that Martha was up against than the cover illustrations on the Canadian Tire catalogue. The catalogue had begun in 1928 as a price sheet, with tires on one side and a road map of Ontario and the Maritimes on the other. The first magazine-style catalogue arrived in 1934 as a 9-by-12-inch, twenty-four-page publication.

The suave gentleman who graced the spring and summer number of 1941 never had a name, but he became a regular fixture for the next three decades. That first illustration showed an older man at a campsite, with two younger men at the side of a stream. The Old Gent had a fisherman's creel hanging around his neck and his hands positioned as if describing the one that got away. By the 1950s Old Gent had taken on the look that would last for the next twenty years: handsome and rotund, with white hair and an upturned white moustache. The situations in which he found himself were slightly risqué, like scenes in a movie that had passed muster with the censor board. In 1951, for example, he trolled for fish from a boat on a river along with the two characters who looked young enough to be his sons; let's call them The Boys. Peeking from behind a Canadian Tire billboard on the riverbank was a blonde. Her shoulders were bare and her clothing was laid out on the grass. Old Gent was unaware of her naked plight because he was facing the other way in the boat. The same cover girl regularly appeared and developed an unusual relationship with Old Gent. She didn't act like a trophy wife; they were more like a father and daughter. Once she tickled his neck, but he was napping at the time, so the activity was hardly erotic.

Would it be too much of a stretch to see the foursome as the Billes family? A.J. and Old Gent were always the centre of attention in their respective worlds. The Boys, like Fred and David, seemed too light for heavy work and too heavy for light work. And The Blonde! Well, Martha was a redhead, but the roles were certainly similar. The cover girl was much more impressive than The Boys, in the same way that Martha was more assertive than her brothers. But both women could also be nags, always trying to achieve goals that others opposed. In 1963 Old Gent's hammock reverie was interrupted by The Blonde, who was thrusting a garden spade at him as The Boys slunk away in the background. In 1969 the four characters were reduced to disembodied heads in separate circles surrounded by merchandise. The following year they were gone, with no explanation of who they were or why they disappeared. The cover girl always had a game plan and the gumption to carry it out. The real-life Martha was the same; she wanted a chance, but A.J. consistently refused.

A.J. focused on making Tire in his own image, a vision that did not include Martha. He put Canadian Tire back into the retail gasoline business, a field the firm had abandoned thirty years earlier. J.W. would have been against such a step, but, with his older brother gone,

A.J. could do as he pleased. He'd been eyeing the profits made by big oil companies, so in 1958 he opened his first gas station in conjunction with the Yonge Street store. At street level a team of employees provided gas from five pumps in nine octane blends stored in twelve underground tanks. They also checked tire pressure, oil, anti-freeze, and battery levels and vacuumed the vehicle. A lower-level open service bay featured a 56-foot-long conveyor belt capable of moving cars along at the rate of 12 feet per minute, as eight men performed chassis lubes and oil changes. By 1961 there were fourteen gas stations in the Toronto area, with nine of them opening in that year alone.

A.J. was canny enough not to tweak the nose of big oil by becoming too competitive. He relied on them to supply Tire with petroleum products. Rather than get into a price war at the pumps, a coupon program was launched to give customers money off their next purchase. The first Canadian Tire money featured the illustration of the happy tire and silver dollar running together, just as they had been doing since the 1920s. On the back there was a grand scene that included a rising sun shining on a Canadian Tire store set among industrial plants and other symbols of the Canadian economy — a freight train, cars, a ship, and an airplane. The printer sought the signatures of A.J. and Fred Sasaki for the bottom of the coupon, in the same way that the governor of the Bank of Canada and his deputy sign Canada's currency. A.J. made a sample of his signature available, but Sasaki did not, so the printer signed his name for him, mistakenly spelling it Saski.

For A.J., the man who had wanted to be a missionary, there was a message in Tire money. "We were trying to show people that credit costs money, and how much 5 per cent could add up to over the years."[1] The coupons expanded to the stores in 1961 and their popularity continued to grow. By the mid-1970s, 80 per cent of all

---

1   *Reader's Digest*, July 1977, 70.

coupons were redeemed by customers on subsequent visits. (The payout, set by head office, has dropped from 5 per cent to 2.5 per cent for cash and has been extended to Canadian Tire credit cards, where it is 3.2 per cent.) The coupons were a tough sell internally. "The idea was very unpopular with the Canadian Tire dealers," said Arch Brown. "They called me a communist for doing it. We were going to destroy the company. As it turned out, it was one of the best merchandising ideas in the history of the Western world. I don't think that A.J. had the vision that it would be accepted as widely as it was."

As Canadian Tire money caught hold with customers, the birth of the concept took on mythic proportions. Of all the family members, only Martha has regularly praised Muriel both for inventing Canadian Tire money and for coming up with the earlier idea that counter staff should wear roller skates. "I guess my mother was also a frustrated female entrepreneur. She felt disempowered by society's expectations around the role of women," said Martha. "A lot of Canadian Tire was her ideas. It all just happened, it was all just part of the family enterprise." David, in contrast, claims that he never once heard his father give Muriel credit for coming up with any ideas. The closest A.J. came to acknowledging Muriel's role in relation to Canadian Tire money occurred, he said, when people would mention the topic and A.J. did not outright deny it. "He wouldn't say no because he was so devoted to her," agreed Dick. Fred went even further and derided Muriel's capacity as an adviser to A.J. on anything to do with Tire. "How would a housewife who never spent any time working in that business know anything about [it so] that she could discuss current affairs? The only business she even worked in was an insurance company. She didn't get far up in that," said Fred.

Of course, memories can be selective, faulty, or both. Martha's recollections of her growing-up years are far different from those of Fred or David. According to Martha, Tire was a constant topic at family meals. By contrast, Fred and David both say that Tire was discussed only in the brief period leading up to the annual convention. Dealers organized events one year, head office the next, so on those alternative years Muriel would be involved in the head office program to entertain spouses. "I can't answer for Martha," said Fred. "I have no idea what goes on in her head. Psychologically some people put a lot more emphasis on some things and I suppose women put a lot of emphasis on the social end. Maybe there was a lot of discussion about women when she was around. There was not very much discussed about the business at the dinner table, strange but true."

OWNERSHIP WAS THE ONE important aspect of the family business where Martha was treated as an equal. In 1958 A.J. established Aldamar Corp., a name devised from the first few letters of each of his children's names — Alfred, David, and Martha. In a legal manoeuvre known as an "estate freeze," ownership of Tire was transferred from A.J. to the three siblings, each of whom was given a one-third interest in Aldamar. In 1963 he implemented another tax-related reorganization known as a "butterfly," a step that allowed Martha and her brothers to own their third of the company on an individual basis, rather than sharing the holding jointly. These steps, although done for tax planning and estate purposes, had an important outcome. The likelihood of blood feuds among the siblings was all but guaranteed, since there was no longer any parental guiding hand. Equally important, the structure meant that one of them could buy out the others.

As part of the new arrangements, the J.W. branch of the family and the Aldamar group could each nominate three directors, half the board in total. A.J. was already on the board: the other two Aldamar seats were bestowed upon Fred in 1965, followed by David in 1966. Despite her equal ownership position, Martha was left sitting outside in the car again while her brothers roamed the aisles at will. Fred's directorship was granted on top of achieving another position to which Martha could not aspire. In 1963 he was named a dealer at the flagship Yonge and Davenport store, a position where his annual income was hundreds of thousands of dollars a year — far more than most corporate presidents of the era.

Martha yearned to be included, but could participate only vicariously through her brothers. "That's where I began, when my brothers went on the board and I didn't, but I'd hear all the frustrations. 'But why don't you do it this way and why can't we do it that way.' Just why you do what you do when you do it in business to satisfy the customer, to satisfy the corporate needs, the strategies to fit the company together — I began to get hooked on this, but was extremely frustrated because I wasn't allowed."

REORGANIZATION AND MARKET pressures were taking their toll on A.J. Gas wars cut into profits, the devaluation of the Canadian dollar in 1962 caused import costs to soar, and net profit that year was flat at $1.4 million — about the same as the previous year. In 1964 doctors told him that he suffered from stress-related diabetes and warned him that he'd have to step down as president to stand any chance of maintaining his health. "It wasn't that he couldn't cope," declared the *Monetary Times* in its August 1966 edition. "Indeed, A.J. Billes, 63, had been largely responsible for many of the bright merchandising ideas that had kept Toronto-based Canadian Tire Corp. miles ahead of its imitators in recent years (most successful: CTC premium money). Still, Billes figured, it was time for younger blood at the top."[2]

When the board of directors met on June 17, 1965, A.J. told them he was stepping down. During his presidency the number of stores had grown from 149 to 224 and sales had tripled to $100 million. "A.J. was a master of human psychology. That was his real forte. He really

---

2 *Monetary Times*, August 1966, 13.

understood the consumer," said Arch Brown, the Barrie dealer. "He said, Never tell in your advertising all the sales points of a product. Always let the customer find a couple of those things out for themselves. If they find something they didn't expect, it makes them feel good." A.J. now designated Dean Muncaster as the next president. "A.J. realized that there was nobody in the family at that time that could perpetuate his presence," said Brown. "This is one of the signs of greatness of A.J., that he went outside the family. Martha wasn't ready, Fred wasn't stable enough, and David didn't have the interest." Muncaster, by contrast, had exhibited the necessary attributes as he moved easily between his father's Sudbury store and the Toronto boardroom. In 1962, when A.J. took a winter vacation, he asked Muncaster to take over. When A.J. returned, he liked what he saw. There had been no schmozzle with dealers this time.

The laying on of hands by A.J. had continued in 1963, when he made Muncaster vice-president and gave him expanded duties that included warehousing, distribution, data processing, and marketing. The company needed Muncaster's fresh insight and his more modern management style. Much of what had happened in the past at Tire was lackadaisical and haphazard. The company had only two annual promotions, Christmas and summer, yet no one seemed concerned if the June flyer was distributed in July and the featured merchandise didn't arrive in the stores until later.

In 1965 Muncaster was given a free hand by A.J. to bring about change. "He had come to realize that the business had grown beyond one-man leadership and, for it to progress, it was going to have to have an organizational framework," said Muncaster. As part of the new arrangements in the Muncaster regime, a bridge was built between the two branches of the Billes family. Dick, who had left in a huff in 1961, was brought back on the board of directors. He was also given a store, at Kennedy Road and Lawrence Avenue in Toronto's east end, to supplement the annuity from his father's estate. Alex

Barron, who had helped take the company public in 1944 and had resigned from the board in 1962, returned as chairman.

Muncaster tapped his university pals for senior management positions. John Kron, who ran the family trucking business in Kenora, Ont., from 1958 to 1964, was named vice-president, distribution. He had lived in the same rooming house as Muncaster while they attended Western. They became friends and later joined the same fraternity, Delta Upsilon, where they met Richard Hobbs. Hobbs, who had run Tire stores in two Ontario centres, was appointed vice-president, dealer relations. Bill Dawson, the new vice-president of marketing, was equally well known to the new boss. He had been a dealer in Muncaster's home town of Sudbury. The three vice-presidents fashioned themselves as visionaries, replacing the seat-of-the-pants style favoured by A.J. "J.W. was the smart one. He was the one that built the company. A.J. was along for the ride," said Kron. "He did the soft stuff. When J.W. died and A.J. took over, he couldn't handle it. Fortunately, he was smart enough to realize that. Dean started to bring some discipline to the company, some financial acumen, and developed a crew of people that could take the thing through for the next fifteen or twenty years."

Within months of assuming office, Muncaster opened a store in Winnipeg, the first Tire outlet west of Ontario. As he expanded the chain, he added product lines, modernized outlets, and launched a more aggressive marketing campaign. His loose management style allowed his executives their individual freedom and gave them broad powers. "Dean was not particularly involved in the operations of the business. It was Dean's strength and his weakness," said Hobbs. "The three vice-presidents were all wilful, strong people. We ran our areas without a lot of direction. He was the outside guy; he was on a lot of boards of directors." (The blue-ribbon companies came to include Moore Corp., Bell Canada, Renaissance Energy Ltd., Royal Insurance Group, National Trust Co. Ltd., and Steinberg Inc.)

There may have been no place for her in the family business, but Martha was no dutiful, stay-at-home wife. After she married Roger, who was then studying for his PhD in engineering at the University of Toronto, she set out to prove herself professionally. In high school she'd wanted to become a lab technician. Now was her chance to pursue that dream. In 1963 she was hired to work in research and development at Lever Brothers in Toronto. Instead of building her self-confidence, that first job was a dismal failure. There were no walls between the factory where detergent was manufactured and the lab where she worked, so particles floated throughout the building. She arrived in the morning to find every surface covered with a dusting of detergent. Martha had never before been seriously affected by allergies, but she began to develop problems. So much for inheriting helpful genes from her soap-making great-grandfather! First came persistent wheezing that turned into emphysema. Next, water blisters erupted on her skin. After four months, she quit. Her body had become so supersaturated by the environmental toxicity that she couldn't drink instant coffee; she'd developed a reaction to the emulsifiers used in its production. Martha worked next in the biochemistry department at the Ontario Research Foundation, where the surroundings were cleaner. In all, Martha spent two years as a research assistant, but was left with allergies that afflict her still. First home, then school, and now the world of work: Would she not fit anywhere?

Martha could only watch from afar as Muncaster instituted changes at Tire that ranged from the mostly cosmetic to the more fundamental. The fleet of one hundred diesel trucks and trailers was upgraded and washed every day so they functioned as mobile billboards. Cash sales, the favoured transaction of the founders, were no longer as popular with customers, so the company created Canadian Tire Acceptance Corp. to handle credit card purchases.

Tire became the largest retail advertiser in Canada through its newspaper ads, flyers, and catalogues. Muncaster expanded the range of leisure-time goods and added new product categories such as cameras and cookware. Stores grew bigger. In 1971 Tire's largest store ever opened in Oshawa, Ont., with dealer Ken Mann presiding over its 88,000 square feet. Computers replaced the by-guess-or-by-golly approach to predicting sales patterns. Tire developed 90 per cent of its own software and, by 1973, orders were being sent nightly from stores to head office on cassette tapes via telephone lines.

Order filling was a far cry from the days of roller skates. A mechanized distribution centre built in Brampton, Ont., was a model of efficiency. A computer assigned incoming merchandise to specific locations in eighty-foot-high racking. Aisles were half the width of the previous distribution centre in north Toronto, so more goods could be crammed into less floor space. The labour force shrank by two-thirds, but efficiency levels were four times higher. Analysts applauded Muncaster's every move and urged him to even greater heights. "The future of Canadian Tire still looks exceedingly bright, because the present market served by the company is not yet saturated and the direction of expansion appears to be western, which will open up new and large markets," wrote Tony Reid in the *Financial Post*. "Also, with its marketing concept, the company may eventually move into the huge U.S. market."[3]

As Muncaster propelled Tire forward, Martha could not even seem to count on her own mother for help in achieving her ambitions in the family business. Given Martha's belief that her mother was intimately involved with Tire, it should have been simple for Muriel to tell A.J. to include Martha in Tire in the same manner that he had included their two sons. But if Muriel did intervene, she must have been rebuffed because nothing came of any such efforts. "She wanted to [get into the business], but the boys resented her," said Kron. "The more you think about it, it was tragic the way that family became

---

3   *Financial Post*, January 10, 1970.

dysfunctional. I think it was because A.J. spent so much time thinking about the business and not thinking about his family. I guess that was the void that caused some of the emotional problems or dislocation problems."

At Tire, women were regarded as little more than baubles to behold. Dealers who attended the 1965 convention were offered personalized *Playboy* calendars. "Posed for you in living colour . . . and not much else," said the notice. Entertainment included a go-go dancer and a scantily clad woman with performing dogs. By 1971 the atmosphere had not changed. As dealers' wives toured Ontario Place, the newly erected tourist attraction on the Toronto waterfront, their husbands were greeted at the welcoming ceremonies by a bevy of barefooted women in tights. Bill Dawson's marketing presentation featured a model who had been carefully picked for her statuesque 38-25-36 figures. Much was made of her voluptuous measurements because they totaled 99, the same as the coded number used internally by the company to designate promotional merchandise.

A.J. did not seem interested in establishing a dynasty that involved Martha; rather, it seemed as though she had fallen off the family tree. He did, however, concern himself deeply with his own place in the Tire firmament, to the point where he reached back into the past and changed the date of the company's foundation. The startup date for the company had previously been stated as 1913, when J.W. worked at Hamilton Tire and Garage. The 1937–38 catalogue had a silver anniversary designation to mark the twenty-fifth year, and the 1953 catalogue declared that particular year as Tire's fortieth anniversary. The occasion was marked by a special announcement in the company's mailings and a ceremonial lunch on March 25.[4]

But if 1913 was the date of foundation, A.J. had a problem. By that count, Canadian Tire had been started when he was only eleven years

---

4   Ross W. Irwin, ed., *The Charlton Standard Catalogue of Canadian Tire Cash Bonus Coupons* (Toronto: The Charlton Press, 1991), 2.

old. To solve the dilemma, he simply changed the official startup date of Canadian Tire by moving it from 1913 to 1922, the year in which A.J. had joined his brother. Eureka! In 1972 Tire could celebrate its fiftieth birthday fully nineteen years after enjoying its fortieth. And so it was that the 1972 catalogue bore a fiftieth anniversary designation, 1922–72. Not since 1582, when Pope Gregory XIII created a new calendar by eliminating ten days from the month of October, had anyone played so fast and loose with time. A.J. wiped out the first nine years of Tire's corporate history as if they had never existed. By the time Canada Post issued a stamp in 1997 marking Tire's seventy-fifth anniversary, A.J.'s revised version of events had long been accepted as gospel.

Such historical revisionism extended to other matters. In the run-up to the 1972 celebrations, Tire hired William Stephenson to write an authorized history of the company. Stephenson's book about the T. Eaton Co. Ltd., *The Store That Timothy Built*, had been published in 1969, so Stephenson looked like the perfect candidate to bring respect to Canadian Tire in general and renown to A.J in particular.

Stephenson's manuscript never saw the light of day. Muriel was unhappy with what he produced. "It showed Muncaster in a better light than her husband. She bought the manuscript," said Arch Brown. "The agreement with Stephenson was that the Billes family could buy the manuscript if they so desired. Nobody ever thought at the time, including Stephenson, that they would ever exercise that." Brown could see why Muriel suppressed the book; he had been asked to review several sections. "I thought they were quite factual. I didn't think they were very smart politically."

A.J. and Muriel went to great lengths to put the spotlight on A.J., but Martha was kept in the shadows. She was rarely invited to social events involving the family business. "Quite a few years later they decided that there was a daughter in the household and maybe they'd invite me to some of the convention activities, too," Martha said. "I was very, very much missing. I was just ignored." Being an outcast only deepened Martha's devotion to Tire as its corporate logo spread across Canada. "Martha was imbued with the triangle," said Mayne Plowman. "She said, 'As long as I'm alive there's always going to be a Billes as part of Canadian Tire.'"

IN 1965, AT THE AGE of twenty-five, Martha decided to switch careers. Tire's doors were still barred to her, but teachers were in such demand that she left the research lab to enrol in a special co-op program for mature students that included courses and on-the-job teacher training. She graduated from Ontario Teachers College in 1968 and taught grades six, seven, and eight in the east end of Toronto. Martha also did some high school supply teaching in chemistry because she had the necessary experience and accreditation. Dalton and Avogadro had come in handy at last, but she still felt unfulfilled. Teaching was not something she had grown up wanting to do.

The frustration Martha felt about her career was accompanied by continued poor relations with her family. In the late 1960s Muriel decided that she wanted to establish a family compound at Shanty Bay. In her romantic notion, all generations should live in harmony. Siblings would again summer in unison, and grandchildren would grow up swimming, playing, and harvesting vegetables together. To achieve this paradise on earth, Muriel proposed that Martha and her brothers should share the property. The boathouse, dock, and the access road would be communal. Muriel wanted Fred to take the eastern side, Martha would occupy the west, and David would live on the middle piece, get the cottage, and act as the buffer between the two old foes. "She couldn't put the two of them side by side," said David.

David did not warm to his mother's idea. "This was totally unfair because I was getting a good deal, I was getting a built house, and there was a lot of moaning and groaning about that," he said. In addition, he wasn't all that keen for his wife, Donna, and their children to share the cottage with his parents. Fred, who was by then a dealer with his own store, didn't give a hoot about the family property or cottage life. His idea of summer fun was boating on Lake Simcoe or Lake Ontario with Barbara and their children on his fifty-foot cruiser. Even if he had wanted a cottage, he would not settle near Martha. "I just couldn't abide being anywhere near that girl, especially not within walking distance," said Fred.

Martha neither embraced the idea nor strongly opposed it, although she expressed concern about the logistics of how they would share the common amenities. David tossed the whole concept back in his mother's lap. As far as he was concerned, only one of the siblings should own the Shanty Bay property. He told Muriel that she should either designate who that would be or oversee a process whereby they all drew lots and the winner would buy out the other two. Once the diplomat among the three siblings had withdrawn, no amicable solution was possible. With neither David nor Fred interested, Muriel decided to give the property to Martha.

About the same time, Martha's marriage was coming apart. In 1968 Martha and Roger moved to Ottawa, where he taught mechanical engineering at the University of Ottawa. In hopes of saving their marriage, they decided to adopt a child. When Fred heard about the decision, he counselled against it. "She had some problems, not that she was sterile," said Fred. "She had yeast infections, or one of those women's infections, but you cure those, you take the pills and then you go on with your life. The marriage was on the rocks before the kid was adopted. The kid was adopted with the speculation that it might save the marriage."

In April their chosen baby boy arrived. Born February 12, 1970, he was called Owen George after Martha's paternal great-grandparents George Orr and Martha Owen. Martha quit teaching to raise Owen, but, within a year, Roger realized that adoption had been a terrible mistake. "I failed to understand her. I missed it, I guess," he said. "Something turned. She had made a decision, I think, and the decision may have been to raise Owen alone."

Nancy Kerr, Martha's bridesmaid and Mac roommate, was not surprised to hear that the marriage had collapsed. "I'm not sure it was really that great to begin with. It was probably a difficult marriage. I don't think she ever said things verbally to me. I'm pretty good at reading signs, so she wouldn't have to."

Almost thirty years later, Roger Henry, now retired and living in Ottawa, cannot talk about Martha without bile coming to his lips. He has even purged from his memory any details about how the two first met. "It was a regrettable part of my life. It's history for me, and I don't want to go back over any of it anymore. The best day of my life [was] when I was rid of her."

Testy relations continued after the divorce. "My sister wanted Owen to have absolutely nothing to do with his father, even though his father had visiting rights and the son went to live with him for certain periods of time," said David. "There were financial restrictions put on her estate relative to her ex-husband. He was not to have any gain from her estate in the event of her death. Stop and think about what would happen to her son in the event she died. The logical thing is he would go to live with the father. Then supporting the son is supporting the father. [To Martha] that would be an unacceptable advantage. Whenever anything came up about her child and her previous husband, it was like waving a red flag in front of a bull."

MARTHA WAS LED to her next male relationship through the purchase of a dog. In 1970, while she was still married to Roger, she contacted a Toronto couple, Dennis and Casey Gardiner, who bred Kerry Blue Terriers. She made several trips before she was able to select her pup. There were also follow-up visits to learn about grooming and to put the animal through obedience training. At Martha's request, Dennis showed the animal in the puppy class at dog shows.

According to Dennis, his marriage was already over when Martha returned to Toronto in 1971. She lived in a condominium on Steeles Avenue in Toronto's north end, busied herself raising Owen, and acted as a private secretary to her mother. Martha began asking Dennis for help with odd jobs around the house. Soon, they were living together. "Martha has her own way of getting what she wants," said Dennis. "I was not chasing her."

Casey Gardiner, the aggrieved wife, saw events differently. In June 1972 a heartbroken Casey and another dog-breeding friend, Sally Vertulia, travelled together on a holiday to England and France. "It was the worst trip I'd ever had in my life because all I heard day in and day out was 'Dennis and Martha,'" recalled Vertulia. "That was for a month. That was in London, that was in all the trips we made, it was in Paris — it was awful. Martha had a very unsettled life as far as finding the right relationship with somebody."

Dennis was nine years older than Martha, a slender and dashing man who had been born in Ealing, near London. He'd apprenticed as a printer, then emigrated to Canada at twenty-three following service in the British Army. His split with Casey was acrimonious and his divorce was slow in coming, so there was no immediate possibility of marriage. Martha and Dennis lived common-law. After a year on Steeles Avenue they moved to 1511 Pinetree Crescent in Mississauga, a suburban community west of Toronto, where the house had a dog run.

For a time Dennis worked as a lithographer for large printing companies, but increasingly he became Martha's devoted househusband. "Obviously I was in love and obviously I thought she was a very terrific lady and, yes, we were very happy," he said. In a most unusual move for a man of that day or any other, Dennis legally changed his name to Dennis Gardiner-Billes. "To save her some embarrassment," he said, "to save myself some embarrassment. We could keep our names. Her name meant a lot more to her than my name." According to Martha, the name change was not legal at all; it was merely done for passport purposes by filing an affidavit that indicated he had used the name Gardiner-Billes for two years. For her part, Martha took Dennis's surname as a middle name and began referring to herself as Martha Gardiner Billes, without the hyphen that Dennis used.

Just as she had switched partners, Martha also moved from Kerry Blues to Lakeland Terriers. Lakelands originated in the Lake District of northern England, where the dog was developed to hunt and protect sheep from predators, particularly foxes. Lakelands have a wiry coat, stand about fourteen inches high, and are athletic, determined, and tough. It has been said that a dog and its owner often look like each other after they've lived together for a few years. In the case of Martha and her terriers, there are character similarities. Lakelands are serious about pack order; Martha also likes to control. The dogs are indefatigable and can run all day with the horses while hunting foxes; Martha is just as tenacious and persistent. At the end of the hunt, Lakelands burrow into tunnels for the kill. Martha has similarly tough instincts. The world of business is no place for weakness, and Martha would prove to be no ineffectual kitten.

FOUR

THE DOGS
OF WAR

*"Her brothers, and to some degree A.J., put her down
because she was a woman. They used to say
some awful things at times to one another."*
— DICK BILLES, MARTHA'S COUSIN

$\mathscr{M}$artha could not sit back and wait for the business world to
welcome women, nor could she expect to bring about swift
change on her own. At the time, women weren't even well represented in television. Newscasters were mostly male. In 1970 Mary
Tyler Moore played the only female character who was given
anything other than a secondary role. Bea Arthur starred as a thrice-
divorced feminist in *Maude*, which debuted in 1972, but prominence
by a female in entertainment would take a long time to wend its way
into business.

Meanwhile, with her father and brothers keeping her far from the
family firm, Martha had to seek experience elsewhere. The skills she
had learned in the laboratory and the classroom did not fit her for any
management role. Martha did, however, have something that few
other females possessed: wealth. The shares of Canadian Tire that she

owned had been paying an annual dividend since 1958. That income, as well as the proceeds from the sale of some non-voting shares, provided the entree she needed to become an investor. After all, money had no gender.

One of the first projects that caught her attention was equipment leasing for railway construction in British Columbia. Next, she invested in Alberta oil and gas properties. Martha did not want to be a long-distance dabbler, someone who turned her money over blindly to others. She wanted to plunge in, become a full-fledged partner, and be accepted for who she was, not just for the resources she represented. As a result of such thinking, she became a 49 per cent owner of Newmat Drilling (Western) Ltd. She also became a director of Shelter Hydrocarbons Ltd. and Saxon Petroleum Inc., so she could not only have a say about where her money went but also benefit by hearing the insights of others. Martha didn't mind being an apprentice so long as she was appreciated.

For her investments in junior oil and gas companies, Martha established Marlore Enterprises Ltd., a company with a fanciful corporate name devised by using the first three letters of her name plus "lore," which in her mind stood for the story of Martha's oil and gas. To her, business was not just about numbers, important though those were; the world of commerce was also a romantic place that had captured her heart. A.J. had demonstrated his devotion to Tire and she would follow his lead — to love amid the capitalists. Martha also created Albikin Management Inc. for other venture capital investments and named herself president and chief executive officer. As a woman, she knew she had to work harder than any man just to stand a chance to change her life.

Many of Martha's investments were in limited partnerships, a structure devised to reduce personal income taxes as well as produce profits. One such partnership began as a flooring company in Toronto that bought a shell company in western Canada that in turn became an energy firm. While Martha cared about the business plans of such ventures, she was more interested in who was running the company. When it came to betting her money, she was more likely to back the jockey than the horse. "Faith in people" was how Martha described her style. "Some of it flies right up the tube and it's gone. But it's a calculated risk. [You] go in beside them and you're adding your chips with their chips and hopefully it'll succeed. A lot of them are failures, but some of them are winners."

The process was a learning experience. Martha listened carefully when geologists talked about the likelihood of finding oil in a certain area or when management reported on specifics, such as the ability to tie in with an existing pipeline. "You don't tell a geologist where he's going to drill a hole, so in that respect [I was] quite silent," said Martha. "But on structuring deals and choosing prospects I would often have a voice, along with other people of course, as to whether we drilled in this section or that section. There are business decisions to be made and I would be part of those, but once made, back right off."

As Martha's oil and gas investments grew in value, they consumed more of her time, and that meant an increasing number of round trips between Toronto and Calgary. In 1978 Martha decided that she, Dennis, and Owen should move to Calgary, where she could keep a closer eye on her financial holdings. She also hoped the cleaner western air would alleviate her allergies. Martha wasn't the first child of a strong father to flee from that towering presence. Like a lot of offspring who have grown up in the household of a strong man, she wanted her own place in the sun.

With 2,000 miles and two time zones separating her from A.J. and the family business, Martha felt free to act independently and, with any luck, achieve results that might eventually meet with his approval. Meanwhile, if she made a few mistakes due to inexperience, she wouldn't feel A.J. was watching over her shoulder, clucking his tongue. Her judgment was so good that Marlore's annual cash flow grew to between $1 million and $2 million. (While most of her investments from that era are long gone, she has remained involved with Universal Explorations Ltd., a company with oil-producing properties in Saskatchewan. In 2000 the Martha Billes Family Trust purchased 44,000 flow-through shares of Sunfire Energy Corp. at $2.25 each.)

In 1980 Martha and Dennis began to discuss marriage. "She had been advised by her legals that she was wide open if anything happened to our association, that I would claim half her estate, so it behove her to get us married and sign a marriage contract," said Dennis. "That was all brought up at the same time. Yes, I did do it, and, yes, I didn't think twice about it because I wasn't after her money anyway. It meant nothing to me."

Fred, who arrived in Calgary that summer to borrow Martha's mobile home for a vacation with his family, was the first family member to hear about the wedding plans. He had previously told Martha that, after her experience with Roger, she should never marry again. Fred saw no reason to change his mind; he didn't like Dennis. He urged Martha to reconsider her decision and remain in a common-law relationship. Fred was not alone in his distaste for Dennis. "Dennis was a real wimp," said Mayne Plowman. "I don't know how the hell she ever tied in with him to start with."

When Fred returned the mobile home after his holiday, he found Martha still resolute about marrying Dennis. Fred's counsel had no more been heeded than his warning against adoption ten years earlier. The wedding went ahead on September 26, 1980. Since he was already in Calgary, Fred attended the ceremony despite his opposition. "They were happy and it worked. As soon as they got married, they weren't happy and it didn't work," said Fred. "Familiarity breeds contempt."

David served as one of two trustees overseeing Martha's estate for Owen. David believed that if Martha died, Dennis, as her new husband, would have a claim on the estate that he wouldn't have had as a live-in, but neither Fred nor Martha bothered to tell David about her change in marital status. David eventually heard about the marriage by accident when Fred made a passing comment about Martha and her husband.

"You mean her live-in?" said David.

"No, her husband," replied Fred.

"They're not married," insisted David.

"Yes, they are."

David was incredulous. "Seriously?"

When David confronted Martha with his new-found knowledge, she just shrugged the whole thing off. "Oh yeah," she said, acknowledging her marriage to Dennis as if it were no big deal. Martha's disregard for the niceties of family life amazed David. "Boy, did that shake me up," he said. "[Fred] just found out because he was in the area. I found out a couple of years later." Beyond the normal courtesies, David was upset because, as a trustee, he should have been informed there was now a stepfather. "She is secretive [and] does not discuss her inner thoughts, at least to me. I have no explanation."

For all her success as an investor living in Calgary, Martha continued to be denied her most fervent desire — a seat on the Tire board of directors. Fred had been appointed in 1965 when he was thirty. David joined him on the board the following year when he was only twenty-eight. On several occasions in the 1970s she asked her brothers to establish a rotation system so she might take a turn sharing one of their two seats. They consistently refused.

Nor did Martha receive support for her goal from the corporate hierarchy. Their prejudiced views were not kept hidden, but were voiced directly. "Alex Barron was the chairman of the board," said Martha. "Alex Barron had thoughts about where Martha should remain and he expressed them to me quite openly." Members of management also opposed Martha's presence in the boardroom. "I never wanted Martha on the board," said vice-president Richard Hobbs, a director from 1966 to 1979. "I felt she didn't understand the business; she'd never been involved in the business." But Hobbs had another reason that had nothing to do with her business acumen. He feared being overpowered by her personality. "I knew that she was pretty headstrong. This probably says a lot more about me than anything else; I always felt more nervous with the female members of the Billes family than I did with the men. Maybe it was because they were smarter. I'd pick Martha over Fred any time."

Denied a place inside the tent, Martha would lob embarrassing questions from the floor at the annual shareholder meetings. "She had a real concern about the company," said George Hartman, a brokerage firm analyst who began following Tire in 1969. "Dean would always look perturbed. She was a member of the family; you're not supposed to make the company look bad. The impression I had was that she was a shrill woman who didn't have the manners to do it privately."

Dean Muncaster appeared to need no scolding from Martha or anyone else. During his first decade in office, annual sales increased from $100 million to $600 million as he expanded the chain in Quebec, Manitoba, and Saskatchewan, reaching Alberta in 1975. By 1976 the empire had 260 stores, and sales were growing by 20 per cent a year. Such success could not last forever. "If anyone had a secret for turning grease into gold, it was Canadian Tire Corp. Ltd.," wrote Gillian Mackay in the *Globe and Mail*. "For nearly two decades, the Toronto-based company raced ahead at top speed, building one of the most profitable store chains on the strength of Canada's love affair with the automobile. Canadian Tire dealers became millionaires and the palace of grease was high on the list of Canadian growth stocks. Then, in 1977, the unthinkable happened and Canadian Tire came through without a profit increase. Suddenly the company that could do no wrong was doing nothing right. Its stores were either too big or too small, prices were up when they should have been down, the product mix was wrong and the advertising was out of date."[1]

Profits suffered for the next three years. Tire had overshot demand in the marketplace by building too many stores that were too large. Dealer profitability declined. In response, A.J. urged a bonus arrangement for the dealers. Hobbs did not agree and felt he received no support from Muncaster for his stance. "I didn't think that Dean was doing the job he should," said Hobbs. "He wasn't combative in any way. He wasn't prepared to go to the board or A.J. and make any demands." Hobbs quit in 1979 and later became president and CEO of MacLeod-Stedman Inc. of Winnipeg, a retailer of five hundred stores operating in small communities. Bill Dawson, vice-president, marketing, also left his management job to go and run a Canadian Tire store in Toronto. Internal strife was depleting management resources.

A.J. COULD DO NOTHING about the downward slide in Canadian Tire. It had been almost fifteen years since he'd handed power over to Muncaster. Even though Muriel's health was deteriorating, he continued to go to the office every day, mostly to promote his profit-sharing ideas. By June 1979 his wife was bedridden, cared for by household staff. She died at home on August 13, 1979.

In her will, Muriel left $6 million to her nine grandchildren. The estate was divided into three equal parts — *per stirpes* is the legal term, by the root, meaning that one-third of the total went to the offspring of each of Martha, Fred, and David, irrespective of how many children there were. As a result, Owen inherited $2 million, David and Donna's three children shared another $2 million portion, and Fred and Barbara's five split $2 million. The money was placed in trust funds for their benefit.

---

1   *Globe and Mail*, July 16, 1979, B3.

Without Muriel, A.J. was bereft. He dismissed the household staff and tried to live on his own, but at seventy-seven he couldn't so much as boil an egg. He fed himself potato sandwiches from an ancient refrigerator that seemed incapable of maintaining food in a safe state. Within a few months A.J. moved in with Fred and Barbara; the house at 24 Old Forest Hill was sold for $400,000.

Muriel's death, followed by A.J.'s household move, seemed to precipitate a change in A.J.'s thinking about Martha's place in the family business. In 1980 Martha was due to turn forty. Some women who are childless have a biological clock that starts ticking louder when they're in their mid-thirties. Martha had a boardroom clock that had been sending off alarms for years. In the process of yielding to Martha's long-standing demands, A.J. employed extraordinary measures. He resigned his board seat in 1980 and designated Martha to be his replacement as a director of Canadian Tire. "Martha was quite insistent," said Fred Sasaki, vice-president, finance and treasurer. "Martha wanted to be on the board. I guess she was that persuasive."

A.J.'s resignation was the only way he could be certain that Martha would enter the inner sanctum. "The number of positions was fixed and there were agreed-to relationships between the various parties — the two families and the dealers," said David. "In order to bring one on in any one group, somebody had to go off or all the parties had to change. At that point in time it was not an easy thing to do." Others argue that the rules governing the makeup of the board were not quite so rigorous. "If A.J. had taken a strong position on it, she'd have been on the board," said Hobbs. "In those days we deferred to A.J. about a lot of things, more than probably we should have."

Marion Stone, who was both a family friend and a cousin to Muriel, understood the dilemma with which A.J. had wrestled all those years. "Maybe he could see the little devil in her at a very early age and therefore he wanted to keep that out of the business," she said. "Maybe she was so prohibited from doing what she wanted to do that it made her that much more aggressive. There was a certain role for her to play and that was it. When she was old enough to rebel, did she do it with a vengeance!"

Fred was aghast when A.J. told him of his plan to make Martha a director. "I tried to influence him not to do it because it was war," said Fred. "It turned out exactly that way and it makes a difference to the company to this day." Fred quoted to his father the famous line from Shakespeare's *Julius Caesar*, the declaration by Mark Antony immediately after Caesar's assassination: "Cry havoc and let slip the dogs of war."

NOW THAT MARTHA HAD the same power as her brothers, she had a platform to gain power over Tire. On her analysis, David was a pushover. His interest in Canadian Tire was so limited that he didn't even want his photo to appear in the annual report. Individual pictures of his fellow directors appeared in the five years 1976 through 1980. David was always listed with the designation, "Missing from directors' photos."

Martha had no such qualms. After so long a wait, she wanted the world to know she had arrived. Her photo in the 1980 annual report showed her in an open-necked blouse and a string of pearls. Her oversized glasses were stylishly large as she stared off camera in the manner of her graduation photo. She used her full name, Martha Gardiner Billes. Her corporate affiliation was listed as president, Marowe Investment Corp., one of her many investment holding companies.

As for A.J., Martha sought to make him her ally. After all, A.J. might have stepped down from the board, but his power remained. He continued to attend all board meetings and sat at the table with the other directors as he always had. "While he may not have voted, once he expressed an opinion it had a lot of persuasion behind it," said

David. "He may have ended up with more control rather than less."

Martha found ways to gain A.J.'s support and play to his fears. Canadian Tire had grown to 327 dealers and $1 billion in sales, but there were some trouble spots, such as British Columbia, where the small-store concept was not working well. "If we had a chance to do our B.C. stores over again, we would build larger stores using our Calgary mode," Muncaster admitted.[2] Another problem was developing in Australia, where Tire had expanded in 1979 after management became convinced that growth in Canada was reaching its limit. Debates about a possible location for foreign growth had persisted for years at Canadian Tire and Australia had always been a favourite candidate. Like Canada, its citizens spoke the same dominant language, the country was large and sparsely populated, and there was the Commonwealth connection. Never mind that it took almost two days to get there by plane.

Martha was aware that A.J. had opposed setting up shop in Australia. For him, the heavily unionized workforce in that country didn't fit with his views on employee profit-sharing, but his only first-hand knowledge came from a holiday cruise he'd taken there with Muriel. In the end, however, management made a convincing case, the board approved, and in 1979 Canadian Tire bought a 10 per cent interest (later increased to 36 per cent) in McEwan's Ltd., Australia's largest hardware dealer, with annual sales of about $150 million. After Tire had made that initial investment, but before Martha joined the board, father and daughter talked about his concerns. As a result of their conversation, Martha made a flying five-day visit to investigate McEwan's for herself. "I didn't like what I saw," she said. "I didn't feel that they were running anything like Canadian Tire. It was quite loosey-goosey. We'd been in it for a while then and it just wasn't coming up to snuff. You could talk to the people and it was not tomorrow

---

2   *Executive*, February 1982, 27.

or the next day; it was kind of like next week or next month would be OK to think about something, rather than implementation. It was very stagnated. It needed a lot more than we could offer from the distance and the level [of investment] we were offering. We needed [to buy] the balance of the investment or get out."

Fred also visited Australia and brought back photographs of McEwan's to show directors what he regarded as poorly maintained stores. As Muncaster watched the boardroom scene, he bit his tongue and kept quiet. "My regret was that I didn't have a similar stack of pictures of Fred's store," said Muncaster. "There were a lot of folks from downtown who had the idea that's the way we thought Canadian Tire should be run. It was just out of control, [but] he was Fred Billes, a big shareholder."

In the end, Martha's unhappiness and Fred's manner were irrelevant to the outcome of McEwan's. Australia's Foreign Investment Review Board denied Tire's attempt to exercise an option that would have given Tire control of McEwan's. In 1982 Tire sold its minority interest in McEwan's and quit the country. Muncaster had been wounded by the failed Australian foray and Martha smelled blood. "Martha grabbed that one and made it her cause célèbre," said Muncaster. "Anytime that Canadian Tire was going to look differently than what the mould had been that her father had cast, that caused her a problem. The whole idea of going international was something that she had difficulty with. She wanted it to remain the business that she thought she understood."

Undaunted by defeat, Muncaster proposed another acquisition: White Stores Inc. of Wichita Falls, Texas. On paper, Whites looked like Canadian Tire. Whites held long-term leases on eighty-one stores and acted as a wholesaler to another four hundred independently owned stores in Texas and a dozen other sunbelt states, such as Oklahoma, New Mexico, and Louisiana. Stores were about the same size as Tire's, at 25,000 square feet, with six to eight service bays. The chain had sales of US$150 million a year in household and hardware items, lawn and garden products, sporting and automotive goods. The United States was so close geographically and Whites looked like such a certain success that, in 1982, Martha and the board approved the US$48 million acquisition and announced plans to spend another US$45 million to refurbish stores and update inventory systems.

During her first few years as a director, Martha failed to win over the old hands. "I wasn't impressed with her, frankly," said Fred Sasaki, who was not a director, but had attended all board meetings since 1960 in his capacity as treasurer. "She seemed to be against what management wanted to do. She had a critical attitude."

Martha's arrival as a director changed the dynamic of the meetings. When the board gathered, the sessions were meant to be the place where management presented its ideas and strategies for debate, discussion, and approval. Martha tended to spend too much time on topics that drove Muncaster and the other members of management to distraction. "It was her insensitivity, her lack of interest in other people, those sorts of things were her shortcomings, not her intellectual capability," said Muncaster. "She's abrasive. She complained about the air quality in the boardroom, just going up one side [of me] and down the other. 'You guys ought to provide better accommodation,'" he recalled her saying as she pounded her fist on the table. In fact, in 1973 Tire had moved its head office from the long-time location above the main store to an office tower further north on Yonge Street. "I thought it was a pretty good office building. In the other place, there probably would have been some merit in [her complaint], but she wasn't around then."

Martha's style as a board member paralleled that of politicians who rely on slim pieces of anecdotal evidence to make sweeping conclusions. She once complained about the poor quality of paint she'd bought in a store, suggesting that this example could reflect a serious problem throughout the organization. After numerous tests were conducted, it came out that she had bought the paint from a clearance table. The contents were beyond the product's normal shelf life. In another typical intervention, Martha reported that she had visited a dealer who told her about a late shipment. "Those are the kinds of things that happen in an organization that's dealing with tens of thousands of products," said Muncaster. As far as he was concerned, the board should deal with more important matters. "It's the kind of thing that aggravates people."

Fred blamed A.J. for putting Martha on the board in the first place. "He knew she was a heller and she performed as a heller." Dick Billes watched the family conflict at the board meetings with dismay, but empathized with Martha. "Her brothers, and to some degree A.J., put her down because she was a woman. She was fighting and trying to establish herself as a woman in industry," he explained. "There was this conflict where her brothers didn't want her there, I could tell that. They used to say some awful things at times to one another, some really bad things. They'd say just petty things, put-down things. I can just remember how unfair I thought the whole thing was. They were building the conflict that was going to end up the way it has."

Martha, her brothers, and her father had only to be in the same room for a few minutes before there was some sort of explosion. "The whole 'fam damily' was on the board," said Kron. "David was his own man. He was a gentleman throughout. He kept a low profile, but when he said something, it was worth listening to. Fred tended to be bombastic and very aggressive. Martha, in my opinion, is the epitomization of the word 'shrew,'" he added.

Whatever the issue, real or imagined, most of the negativity towards Martha flowed from the fact that she was a woman in a man's world, doing what men do. In some cases she did it better than any man, so they felt threatened by a force they did not understand. "Her strength, or her weakness, I guess, [was] she did all her manoeuvring behind the scenes," said Kron. In that regard, Muncaster saw that

Martha was cut from the same cloth as her father. "He liked to see quite a bit of conflict around him. When A.J. had something in mind, he'd go after it very hard. She's clearly that same way. They want to be winners, maybe not at any cost, but at considerable cost. She has to win."

The divided nature of the board after Martha's appointment was illustrated by the 1983 annual report. In any company, directors should offer savvy oversight of management's plans. A chief executive officer should even be made to feel that his undated resignation is always on the boardroom table, so directors can demand top performance. But directors and management must work cooperatively. At Tire, increasingly, there were two camps: Martha and the family on one side and everyone else on the other. Even the photograph in the annual report that year seemed to reflect that divide. On the left-hand page were Martha, A.J., her brothers, and their faithful retainer, general counsel Robin Law. On the right-hand page were Dean Muncaster, Alex Barron, John Kron, A.H.D. Crooks (a Tire dealer), and A.L. Sherring (a former National Trust executive).

OUTSIDE THE BOARDROOM, Martha was an activist director. In the early 1980s many directors of public companies did little or no homework. They simply attended board meetings, spoke their minds infrequently, and dined contentedly on a free lunch. Martha was not that sort of do-nothing steward; she desired first-hand knowledge. She cruised through Texas in her mobile home with Dennis and Owen in tow, visiting stores just as her father had done. This time, however, she was the one who went in and talked to the dealers. Dennis was the also-ran. "She was quite obviously the leader in the pair," said Kron.

Martha also visited stores in Canada, but she was not well known in the trenches. Steve Groch ran a store in Saskatoon when Martha showed up unannounced in 1984. "She walked into my office. I didn't recognize her," said Groch. "I assumed she was trying to sell something." Martha did not introduce herself, even though she must have known that Groch was baffled about her identity. A few awkward seconds passed before Groch finally realized who she was. The incident became a standing joke between the two. When Groch was named a dealer representative on the board in 1986, he assumed he was picked over other possible candidates because Martha had previously met him.

Martha promoted the presence of other women on the board and sought their help. Jean Pigott, chair of Morrison Lamothe Inc., an Ottawa-based family baking business, was named a director in 1984, but resigned after a few months to take a position in the office of the newly elected prime minister, Brian Mulroney. In 1985 Martha succeeded in having two women appointed to the board: Maureen Sabia, a lawyer, and Lynne Hall, president and chief executive of F.S.G. International. "It was a private agenda of Martha's and that was all done behind the scenes," said Kron. "Dean and Alex went along with it primarily to shut her up."

Sabia took her cue from Martha's hands-on style and spent two weeks in a store to learn about the business. Unlike Martha, who grew up in a household where she was supposed to know her place, Sabia had been encouraged to get involved in debates with her parents. Her mother, Laura, was the founding president of the National Action Committee on the Status of Women, and her father, Michael, was a surgeon. "I'm quite comfortable being a minority of one," said Sabia. "It has cost me in my career by making me less attractive to a lot of people. I can be arrogant. I'm not everybody's cup of tea. I am not a compromising person. I'm already a freak in a society obsessed with mediocrity. It's who I am and it adds to my courage. It gets you noticed, not always to your advantage." Sabia, who was a year younger than Martha, became both a firm friend and a useful foil for

Martha. She also offered proof to their fellow directors that there were other competent women in the world in addition to Martha. "Men were not used to women as competitors. They were used to them as nurturers and companions," says Sabia. "I'm a change agent, which makes me unattractive in many quarters because a lot of institutions want persons who do not rock boats. I rock boats." Among the directors aboard the good ship Tire, only Martha and Maureen revelled in the turbulence they caused.

MARTHA'S FIRST MAJOR FIGHT over ownership of Canadian Tire showed her capacity to forge whatever alliance was needed to achieve her goals. Despite a lifetime of feuding with Fred, Martha made common cause with both Fred and David to buy the shares that had been owned by the J.W. Billes branch of the family. By so doing, Martha helped to create the control block of shares that she alone owns today.

Martha's manoeuvrings began in the late 1970s when some of the charities that had been bequeathed shares in Tire after the death of J.W. became concerned that they had too much money tied up in one investment. In 1979 the Toronto Humane Society took the lead by officially requesting the freedom to sell its shares in Tire. Initially, none of the trustees — National Trust, J.W.'s widow, Gladys, and their son Dick, a director and dealer — agreed with the demand. By late 1980, however, National Trust believed that selling was appropriate. Dick was unhappy about the prospect of losing what little say he had. He and Gladys continued to oppose any change in the arrangements. "[He] has been close to Canadian Tire all his life. He and his family just hate to sell Canadian Tire. It is like selling the old family mare off on the farm,"[3] said J.J. Robinette, the lawyer who was acting for National Trust.

---

3   *Globe and Mail*, May 27, 1983.

At first, Martha and her brothers could do nothing about the impasse, which finally went before the Supreme Court of Ontario. On June 15, 1983, Mr. Justice John Holland ruled that the charities could sell their holdings. By then, the values involved had seen phenomenal growth. J.W. had left an estate worth $6.2 million in 1956. Even after disbursing $2.6 million for debts, taxes, and executors' compensation, plus a further $3.4 million in payments to his widow and their children, the value of the shares that made up the estate had grown to $51.6 million in 1983. If Martha, Fred, and David could put their shares together with the J.W. holdings, that would total 61 per cent of the voting shares and give them control of the company. The next largest shareholder was the employee profit-sharing plan, with 12 per cent, followed by the dealers, who had 9 per cent.

The ruling generated immediate interest from an outsider buyer, Imasco Ltd., which was controlled by B.A.T. Industries, the British tobacco giant. Imasco, owners of Shoppers Drug Mart and Imperial Tobacco Ltd., offered $1.1 billion for all the shares of Canadian Tire, voting and non-voting alike.

Once the Imasco bid was announced, trading in shares of both Imasco and Canadian Tire was halted for three days, awaiting official response. Martha rejected the Imasco bid on behalf of herself and her brothers. "The Billes family (which also holds 30 per cent) intend to exercise their right to purchase the voting trust certificates when they become available," she said in a prepared statement. "The 60-year-old Canadian Tire Corp. philosophy, the sharing of toil and profit, has evolved a unique Canadian corporate family from a small family store. Employees have become owners. First-, second-, and third-generation Canadian Tire Corp. 'family' members are working together within the corporate structure," said Martha.[4] "Our goal

---

4   *Globe and Mail*, May 27, 1983.

is to stay with Canadian Tire, to watch and help it grow. That has always been our intention, and hopefully it always will be," she told the *Financial Post*.[5]

Martha's opposition did not deter Paul Paré, chairman of Imasco. He ordered the offer mailed to Tire shareholders, hoping they would put pressure on the family. Martha remained unmoved. "I'm not interested in his offer, whether it be friendly or unfriendly. I'm in there for keeps," she said. "I'm not interested in money. I'm interested in the corporation. [N]o outside takeover would make me happy in any way."[6]

Martha and her brothers were supported by senior management, which announced that it was rejecting Imasco's bid. The trustees of the employee profit-sharing plan and the dealers also closed ranks behind Martha, Fred, and David, fearing that Imasco might upset their lives and their livelihood.

The Imasco bid made two things clear. First, A.J. still had power over his offspring, although this would be his last hurrah. He was able to keep Martha, Fred, and David together by exercising his moral authority. "The dealers rejected the offer after they were assembled by A.J. Billes," said Paré. "He was called into the fray and said to the employees and dealers, 'Let's stay as a family.'"[7] Imasco abandoned its bid. Second, the Imasco bid briefly pulled back the cloak to reveal something of the behaviour of Martha and her brothers. For all their stated dislike of conglomerates such as Imasco and their jingoistic patriotism about not wanting the company to be owned by a foreigner, Martha and her brothers didn't take into account the Class A shareholder, those without a vote. At least the Imasco bid included an offer to buy the same proportion of non-voting shares as it was able

5 *Financial Post*, June 25, 1983.
6 *Globe and Mail*, June 23, 1983.
7 *Maclean's*, January 26, 1987, 29.

to buy of the common (voting) shares from various members of the Billes clan.

With Imasco out of the running, the court ruling meant that the 1,050,000 voting shares from J.W.'s estate could go up for auction. Under this approach, non-voting shareholders did not participate or benefit. There was no question that Martha, Fred, and David would bid for the shares, if only to protect their position. "It could have been the end game," said Fred. "If those shares had been bought by somebody else, our shares would have been worthless, or certainly downgraded. We had our interests to protect."

As they prepared for battle, Martha and her brothers signed an agreement on July 20, 1983, which said that if any of the three decided to sell his or her individual holdings, that person had to offer the shares to each of the other two first, before going outside the family.

David was the least interested in buying the J.W. estate shares, but he went along with Martha and Fred. "I made an agreement that I would put up a third of the securities and the cash to do it on the understanding that I would only support it as long as my sister and my brother were involved," said David. "If one or the other dropped out, I was out, because I felt together their two opposites combined had real force, knowledge, the right combination. Neither one of them alone was the right person to manage Canadian Tire."

Dick, J.W.'s son, had the behind-the-scenes backing of Dean Muncaster and Alex Barron, who helped him arrange bank financing for his competing bid. Barron and Muncaster preferred the three-legged balancing act of the two families and the dealers over one dominant owner. This support riled Martha, David, and Fred, who felt that such favouritism — particularly when it helped their family foe — was tantamount to back-stabbing.

On October 3, 1983, all the bidders gathered in the downtown offices of a Toronto law firm designated to oversee the auction.

Through Aldamar, Martha, Fred, and David bid $63 a share, Dick bid $64, and the employee profit-sharing plan bid $65. Once the initial positions were established, Aldamar proceeded to top the other two with a bid of $73 a share, a total of $76.7 million. Dick couldn't bid any higher because he'd reached his limit on the loan he'd arranged, and he didn't have the same personal financial resources that they possessed. Martha and her brothers were victorious. Combining J.W.'s 30.4 per cent of Tire's voting shares with their similar holding gave them 60.9 per cent and absolute control. No follow-up bid was required to other shareholders, voting or non-voting, declared the Ontario Securities Commission, because there had been no change of control.

Martha, Fred, and David won; Dick Billes had lost. "The Dick Billes thing was a travesty," said Richard Hobbs. "He ended up on the outside looking in and was never allowed to get back in. That was a shame because, of all the family members, I had more respect for Dick than any of them. As difficult as it was for him on a personal basis, that he was not able to stay in management because of A.J. and the family, I think he handled himself very well. He handled himself like a gentleman." The charities got what they wanted: cash. After taxes and legal fees, $13 million flowed to University of Toronto; $5 million to the United Way, the Hospital for Sick Children, and the Canadian Mothercraft Society; $4 million to the Canadian Red Cross, the Salvation Army, Bloorview Children's Hospital, the Boy Scouts of Canada, and the Ontario Society for Crippled Children; and $2 million or less went to each of the other fourteen organizations and institutions. J.W.'s wife, Gladys, and their three children — Gwen, John, and Dick — shared 5 per cent of the proceeds of the sale, or about $4 million.

Martha wrote to the employees in an attempt to reassure them that she and her brothers intended "to continue a policy of leaving the day-to-day operations with management. You can be assured that control of Canadian Tire remains unchanged; if anything, it is solidified."[8]

It certainly was. Control of Canadian Tire was now in the hands of Martha, Fred, and David. That silly old Dick, the cousin nobody liked from the other side of the family, had been dispatched. Forever.

---

8 *Financial Post*, October 15, 1983.

FIVE

THE POWER
OF ONE

"Martha had an incredible need to be loved.
At that time, women were emerging as individuals,
but they weren't taken very seriously."
— JEAN PIGOTT

With the auction over and ownership secure, Martha and her brothers now had to pay for their purchase. They proposed a share split, which meant that each voting share became one voting and five non-voting shares, or six shares in all. Canadian Tire had previously issued non-voting shares as a way of raising money from the public for its capital needs. This technique, followed by other Canadian companies with dual share structures, such as Magna Inc. or Rogers Communications Inc., does not change the ownership balance. In this case, however, the effect of "splitting" each voting share into one voting share and five non-voting shares was to create value for the holders of the voting shares (namely, Martha, Fred, and David) out of thin air. They'd be left with the same number of voting shares, plus a flotilla of new non-voting shares with immediate worth.

To convince the board and the non-voting shareholders that this fancy arabesque was in everyone's interest, Martha and her brothers promised that non-voting shareholders would participate in any subsequent takeover bid for the company. "Takeover protection (not presently enjoyed) will be granted to the A shareholders in the event of a sale by our family of a controlling interest in the Corporation resulting in a follow-up obligation to all common shareholders," the siblings said in a letter of undertaking to Muncaster. "We believe this is an extremely valuable addition to the rights of the Class A shareholders and will be well received by the market." Muncaster and Barron didn't like the family's plan, but they welcomed the idea of protecting the Class A non-voting shareholders. The arrangement, known in investing parlance as a "coat-tail," meant that if the Billeses sold out at some point in the future, the non-voting shareholders tagged along and also received the benefit of the higher share price.

Negotiations with the family to preserve the coat-tail meant that the share split was altered. Each voting share became one voting share and four non-voting shares, while every non-voting share was split five-for-one. The family also agreed to a board where the majority of the directors were independent of the family. The immediate impact was a windfall for Martha, Fred, and David. Their 2.1 million voting shares became 2.1 million voting shares *plus* 8.4 million new non-voting shares. These new shares, which hadn't existed before, could now be sold on the open market without in any way changing their powerful position as controlling shareholders. They sold five million of those non-voting shares and raised $58 million towards the $76.7 million they had paid for control. The money was in the deal. Easy money, Canadian Tire money, you might call it. Equally important, the creation of the 61 per cent control block meant that it was now possible to see the day when one powerful person could rule the kingdom on her own.

⮾

WITH MARTHA STRONGER than she had ever been before, Muncaster feared that his world would be forever changed. "Seeing this institution going under the auctioneer's gavel was a very strange sensation," said Muncaster. "There was some degree of consternation with the way things were going. There were quite a few people who thought that this thing had worked pretty well for a long time, having two sides of the family with control. They were apprehensive what the outcome would be after the Aldamar group had absolute control."

The first casualty under the new regime was Canadian Tire's chairman, Alex Barron. He had backed the wrong horse in supporting Dick, and he made matters worse by constantly reminding Martha, Fred, and David that he did not approve of their tactics. "He was grumbling and griping," said David. "When you have a chairman of the board who is sniping at what's gone on and making snide remarks, that's not comfortable. [He said] that it was inappropriate to finance the deal the way we financed it."

As far as Martha and her brothers were concerned, there was nothing nefarious or unfair about their actions in creating new non-voting shares for themselves. "We didn't invent the concept," said David. "There was complete disclosure. The shares were used for the purposes set up by the founding shareholders. The whole concept as it was explained to me was that, in the event that one of them died, the other would have a means of buying them out."

The siblings were fed up with what they saw as Barron's obstinate insubordination, so they fired the man who had been present at the creation of the modern Canadian Tire when the company had gone public in 1944. It was an ignominious end to an illustrious career. "It was not personal, it was not vindictive, it was just a disagreement on some concepts, how the company should be managed," said David. Others saw the action differently. "Fred and Martha had concluded that Alex was not as sympathetic to what they saw for the relationship between the family and the company," said Hugh Macaulay, who had just completed a four-year term as chairman of Ontario Hydro before being named to replace Barron as chairman of Tire. "At a time like that it's easy for the three offspring to feel it's sort of 'them and us.'" There was little anyone could do about the power putsch. "Alex Barron was a real gentleman, a classic chairman, and a classic businessman with a capital B, above reproach, morally and ethically, and they decided to turf him," said John Kron, a director and officer.

Martha and her brothers stopped short of firing Dean Muncaster at the same time. "They felt the same way about Dean, but he was almost indispensable to the activities of the company," said Macaulay. "They tried to work with Dean and he tried to work with them and we all tried to make it work." Muncaster's public profile had become even more prominent since the days of the laudatory Stephenson manuscript in 1972. Muncaster was given all the credit for the success of Tire, leaving no plaudits for anyone bearing the Billes name. He was regularly interviewed in the media and was always shown grinning like the Cheshire cat. In addition to his outside boards, he was also a member of the Young Presidents Organization, a prestigious group limited to executives who had made their mark before turning forty.

Muncaster had transformed the family business beyond recognition in the time since A.J. had hand-picked him almost two decades earlier. When Muncaster became president, the 12,000 square foot Sudbury outlet run by his father was the largest in the company. By 1984 most outlets were twice that size; some of them ran to 40,000 square feet. Muncaster had also diversified the product mix. In the 1960s, 50 per cent of the inventory was auto parts and accessories; twenty years later two-thirds of all goods were hardware, household, or leisure-time items, a transformation aimed at attracting more female shoppers.

Along the way Muncaster had also altered the relationship between head office and the dealers. When Canadian Tire expanded to British

Columbia in 1980, for example, Tire did not set out to find ten dealers for the first ten stores. Instead, two dealers were designated as master owners of all ten locations, with the expectation that the number of stores would double under their stewardship. Distribution arrangements were also unique. Muncaster argued that transportation costs from central Canada made supplying individual stores too expensive, so all the new outlets were fed from a single 60,000-square-foot warehouse in Burnaby. Just-in-time shipping meant that individual stores didn't need as much storage space, so each store could be as small as 10,000 to 13,000 square feet. A similar approach was followed on Vancouver Island, where a 53,000-square-foot distribution centre was built in Victoria in 1981 to serve an initial group of four stores.

Martha, Fred, and David chafed at Muncaster's methods. "They were concerned about breaking the mould, with some justification. It was an unusual step," admitted Muncaster. Still, he was riled by the rigidity in the family's thinking. "If it was different, they were likely to be against it."

With Muncaster regarded as untouchable — for the time being — Fred and Martha were forced to exert their influence elsewhere, so in December 1983 they reorganized the board. Cousin Dick and Robin Law were ousted and seven new directors were elected. Now Martha and her brothers could put people in place who were more amenable to the family's views.

With the auction over, Martha's power began to increase. "There was a widespread assumption that Fred would be the leader if there was to be a leader of the three siblings," said Macaulay. "But Martha is a very strong personality, with some very strong ideas of her own, and also with a feeling that she had not had the opportunity that the two boys had to become involved in the business, particularly Fred, and was determined to see that she did." Despite Martha's obvious talents, some of the male board members tried to limit her involvement. "She was always underrated by Macaulay and the boys," said

Jean Pigott. "Martha had an incredible need to be loved. At that time, women were emerging as individuals, but they weren't taken very seriously. She had a vision. She understood the franchise. Martha has a gut feeling about making a deal. She liked business; she enjoyed business. She had a shrewdness to her that I think was genetic — it came from the old man." But Pigott was also well aware that family businesses have their own specific perils and special pitfalls. "I come from a family business," she said. "There's nothing new under the sun in a family business. Either you are happy and perfectly content to be part of a family and take the good with the bad or you rebel. I've seen that so many times."

Yet for all Martha's abiding interest in Tire and her celebration of the company's heritage, she did not seem interested in passing along her love of the business to her son, Owen. In his younger years, Owen was kept blissfully unaware of his familial link to Tire. The closest he came to figuring out the connection was through the Cadillacs owned by his grandfather A.J. and his uncle Fred. Their cars each had the Cadillac "flying V" logo on the trunk, so, in his childish way, Owen concluded that, since the Tire triangle was similar in design, there must be some correlation between the car and the company.

Owen attended the Toronto French School for kindergarten and grade one when he lived in Toronto, went to public school after Martha and Dennis moved to Calgary in 1978, then boarded at Brentwood College School near Victoria for grades eight through ten. He returned to Calgary for grade eleven as a day student at another private school, West Island College.

Owen was not born with the natural dexterity that ran in the Billes family. One Christmas he was given a wooden hammer and pegboard. A.J. held the pegboard for Owen's first attempt to bang the pegs into place. "I hit his thumb with the little hammer," recalled Owen, now thirty-one. "He must have been so disappointed that day. I just didn't have it." In grade seven Owen failed a simple test because he was unable to identify tools by name. While the other students in shop classes were making useful furniture, Owen managed to produce only rudimentary items such as a leather bookmark and a pencil holder with drilled holes.

Nor had the family wealth trickled down to him. At Brentwood, for example, fellow students owned numerous items of attire from the popular Ralph Lauren line. Everyone seemed to smell of the Polo cologne. Owen owned only one Polo golf shirt, and it had been bought on sale. He finally became aware of his family's riches when a fellow Brentwood student pointed out a newspaper story describing the 1983 auction of the J.W. Billes shares. Owen assumed that whatever vast sums might have existed had been donated to charity and that he'd missed his chance.

But Canadian Tire also provided him with a home away from home. From the time he was four, Owen had split his summer holidays between Shanty Bay and camp. When he at last learned about his connection to Tire, he decided he wanted to work there. With no prompting from Martha, he wrote a letter to Arch Brown, the dealer whose store in Barrie, Ont., was closest to the cottage, saying he would take any summer job offered. Brown hired Owen and dispatched him to the warehouse, where he swept floors for two days before being assigned to the paint department. Although Owen tried several other departments and fielded complaints at the customer service desk, mixing paint colours became his favourite role during the eight summers he worked in Brown's store.

The happy independence Owen enjoyed at the store was in stark contrast to his life at home, where he and Martha fought constantly. "She's obviously very strong and determined," said Owen. "I can dig my heels in. It's like a scorched earth policy with me sometimes. If I can't have what I want or something doesn't work out, then that's it for everybody, you're all going to lose. I used to do that a lot when I was younger."

Martha also caused the teenaged Owen some mortifying moments. He rarely invited anyone home, but there was one occasion when several of his friends were using the Shanty Bay cottage as a meeting point before heading out together. "My mother chose that night to repair the toilet in one of the bathrooms," said Owen. "She came walking through the living room with the floater and the whole mechanical guts of the toilet tank and said 'Hi' to everybody. When you're seventeen [you think], 'Why did you need to do that just right now in front of everyone I know?'"

Martha might have been an embarrassment, but Dennis was a martinet. After 1980 Martha's duties as a director on the board of Canadian Tire meant frequent trips to Toronto. As a result, Dennis was often left in charge of Owen, who was constantly at loggerheads with his stepfather. "I don't think we ever really got along," said Owen. "He was very strong and controlling. He was a very strict disciplinarian in the old-school British sense. I never considered him my father. I don't think he was ever interested in me." Owen was a chunky child and he recalls Dennis making a particularly cruel comment about his weight. Once, when Owen was in his mid-teens, they went shopping for back-to-school clothing, but the store seemed unable to produce the proper fit. "You probably don't have anything his size," said Dennis to the clerk. "You don't have size obese." Owen slunk away into the mall.

Dennis sees it differently. "As far as I was concerned, he was my son. I looked after him and changed his diapers and did everything else the same as any other father. I don't even remember him being fat at that time. I think he started putting on weight when he was about fourteen. But up to then he was just a normal kid with puppy fat."

Owen lived in constant terror of Dennis. When Owen visited his grandparents as a young boy, he enjoyed pounding on the keys of the Steinway baby grand piano. Muriel showed him how to play simple tunes and, when she died in 1979, bequeathed the piano to him.

Owen took lessons, but didn't like practising, and the piano became just another bone of contention between Owen and Dennis. Dennis would stand on the landing of their Calgary home and holler up at Owen in his room to come down for his daily practice. Owen was so intimidated by Dennis that, as he passed his stepfather on the stairs, he would try to dart by him on the way to the dreaded piano.

By the time Owen was sixteen, tensions had reached such a fever pitch that Martha wanted Owen out of the house and sent back to boarding school. Owen had not enjoyed his time at Brentwood and preferred to continue as a West Island day student. That way, he told his mother, he could graduate from high school in Calgary with his friends. Martha insisted that he attend Appleby, in Oakville, Ont., the same institution that Fred had detested more than forty years earlier. Martha had applied on Owen's behalf and he had been accepted. "I didn't think he needed to go there and I didn't think he should go there," said Dennis, "but that was part of my duties to back her up, which was what I did." Owen refused to comply, so he was given a choice: go to Appleby or get out of the house.

Owen ran away from home and showed up unannounced at Roger Henry's door in Ottawa. Owen's sullen presence around the house, where Roger lived with his second wife, Sharon, and their five-year-old child, was disruptive, but the family dealt with it as best they could. Owen seemed like a lost soul who needed solace. "What shape is any sixteen-year-old in? I think he was extremely confused," said Roger. Jean Pigott, who lived two doors away agreed: "He was a troubled boy. You knew that something was wrong."

Owen worked briefly at Eaton's, then quit. Roger suggested he get a job at Tire rather than hang around the house. But despite who his mother was, Owen could not seem to find work at Tire. Roger called Fred to ask him to intervene, and Owen was hired at the Tire outlet in Bell's Corners, on Ottawa's outskirts. "Fred had a little more power than her at the time. Fred was fair," said Roger. Explained

Fred: "I feel sorry for him. He was browbeaten by his mother."

After a year in Ottawa, Owen returned home to Calgary. Roger says that when Owen got home, Martha gave him a new car, a trip somewhere, whatever it was that he wanted. "He's been made to live in a certain luxury that he's chosen he's going to go after. But it's not his fault, that's the way he was brought up." In both cities, Owen felt unwanted and the cause of all the problems. "I had a magical effect on everybody," said Owen. "I wouldn't say I have an over-abundance of self-confidence."

THE RECESSION THAT BEGAN in 1981 had turned into one of the worst economic downturns in modern memory. Corporate directors and owners like Martha and her brothers might overlook management foibles during profitable years, but they could become unforgiving in the face of financial losses. Differences in personal style between Muncaster and the family, issues that had not mattered when the economy was strong, now took on new relevance. "A.J. was totally intuitive in his decision-making," said Robin Law. "That was really where the clash was between the family, who were intuitive, and Dean, who was so analytical."

For his part, Muncaster was irritated because the family's control was based on owning such a small proportion of the total number of shares. "I didn't think that gave them the right to determine how everything was going to happen," he said. "We got into quite a lot of conflict over the fact that 96 per cent or 97 per cent of the shares were in other people's hands. Doing the right thing by those folks was very important." For Martha and her brothers, the interests of the family and the other shareholders were synonymous. If the family was happy, well, the public should be happy too. Why should beneficence be so baffling?

Muncaster also found himself increasingly at odds with A.J. In 1984

A.J. had presented a plan to Muncaster that A.J. argued would make the stores in British Columbia more profitable for dealers. Muncaster dismissed A.J.'s idea to institute a new accounting method, saying it was "impractical and would detract rather than encourage the entrepreneurial spirit."[1] A.J. asked if he could visit British Columbia, but Muncaster wasn't interested in permitting any such investigation. A.J. went anyway, visited five stores, and claimed that he found support for his concept.

Muncaster was also at odds with A.J. about his revered profit-sharing program. A.J. had moved beyond extolling the theory that profits should be shared with employees in the form of annual bonuses. Now he wanted the dealers to do a fifty-fifty split of their personal compensation — that 6 per cent portion of total sales that was designated as their own income — with their employees. Muncaster believed that it was wrong to impose such an arbitrary split on the dealers. Over the years, Muncaster argued, the company had assumed more and more of the dealers' duties. The only real role left for them was in deciding whom to hire and how much to pay them. If there was a fixed formula for profit-sharing, then managers would be no more than puppets on strings run from home office. "I felt that was going that one step over the edge. The kind of people we could attract into the business would change," said Muncaster.

A.J. was undeterred. "It became almost a religious type of objective," said Muncaster. "He thought this was something that should happen, no matter who thought it was wrong. It was very divisive. It was one of the things that changed the relationship I had had with him. I just wasn't prepared to endorse that. He went away feeling I was not being properly respectful."

Martha and Fred backed A.J., but the fifty-fifty idea found little favour elsewhere. The dealers, of course, were apoplectic, but A.J.

---

1   University of Western Ontario, Canadian Tire Archives, J.J. Talman Regional Collection, box CTP0832, letter from A.J. to director Selby Sinclair, August 29, 1984.

was a zealot about profit-sharing. "As he got older, he realized you've less time to do whatever it is you still have to do, so it got to be a much more proactive thing," said Muncaster. "In his mind, this was the answer to communism, that the people who are working in the enterprise should benefit proportionately to how effectively they're doing."

Along with all these other problems waiting to crash on Muncaster's head, there was Whites, the Texas-based chain that Tire had bought in 1982. Founded in the 1930s, Whites prospered until the 1970s, when the chain lost its way by diversifying into so many products and services that the public became confused. Whites was known locally as "the furniture store where you could get your car fixed."

When John Kron was posted to Texas as president, he expected an easy ride. "Essentially, we're just going to acclimatize the CTC style for use here," he said at the time. "The product mix is already established in Canada — I'll just toss out block heaters and replace hockey equipment with baseball supplies."[2] Kron took with him key personnel in marketing, dealer relations, and computer systems. Canadian Tire money, called Whites money, was also transplanted, along with plans to convert Whites into the dealer-owned philosophy followed in Canada. Improving overall performance of the money-losing chain looked like such a piece of cake that thirty Canadian dealers expressed an interest in expanding their arrangement to include a Whites store.

But Whites was already in deep trouble. The average Whites store generated only $1 million in sales, compared with $3 million for a similar-sized Tire store in Canada. Whites had not grown at the same rate as the population in either Dallas–Fort Worth or Houston, but Kron and Muncaster blithely believed expansion through additional stores was possible. The four existing warehouses appeared to be capable of handling several times their current volume.

---

2   *Canadian Business*, August 1982, 33.

Whites would become a weapon Martha and Fred would wield against Muncaster, but in the beginning even the brokerage firm analysts wholeheartedly supported his strategy. "With this acquisition, Canadian Tire has paved the way for eventual dramatic improvement," said Martin Kaufman of Nesbitt Thomson Bongard Inc. "Looking longer term, I love this stock." Added Ron McTear of Walwyn Stodgell Cochran Murray Ltd., "Given Canadian Tire's expertise in merchandising, I don't think it's unreasonable to expect they'll be able to at least double, if not triple, Whites' retail sales figure. I don't think it'll be long before we see a stock split and dividend increase."[3]

But Kron was the wrong man for the job. "I took on the Whites thing because I was the only one willing to do it," he said. "I went through hell for three years. My family didn't move; I commuted back and forth. I wasn't properly equipped to do the job, and I said that after the first six months. But we couldn't find anybody. I was taking on the corporate responsibilities that perhaps I shouldn't have, but I did try to do my best."

The acquisition was doomed from day one. If only Martha and Fred had forced Muncaster to follow his own advice, tendered in April 1982 at the Conference Board of Canada's seventh annual marketing conference. There he told delegates that any firm contemplating a new acquisition should take into account the possibility of sky-high interest rates. "I would suggest that you work through the impact upon your investment of prime rates of 20%, 24% or perhaps 30% just to establish the possible exposure. And then make your decision," said Muncaster. "For the 1980s, I believe that lean and mean will become the standard."[4]

If only. Whites became a money pit. The forty-five-unit truck fleet had to be replaced. Renovations were costly and store closings

---

3   *Financial Times of Canada*, January 18, 1982.
4   *Financial Post*, April 10, 1982, 16.

during construction reduced revenue, so profits plummeted. The conversion to dealer-operated stores was sluggish; there were only twelve handovers in the first year. Competition laws in some states did not allow Tire's Canadian practice of using a central distribution and price-setting system. The point at which Whites was expected to turn a profit was regularly postponed. In the first quarter of 1984, Whites lost $11 million. By year-end, Martha and the other directors were handed even bleaker numbers. Net losses due to the Whites acquisition and rehabilitation were almost US$100 million. More than half of the eighty-one stores had been turned into dealer-run outlets, but all were losing money. In a last-ditch attempt to achieve a turnaround, the Whites signs were replaced with banners saying Whites Autocenter Plus, to stress how the old Whites had replaced its multiple product lines with a more focused approach. A new ad campaign was launched with the slogan "We've got it or we'll get it." The plan to provide any individual auto part that a do-it-yourself mechanic might possibly need was a costly gambit, given the losses the company had already endured.

For Dean Muncaster, the end was nigh. Martha and Fred now had him in their sights. "It got to the point where very large amounts of cash were going down to Dallas — and without positive result," said Hugh Macaulay. "The conclusion the family reached was that Dean was too closely associated with what was now threatening to do some serious harm to the company and for that reason should be invited to depart." Fred claimed he had been opposed to investing in Whites from day one and had voted against the acquisition when the idea was first presented to the board. "That's when Dean got himself fired," said Fred. "He didn't know it, but that was his death knell. Dean's a numbers man. He doesn't know about people and not a whole lot about product."

Hindsight is always 20/20, and the investment in Whites was no exception. By 1985 Martha and everyone else — even Muncaster —

had come to wish that Tire had never heard of Texas. "The very substantial error we made was underestimating the intense nature of the competition in that particular area and the fact that we were not prepared to put the kind of money in to bring the asset up to the kind of level where it could be truly competitive," Muncaster said. "That's where the whole thing really came apart. It was an improper decision to start with."

Muncaster later admitted that arrogance had clouded his vision. "Things had gone along awfully well in those last number of years here in Canada. You get the feeling that maybe you're capable of doing things that subsequently turn out not to be the case," he said. Martha and her brothers were also at fault. "The whole Whites experience illustrated the very nature of the family's reaction to business," said John Kron. "We went into that thing, maybe a little bit naively, but with the full understanding that we bought a bankrupt company. We thought that the turnaround would be in the third year, but, in point of fact, the U.S. market is very competitive and it was going to take five. The point is, it was going to come. The family used this as an excuse to get at Dean, who they felt very jealous of. He was Mr. Canadian Tire, where the Billeses felt they should be Mr. and Mrs. Canadian Tire." Muncaster agreed that Martha and her family envied his profile. "The A.J. Billes family viewed Canadian Tire as *their* business, but in the minds of most everyone they'd run into, Muncaster was identified with Canadian Tire, not Billes," he said. "That caused them, the children in particular, a lot of difficulty."

Martha and Fred now had three reasons to fire Muncaster: Whites, McEwan's, and British Columbia. At least one director warned Muncaster early in 1985 that his position was at risk. Selby Sinclair, chairman and CEO of Toromont Industries Ltd., told him: "This thing's rapidly coming to a head and you've got to decide whether you're going to play the game the way they want you to play it or not." Martha and Fred put Muncaster on a short leash. "There wasn't anything that was going on at that stage that Fred and Martha weren't involved in," said Muncaster. "They'd have meetings with me before the board meetings, which is highly unusual." The purpose of the gatherings was to give Martha and Fred a sneak preview so they could express any contrary views privately to Muncaster. After a few such sessions, Muncaster said he was unwilling to participate any further.

In an attempt to defend himself, Muncaster prepared a report for the board that included his own complaints about the family and how they were interfering in the business. In making his case, he cited comments by A.J., who had called the dealers "greedy" and management "spineless." Muncaster found little board support. "I came away with the feeling that being a director of a big company was more important to them than actually saying what they believed."

The board asked Muncaster to devise a new business plan for Whites. In April he retained Stephen Garrison of Ward Howell International Inc., a Dallas-based recruiting firm, to replace John Kron with a new president at an annual salary of US$300,000.[5] The rest of Muncaster's proposal, however, lacked detailed ideas. "By year-end," he told them, "we've got to decide whether we're prepared to grow and invest money or get out." For Martha, such fence-sitting was proof that it was Muncaster who had to go. "The board asked for benchmarks and performance against benchmarks," said Martha. "The performance that the board saw did not get anywhere near the benchmarks and Mr. Muncaster didn't have the solution."

The two sides were at an impasse. "They weren't prepared to put more money in," said Muncaster. "At that stage, I wasn't prepared to say only another $100 million will get it done." For Muncaster, the family seemed to have become stricken with selective amnesia. "They were not people who were very eager to acknowledge that they had been wrong or that someone they found themselves on the other

---

5   Canadian Tire Archives, box CTP0870, engagement letter, April 4, 1985.

side of was right. They'd got pushed and shoved and reluctantly said OK. They'll tell you Vancouver, McEwan's, and Whites. [To them] it happened at least three times."

According to David, all available information had not been presented when those decisions were taken. "The board did not see all the analyses in detail," he said. "When you have the president saying yes, the vice-president saying yes, the chief financial officer saying yes, the chairman of the board saying yes — these are experienced businessmen with very good track records — you've got to say, 'Can all these people be wrong?' Well, they were, unfortunately. They were bad decisions, not properly researched. Decisions were obviously not made on good analysis. The relationship was going downhill and it became essential that he had to go."

Even as Muncaster's demise drew closer, Martha positioned herself safely above the fray, just in case the tide turned. "Martha never wanted to take a position on anything," said Muncaster. "She wanted to be in a position where she could criticize, but to get her to say yes or no didn't happen very often. She had this desire that she was going to end up on the right side of things, but let's figure out where they're going [first]." In business, as in war, such a strategy is called "keeping your powder dry." The canny approach was well suited to Martha, who had spent a lifetime waiting for the right moment before taking action. She could not afford any setbacks. Victory had to be certain before she made her move because, for her, there were no second chances. Once her foes knew her views, they'd be better prepared the next time and she might never achieve what she wanted.

Matters came to a head during a spring board meeting when Dean Muncaster, John Kron, and Robin Law were asked to withdraw. They retired to a nearby room to await the outcome of the board's deliberations. The minutes stretched into hours. Every so often someone would come by to tell the trio that matters would take just a little while longer. "That continued on for half the day at least," said

Muncaster. "Then the decision was [announced] that they were going to delay the annual meeting. By that point it was obvious that something was afoot."

To Martha, poor financial results were not Muncaster's only problem. Dealers and employees were telling her that he was indifferent to their concerns and spending too much time on his outside boards. "I did receive a number of complaints from dealers at the time and from corporate employees [that] they could never get to talk to Dean, that he just went totally inaccessible to them," said Martha. "He became a different man. The torch was passed." Said Fred: "The fight came out of him real quick. As soon as he realized the whole board was against him, he sort of caved."

Muncaster fulfilled his public commitments. "It is quite clear that we are not going to be prepared to lose $55 million a year for very long," Muncaster told a group of analysts in a May speech. Asked if throwing in the towel was possible, he answered: "If we are not encouraged by the prospects of being able to return [Whites] to profitability within a reasonable period of time, then that is one of the alternatives."[6] Arguing his case in other venues was of little value. Muncaster had lost the confidence of his most important constituency, the family. The directors established an executive committee that included Martha, Fred, Hugh Macaulay, and Pierre Côté, chairman of Celanese Canada Inc., to negotiate a severance package and send Muncaster packing. Muncaster initially said that he'd help the committee find a successor, but on June 5, 1985, the day before the postponed annual meeting, he had a change of heart. Muncaster told them that he would leave in ten days.

Shareholders attending the meeting were stunned when Macaulay announced that Muncaster had "relinquished" his duties. Despite that changed status, Muncaster delivered his speech as prepared.

---

6   *Financial Post*, April 13, 1985.

Obviously shaken by events, his voice broke throughout his remarks. "If you want a definition of class — there it is," said Macaulay to the shareholders as Muncaster took his seat. Muncaster was given a standing ovation. He had been president since he was thirty-three and had taken the firm from revenues of $100 million to $2 billion. Now, at fifty-one, he was gone, along with his annual salary of $450,000, although a $1 million severance agreement eased the departure.

Gone, too, were eight of the ten district managers at Whites. Also turfed was John Kron, Whites president and chief executive. (He has since worked as a consultant for Stevenson Kellogg and has been a director on several boards.) Kron saw a way Tire could have cut its losses, but Tire chose not to follow that route. Tire had paid for Whites by using what, in financing terms, is called the "double dip." Tire loaned the money required for the purchase of Whites to an offshore company in the Netherlands, which then loaned the money to a firm in the Dutch Antilles, which in turn loaned the money to Whites. "I guess we thought we were being clever doing the double dip," said Kron. "Of course by doing it this way, Canadian Tire could not 'tax effect' any losses because it was only a question of lending money to an offshore party. Canadian Tire could have reversed a large portion of the losses and thereby reduced the dramatic losses to half. It could have been done, but they wouldn't even consider it — the family wouldn't — because they wanted to hang Dean on this whole issue."

The result of not unwinding the double dip stranded US$150 million worth of tax losses in the United States with no ongoing operations against which those losses could be applied. If the double dip had been reversed, then some of the tax losses could have been repatriated to Canada. The losses could have reduced Canadian taxes payable in future years, thereby cutting the overall loss caused by Whites. "What we did was just let it go right through until Dean was fired and then they just dumped it all and 'fire-saled' it," said Kron.

"That's not responsible corporate governance. It was a vindictive act, in my humble opinion."

A.J. was unrepentant about the departure of Muncaster, his former boy wonder. "We were like the drunk that has to hit bottom before he can pick himself up," A.J. said at the time. "We hit bottom when Muncaster left. Texas is a real mess. He was good for the company for the first ten years, but then he began to get a bit full of himself." Muncaster was equally dismissive in return. "There were some of us," he said, "who liked to think we worked for *all* the shareholders."

The dealers were quick to turn their backs on their former leader. "Dean was a friend to many of us for a long time. He took us to $2 billion in sales, but we're in a changing world," said Ian Van Norman, a dealer in Saskatoon who was president of the dealers' association. "Dealers don't need direction on a day-to-day basis. The president is our leader, but, on retail street, we're out where the rubber meets the road."[7] Naysayers conveniently forgot that the U.S. retail market was tough. Canadian Tire was hardly the only foreign interloper to commit the same blunder. Other high-profile failures included forays by Peoples Jewellers, Dylex, and Reitmans.

Muncaster spent the summer of 1985 travelling in England and sailing his thirty-nine-foot ketch on Georgian Bay with Brenda, his third wife. He was, for a time, chairman of Electronics Distributors. Then, in 1989, Barry Setnor, who had been Muncaster's executive vice-president, marketing, at Canadian Tire, asked him to become involved in buying Bargain Harold's Discount Ltd., a cut-rate retailer with 160 outlets in seven provinces. Muncaster agreed to join as a part-time chairman, but attempts to spruce up the stores failed. In 1992 Bargain Harold's filed for court protection under the Companies' Creditors Arrangements Act. Muncaster was left holding the bag and dealing with angry creditors. He believed fraud was involved, but

---

7 *Toronto Life*, January 1986, 18–19.

was never able to prove anything, and he lost his own investment. "It didn't do me, my reputation, or my health any good. It was really what lay beneath the breakup of the marriage between me and Brenda. We had to sell the big house that she had designed, built, and furnished." He now lives in Collingwood, Ont., with Joan Cameron.

By comparison with the fiasco of Bargain Harold's, being fired from Canadian Tire had been a breeze. "The Canadian Tire thing was a blow, but at least I came away feeling good about myself," Muncaster said. More than fifteen years after his firing, Muncaster still shops at Tire and keeps an interested eye on the company. Once he was in the Collingwood store when a loud voice called "Muncaster, I thought they threw you out of this place." It was Bill James, then CEO of Falconbridge Ltd. Admitted Muncaster, "I do miss the business."

In September Martha and the other directors were treated to a first-hand look at a corporate sponsorship that had been in place for four years. Grand Prix race-car driver Jacques Villeneuve, with only seventeen laps left in the 225-lap race at St.-Pie, Quebec, tried to pass Bobby Rahal, but the two cars touched and spun out of control into the wall. The drivers were not injured, though both vehicles were destroyed in the crash. That November, after spending $10 million on the marketing program, the deal with Villeneuve was cancelled. With Muncaster gone and Martha's hand increasingly on the wheel, driving at Tire would become safe again.

SIX

THE LITTLE
RED-HAIRED DEVIL

"I tried to cultivate a relationship with her,
but I couldn't break through the ice or
break through the shield, or whatever it was."
— DEAN GROUSSMAN

*B*efore Martha could make her next move, Fred, her life-long nemesis, took one final look at the top. He headed for the southern United States in August 1985 and took charge of the debacle that was Whites. There he closed a warehouse in Georgia as well as twenty-eight Whites outlets, a task aided by a tornado that flattened one of the stores. He also fired 30 per cent of head office staff to cut costs. "It's not their fault," Fred said. "They should never have been employed in the first place. The whole operation was twice the size it should have been."[1]

Fred introduced himself to the remaining Whites dealers via a videotaped monologue that was recorded as he stared into a fixed camera and rambled on for more than three hours. "I don't hold much on ceremony," he said. "I don't hold very much on clothing,

---

1   *Financial Post*, September 14, 1985.

dress, or appearance. However, you sure as heck can tell a company by its profit-and-loss statement." Fred boasted that his Yonge Street store had made as much in the first six months of the year as all the Whites stores put together had lost. Whites "did some damn fool things in the immediate past," he said, and told the dealers that "prices are going to go up right now." To restore employee morale, he advised dealers to reward overtime work with chicken dinners, preferably Swiss Chalet. "It's much better than anything Colonel Sanders ever thought of." Fred planned another video until someone said, "Fred, you're no Clint Eastwood."

In fact, Fred had been looking forward to this moment ever since he was five and had run through the store aisles shouting "This is mine."[2] He had previously told David that he wanted to be chief executive of Canadian Tire, a step that Martha almost certainly would have fought. Fred's public image, however, had tarnished his reputation and diminished his chances. "The store he owns in the ritzy Rosedale area of Toronto . . . would not be termed as one of the company's showpieces," wrote Frances Phillips in the *Financial Post*. "It is old, and needs a good lick of paint. 'Fred Billes would not be a popular choice,' one retail analyst says curtly."[3]

Such criticism didn't stop Fred's colourful pronouncements about Whites. "We have to cauterize the devil," he said. "Once it is cauterized, we can make some decisions. It will give us some breathing space." In one interview, Fred declared his long-standing philosophy about growth outside Canada. "I would have preferred to see us expand to the U.K., or Ohio, or any market that is similar to our own — with the same climate, the same autos, and the same kind of products. A place that is close enough that, if there's a problem, we can do something about it."[4]

---

2   *Globe and Mail*, June 27, 1987.
3   *Financial Post*, June 15, 1985.
4   *Financial Post*, August 3, 1985.

Despite all the bombast, Fred came to the conclusion that he did not want to be boss. "He realized that it was not appropriate and it never really went any further than that," said David. Fred concluded that his ownership position and the money he'd earned as a dealer was more than sufficient to see him out. Why take on new headaches? "I'd made my marbles," recalled Fred. "That [job] would have been a killer for me."

David believed that the combination of Martha and Fred as joint chief executives could have worked, a sure sign that Martha's talents were at last becoming more admired and more admitted. "Fred is very outgoing as a person. He had the ability to talk to people, get information from them, and assess a business situation quite well," said David. "Martha was more quiet, but very sharp and quick. She never had the same people skills that Fred had. This was really my father's forte, dealing with people. He was a real people person. J.W. was very stern, very good with numbers. The two of them worked together and I think my brother and sister could have worked together if they hadn't clashed quite as much."

Tire set out to find two new bosses, one for Canada and one for the United States. In October 1985 Dean Groussman was hired as president and chief executive officer of Whites. At forty-seven, he was an experienced U.S. retailer who had worked for Target Stores, Dayton-Hudson Corp., and the May Co. Most recently he had headed several divisions of Zale Corp. of Dallas, including Zale's 170 drugstores, catalogue showrooms, and the 320-outlet fine jewellery divisions. Groussman didn't come cheap; he signed a three-year employment contract worth about US$1 million. "It could be considered generous, but pales by comparison to recent losses," said Hugh Macaulay in a September 27 letter to members of the Tire board.[5] Indeed, Whites was by then losing $2 million a week.

---

5   University of Western Ontario, Canadian Tire Archives, J.J. Talman Regional Collection, box CTP0832.

Groussman recommended to Martha and the other directors that Tire sell most of the Whites outlets, leaving a few as the nucleus for a new operation. Wesray Capital Corp., a New York investment firm headed by William Simon, secretary of the Treasury in the Richard Nixon and Gerald Ford administrations, had acquired Western Auto and was looking for more locations. Tire offered Wesray all but fourteen stores. In January 1986 the board concluded that Tire should sell everything to Western Auto, get out of the United States entirely, and halt the losses at $250 million. With Whites gone, Groussman had a generous contract but no role. When Macaulay relayed the board's decision to Groussman, he asked him, "Have you ever thought that you might like to relocate to Canada?" Groussman did a version of the Texas two-step. In July 1986 he was named Tire's president and chief operating officer. In 1987 he was elevated to CEO.

Martha was not amused. "Martha never wanted me to come to Canada," said Groussman. "She fought hard to prevent the board from appointing me to become the CEO. Martha and I never had different views about wanting to have the best for the company, but frequently Martha's views as to what was best didn't coincide with mine and most often it didn't coincide with the rest of the board. She sometimes marched to a different drummer. I tried to cultivate a relationship with her, take her to lunch and have other discussions with her, but I couldn't break through the ice or break through the shield, or whatever it was."

According to Martha, it wasn't that she disliked Groussman as an individual. Rather, she was opposed to what she saw as a short-circuited executive search. Tire had started out looking for two chief executives, one for the United States and another for Canada. Groussman had been hired to handle Whites, but then that job disappeared. Since he already had a contract with Tire, in her view he was simply shunted to Canada. "I felt our corporation deserved an appropriate search, and that did not take place," Martha said. "There are times when an individual from inside a corporation is absolutely the right person, but, still, you owe the corporation, you owe the shareholders, a search, a look-see at what is available. It doesn't necessarily mean a headhunter search, but a proper and appropriate search process to sort through. That was not done."

Fred disputed Martha's perspective on events. "We did have a search and we did interview people. We did a reasonably good search and got a reasonably good guy. Groussman was familiar with retailing," he said. Of course, Fred was a fan. Groussman had been his choice to run Whites. Moreover, Groussman got along with Fred. "When Fred would say something and I didn't agree with him, I could just come right back without worrying about being tactful and say, 'I don't agree and here's why,'" said Groussman. "With Martha you had to be careful of words and choose your words because they might be played back incorrectly. I'm not sure I ever understood Martha."

THE LIST OF PEOPLE with whom Martha was unable to get along was growing longer. First there were her brothers, followed by Alex Barron and Dean Muncaster, then Dean Groussman. In the spring of 1986 Carling O'Keefe expressed an interest in buying Tire, and Fred saw his chance to escape Martha's clutches. "We could see that Martha was a loose cannon," he said. "Martha thought we should take her commands. She's not controllable and it's not worth the fight."

Of the two, Fred was the more interested in selling, but David went along with the idea so he could have more time to concentrate on Performance Engineering, the business he had started in Barrie, Ont., where he built racing cars and engines. "Canadian Tire was never really that important to me," said David. "It's not my desire, my interest. I'm a mechanical engineer, I love things mechanical, solid. Working with people is a necessary evil as far as I'm concerned. I do not enjoy publicity and negotiations. I was on the board for twenty years, but I can never say my heart was in it."

Initially, it looked as if Martha was interested in selling her shares too. The three siblings met on June 2, 1986, with R.B. Matthews, Peter Beattie, and René Sorell of the Toronto law firm McCarthy & McCarthy. At the meeting, someone suggested a way the family could get around the OSC's coat-tail ruling. A purchaser could acquire effective control by acquiring only 49 per cent of the voting shares — a step that would not trigger the coat-tail.

Martha and her brothers retained investment banking firm Merrill Lynch Canada Ltd. to discover if there were any other prospective buyers in addition to Carling O'Keefe. As the summer wore on, Martha looked as though she might not want to sell after all. She claimed that the main reason she had participated in the talks was to learn the value of her shares. She used the analogy of owning an antique watch and kept repeating, "I want to know what my watch is worth." David was surprised and upset over her apparent change of mind. Relations between Martha and her brothers deteriorated to the point where the tensions became obvious to others. "There was more animosity," said Groussman. "You could see that the chemistry wasn't there."

Such perceptions didn't matter to Martha. She neither wanted nor needed the help of her brothers or anyone else to achieve her goal — control of Canadian Tire. In fact, the more the others fought, the fewer players there would be on the field as they fell, mortally wounded. The heller was hatching a plan.

THE GATHERING OF THE CLAN on a fall evening in 1986 at A.J.'s penthouse condominium in North York was supposed to be about keeping the family and the family business together. A.J. did not want Martha, Fred, and David to sell Canadian Tire, so he asked

Fred Sasaki, his trusted adviser, to attend and make a final appeal on his behalf. "A.J. was quite upset," said Sasaki. "What A.J. wanted was that the children would let him vote the common shares so that he could keep the company as it was."

Sasaki had written down his thoughts and read them aloud to the assembled offspring and their spouses. As Tire's treasurer and A.J.'s confidant, Sasaki might have made a financial argument. Instead, he delivered a plea about the loyal employees and the sacrifices A.J. and J.W. had made on behalf of their families as they built the business.

Sasaki had a very different view of family from that of Martha and her brothers. He had been living in Vancouver with his parents and siblings in 1941 when Japan attacked Pearl Harbor. Sasaki's father was among the first of many Japanese Canadians to be rounded up by the police, classified as dangerous, and placed under arrest. The family was split up and the young Sasaki came to Toronto, where he was unable to find work because of his ancestry. In October 1944, while the Second World War still raged, Sasaki walked into Canadian Tire and A.J. offered him a job on the spot. The money Sasaki earned allowed him to reunite his family. As a result, he was forever grateful and loyal to A.J.

In his remarks to the meeting, Sasaki described the history of the company and his view of the importance of family and respect for elders. "I appealed to their emotions as children and the duty of children to their father," recalled Sasaki. "I said that they should accede to their father's wishes. He had built the company and it was his life. In the closing years of his life he should do what he wanted."

Fred spoke next, but his remarks quickly deteriorated into little more than a flurry of insults aimed at Martha. She had become hardened to Fred's taunts over the years, so she didn't rise to the bait, but Dennis leapt in to defend her. Tempers flared further when Martha spotted a tape machine under the Kawai piano near the sitting area. (Furtive taping seemed to run in the family. Fred and David once met with Martha and realized she was taping their conversation only when they heard the squealing sound of the tape running out.) Fred said he'd make copies of the tape available to everyone, but Dennis was not mollified. "I was trying to say something, but he would not shut up," said David. "He kept interrupting when I was trying to speak. I shouted at him." Dennis continued to interrupt until David, who would not normally say boo to a goose, confronted Dennis, who was by then standing. "Sit down and shut up," said David as he pushed Dennis, sending him flopping back into his chair. That action effectively ended the discussion. Martha and Dennis marched out, arm in arm. "[The meeting took an] inappropriate direction that I wasn't going to stay for. It reached the point where it was off topic and I left," recalled Martha, who would not elaborate.

As far as Fred was concerned, Martha had no intention of allowing the meeting to accomplish anything and had seized upon the tape recorder as an excuse to bring the session to an abrupt end. "I tried to restrain her and her friend, but there never was a discussion between Martha and Fred and David," said Fred. "That leaving was choreographed long before the meeting ever took place. We tried to get the buggers to sit down. This was a meeting that might have made some decisions, might have been important, might have done something positive, but it didn't. The heller left. Martha would sooner have had us in a fighting mood than in a reconciliation mood. She would sooner have divided and conquered."

The meeting lasted less than ten minutes. A.J.'s final attempt at family reconciliation had been a ridiculous fiasco. After everyone had left, Fred Sasaki and A.J. sat quietly together, lamenting what might have been. "They wouldn't listen to him," said Sasaki. "I can't understand it. I think it's very selfish. To me it's beyond belief that they would take that attitude, the three of them. From that meeting I could tell that they would never get along, Freddy and Martha. Dave didn't say too much, but you could tell that he and Freddy were together.

It was so disappointing to me, and I think to A.J. too, that we just didn't say very much. It was a lost cause. Immense wealth creates more discord than happiness."

AFTER MURIEL'S DEATH in 1979, A.J. had moved in with Fred and Barbara. There he grew closer to Barbara's mother, Marjorie, and, following the death of her own husband a year later, the two of them married in 1984. A one-hour video of the wedding ceremony and the celebratory aftermath aptly captured the vastly different characteristics of the three Billes siblings. Fred was his usual ebullient self, giving a speech and saying to Marjorie, "You're now my mother." David offered a quiet handshake and stayed in the background. Martha, dressed to the nines in a wide-brimmed hat and polka-dot dress complete with shawl, noisily played sergeant-major and tried to herd everyone into what she regarded as their proper places for the official portrait.[6]

Having a stepmother is awkward at the best of times. The children want happiness for their father, but no one can ever replace a mother. Martha could not seem to settle herself with Marjorie's new role. She would get upset when A.J. and Marjorie failed to send Owen a birthday card. Muriel had always remembered such special occasions. The marriage of A.J. and Marjorie also meant that Martha could not talk freely about her plans for Tire with A.J. for fear that he might tell his wife, who would talk to Barbara, who would, in turn, pass the information along to Fred, her foe.

As a result, the strategy she was devising to take control went forward without his full knowledge. "My father was apprised of what I was doing and he was very much in favour in his discussions with me of my basic concept and precept and what my goals were," said

---

6   UWO, Canadian Tire Archives, box CTAV033.

Martha. "He came from a different era, and he wasn't privy to all the counsel I had. He couldn't be. He was older and out of the business, and he was married to Freddy's mother-in-law. There are expressions about loose lips and that type of thing. My father knew my basic plans. He didn't know all the details. But he always called me Marth and he was the only person that called me Marth. And I heard Marth many, many, many times during those weeks, months."

Yet for all Martha's stated closeness to A.J. at that time, he was not reluctant to make public his unhappiness with the decision by Martha and her brothers to sell Canadian Tire. "You don't really like to see your baby put up for sale," he told the *Toronto Star.* "You give something to people and it's up to them to use it to the best of their abilities. It hasn't been discussed with me at all. I've divorced myself from that, from the business."[7] *Maclean's* quoted him as saying, "My children have excluded me completely. I pray to God they come to their senses."[8] "Be careful what you give your kids," he warned other parents through the pages of the *Globe and Mail.*[9]

Two of the kids were selling their heritage. On October 2 Merrill Lynch told Fred and David that, in their estimation, the per share value ranged between $67 and $91. By then, Martha had changed her mind and the original buyer, Carling O'Keefe, had lost interest, but Fred and David still wanted to sell. They thought the shares were worth more than Merrill Lynch had estimated, so they set a price of $99.95 per share, just as though each share were another item on the store shelves.

Under the terms of their 1983 agreement, Martha had the right of first refusal. At $99.95 per share, buying them out would have cost $140 million, so she declined. "I didn't have the money," she said, "simple as that." Fred and David were then free to sell to anyone they

---

7   *Toronto Star*, October 17, 1986.

8   *Maclean's*, January 19, 1987, 38.

9   *Globe and Mail*, June 30, 1987.

chose. The dealers, who owned 17.5 per cent of the voting shares, worried what would happen to them if Fred's and David's shares were bought by an outsider. The dealers decided that the only way to ensure continuity was to buy the voting shares themselves. The 348 dealers in CTC Dealer Holdings Ltd. retained investment banker Gordon Capital and, on November 22, signed an agreement to buy the shares owned by Fred and David. To guarantee the arrangement with the brothers, the dealers promised them a $15 million deposit. Half of that deposit was non-refundable, so if the sale to the dealers was not completed for any reason, the two brothers would share $7.5 million. Fred insisted on such a deposit because he had doubts that the deal would ever be completed. "I always considered this a very suspect offer," he said. "I didn't think the dealers would come up with the money."

The sound of money caught Martha's attention. "Martha was doing her usual thing, which is not signing until everybody else had signed," said Fred. Martha told Gordon Capital that she, too, would sell, but demanded the same $15 million deposit the dealers had promised to both her brothers — with the full amount non-refundable — if the sale did not go through. The dealers agreed; they needed all the shares they could get to ensure control. Once Martha signalled her consent, Gordon Capital had to act quickly. Martha was at Shanty Bay and didn't want to drive to Toronto, but her signed consent was required before 6 p.m. or the deal was off. It was by then past noon. Robert Fung, Gordon's vice-chairman, decided he couldn't risk taking the time required to drive to Shanty Bay, so he chartered a helicopter. Three men clambered aboard for the mercenary mission: Fung; Peter Dey, a securities lawyer at Osler, Hoskin & Harcourt and a former chairman of the Ontario Securities Commission, who had been retained by the dealers; and John Stransman of Stikeman, Elliott, Martha's lawyer.

The trio took off from a helipad near Ontario Place, west of downtown Toronto. Fung directed the pilot, using a crude map he'd drawn based on Martha's description of her cottage and her dock, jutting out into the water. As the craft circled over what they presumed was their destination, Martha came out of the cottage and waved, as she had said she would once she heard the noise of the approaching helicopter. The Bay Street bunch landed safely on the concrete dock.

So unusual were the circumstances that the participants took photographs of themselves with the chopper to commemorate the hurry-up moment and its historic meaning. Within twenty minutes the flying circus was airborne again for the return trip to Toronto. Martha was so tickled with their extra effort that those photos remain a prized possession to this day, a reminder of the lengths to which the dealers' representatives had gone to include her. They made Martha feel that she mattered; she preened in that prominence.

But Martha claimed to be saddened by what she had done. "That was probably the low point of my life. I had my fingers and toes crossed for many months there that [the sale] wouldn't happen. I'd be driving from Barrie down to Toronto and a Canadian Tire truck would go by and I'd say to myself, 'That used to be part of my existence.'"

Still, Martha had outfoxed Fred and David; she got the deposit she demanded and her participation was announced December 4. Four days later the brothers renegotiated their deposit arrangement with the dealers. The dealers agreed to do for them what they had done for Martha and to make the full deposit non-refundable, but they refused to change the amount. Martha still came out on top. If the deal did not go through, Fred and David would split $15 million, while Martha would get $15 million all to herself. In the scorecard of the business world — money — Martha was pulling ahead.

ON DECEMBER 9 the dealers made official their bid to Martha and her brothers for 49 per cent of the voting shares of Tire. The price they offered was $160.24 a share, four times the value at which shares had been trading only ten days earlier. The dealers could certainly afford the acquisition. The typical Tire dealer joined at age thirty-five and stayed twenty years, working his way through three or four stores, from a small store in a small town to a larger outlet in an urban centre.

A prospective dealer had to raise $150,000, undergo nine months of training, then move to whatever backwater location he was assigned. His money and a bank loan gave him ownership of the inventory, fixtures, and equipment. The company owned the real estate, charged rent, supplied the goods, and set the prices. From every dollar of sales, the dealer had 22 cents to pay employee wages, rent, advertising, administration, loan interest, principal payments, and compensate himself. A dealer with a store doing $20 million in annual sales earned an annual pre-tax income and return on his investment of $1 million, three or four times more than a chief executive of a major public company was paid in that era. Every dealer also built personal net worth that might run to $5 million through ownership of the inventory and the store fixtures, which were bought by the next dealer to come along and replace him.

The dealers' offer was seen as a scandal and was roundly denounced in newspaper editorials and business pages. If Martha and her brothers sold their shares to the dealers, thousands of individual shareholders who owned non-voting shares would be stranded, unable to tender their shares and earn the sort of premium that Martha would receive. "It's a black eye for investing, probably bad for Canadian Tire itself, and a warning to non-voting shareholders in other companies that they'd better scream for iron-clad protection in takeovers and other big decisions," wrote *Toronto Star* columnist Jack McArthur. "Most of all, it's a striking lesson in the need to limit the use of non-vote and no-vote shares. Talk about the tail wagging the dog!"[10] Even Tire's

---

10 *Toronto Star*, December 5, 1986.

directors, most of whom owed fealty to the family, expressed "grave concern" that the rights of non-voting shareholders had not been dealt with equitably. In a rare display of mutual outrage, pension funds and other institutional investors banded together against the proposal and published a newspaper advertisement with a mail-in coupon to encourage support from shareholders who owned the Class A non-voting shares. Declared the ad: "This is a fight for fairness." Sponsors of the campaign included such blue-chip corporations and big-name money managers as Air Canada, Allenvest (a shareholder rights firm now called Fairvest), Beutel Goodman, Canada Trust, Metropolitan Life, National Trust, and Standard Life. Said ringleader Stephen Jarislowsky of Jarislowsky & Fraser, a Montreal-based pension fund manager: "I didn't want to get gypped and I didn't want the dealers in control either because I knew what they would do to us. They would eat us up alive. They had no interest in the A shareholders."

Once Fred was prepared to sell, then David, who had always deferred to his older brother, was also willing to go along. But why was Martha so eager? She might not have been able to afford to buy out her brothers, but why not hang on to her shares and the heritage she claimed mattered so deeply to her? Even those who, for years, had watched the family at close range were puzzled about Martha's involvement. "Their willingness to sell was inconsistent with what I perceived Martha's view of the grand plan to be and that is 'This is the Billes company,'" said Dean Muncaster. "It must have been the size of the money that got her on side." Jarislowsky agreed. "I always had the feeling that she was a lukewarm seller and that she basically wanted to respect her father's wishes. She basically had her father's confidence more than the brothers did. Her brothers seemed to be only interested in money." Still, Martha put her shares up for sale too. "Greed is a great motivator," said Jarislowsky.

But greed was not the only reason. Martha was putting into motion a long-term strategy that allowed her to use the situation to advance her ownership cause. She neatly created a position for herself where she could not lose. If the deal went through, she would be wealthy beyond her wildest dreams. If the deal did not close, the status quo would be preserved and she would be ahead $15 million. "It's very possible that she knew it wasn't going to go through and she just wanted more in her pocket," said Dean Groussman. "Maybe that's why she asked for twice the non-refundable deposit. Our attorneys felt very strongly that the sale probably wouldn't go through, and Martha was probably getting the same advice."

Martha later claimed that her father encouraged her to sell. "He had his moments where he said, 'Why not throw in the towel? Take the money and go.' I did, but I was able to keep a little powder dry." To do so, Martha served legal notice on Fred and David in November that they had failed to follow the 1983 Aldamar agreement when they jointly offered their shares to her. She claimed that each of them should have made her a separate offer. While her point seemed picayune, that manoeuvre, lost in the hurly-burly of battle, was an important element in her plan for the future control of the company.

Everyone else was too focused on the bid and the battle to see what she was up to. "I don't really blame the dealers," said A.J. "They are like children anyway. We're all like children right now. Children need to be told what to do. And for the past few years the corporation hasn't been telling the dealers what to do. They've forgotten their role in the company. I am very unhappy about what's been happening to the company. It's not the way things were meant to be. It's not the way things started out."[11] In an interview with Theresa Tedesco of *Maclean's*, A.J. referred to Martha as "always being a little red-headed devil" with fixed ideas about the way she wanted Tire to operate.[12] In private, he tearfully told a friend: "This is the biggest disappointment

---

11 *Globe and Mail*, December 6, 1986, A1.
12 *Maclean's*, January 26, 1987, 33.

of my life. I'm just going to have to disavow my children. Because this is one family I never wanted to see broken up — the Canadian Tire family. How can I dislike my own children?"[13] In the past, whenever there had been rumours of a takeover, A.J. had rallied Martha and her brothers and convinced them not to sell. This time around, he had no such clout. "It was not what he wanted and he could not control it," said David. "It was probably the first major thing, relative to the corporation, that he could not control and he was very frustrated about that."

With the dealer offer making headlines and arousing investor ire, the Ontario Securities Commission stepped in. The OSC announced that, on December 18, it would hold a joint hearing with the Quebec Securities Commission. Fred testified that he, David, and Martha could no longer act in concert; that's why they were selling. "The company was too big to control, too complicated," said Fred. "Since we could not agree, it seemed better to have someone else operating the company."[14] OSC staff cited the conflict of interest that would exist if the dealers were owners, and pointed to a 1983 letter to shareholders from Dean Muncaster promising that they would be protected if there was a change of control. "What the shareholders actually got was something you could drive a Canadian Tire truck through," said Joseph Groia, an OSC staff lawyer.

Former directors and executives — Alex Barron, Robin Law, Dean Muncaster, and John Kron — all testified that they believed equal treatment for all shareholders in the course of a takeover had been assured. "I thought we had provided adequate protection at the time," said Muncaster.[15] "I would have been embarrassed voting for something that could be turned over so easily," said Barron. As for the Billes family deciding to sell, "It was just something I never contem-

---

13 *Globe and Mail*, January 17, 1987.
14 Ontario Securities Commission, Hearing Update, January 6, 1987.
15 *Toronto Star*, December 20, 1986.

plated."[16] OSC staff counsel argued that the intent of the coat-tail was to ensure that any premium paid for control should be shared among investors who held either voting or non-voting shares. Groia urged the four-member panel to "not look favourably upon cleverness, avarice and artificial transactions."

In support of this view, the OSC called Tom Kierans, president of brokerage firm McLeod Young Weir Ltd., as an independent witness to comment on Bay Street's view that the proposed acquisition was unfair. Kierans declared that the whole investment climate would change if the OSC allowed the deal, because regulators would be sending a message that no shareholder protection measure need be honoured. "The transaction constitutes a violation of the *de facto* agreement between the issuer and investors," he said.

After testimony from ten witnesses and nine days of hearings that stretched into January 1987, the OSC ruled on January 14 that it would block the deal, declaring that the bid was designed to circumvent the coat-tail provision and was "contrary to the public interest."[17] Kierans's view had been crucial to OSC chairman Stanley Beck. "In the end Stanley's judgment turned on a legal dime, so we can't over-rate my role, but what I provided was the cladding within which you could insert that dime," said Kierans. "It was the dime that did it. I made life-long enemies of a lot of people, but it was worthwhile. You pull a stunt like this and you're wrecking capital markets."

The full 109-page ruling released in February was caustic about what Martha and her brothers had attempted to pull off. "For the Billeses to engage knowingly in 1986 in a transaction which is specifically designed to circumvent the coattail while, at the same time, providing them the total consideration that they want for sale of their control block, is a breach of their duty as controlling

---

16 *Globe and Mail*, December 19, 1986, B1.
17 Ontario Securities Commission, *Decisions, Orders, Rulings*, February 13, 1987, 3-107.

shareholders and directors."[18] The ruling continued: "If abusive transactions such as the one in issue here, and this is as grossly abusive a transaction as the Commission has had before it in recent years, are allowed to proceed, confidence in our capital markets will inevitably suffer and individuals will be less willing to place funds in equity markets."[19] The panel also poured scorn on the argument put forward by Martha's lawyers that she was somehow a victim whose hand had been forced by her brothers. "Martha knew about the 49% scheme in early June," said the ruling. "There is no evidence whatsoever that she objected to that form of transaction, or made any statement with respect to the rights of the Class A shareholders. When faced with a transaction that was advantageous to her, and a buyer that wished to lock up her important 20% position, she negotiated the best deal she could — indeed, a better deal than her brothers had."[20]

The OSC's decision created new law affecting other potential changes of control in companies with dual share structures. A.J. was delighted. "I'm glad for one reason only: because it could bring the idea of real profit-sharing back," he told the *Globe and Mail*. "If the deal had gone through, that couldn't have happened. But now it's still possible because perhaps there's more money that can be left aside." As for the participants, he said: "The dealers are greedy just like you and me. And, in fact, the three [Billeses] were probably even greedier."[21]

Martha, her brothers, and the dealers appealed the decision to the divisional court of the Supreme Court of Ontario. Justice Robert Reid focused, among other matters, on the contention by Martha's lawyers that she was somehow a bit player. "Martha could not, by any

---

18 Ontario Securities Commission, *Decisions, Orders, Rulings*, February 13, 1987, 3–77, 3–78.
19 OSC, 3–108.
20 OSC, 3–122.
21 *Globe and Mail*, January 16, 1987.

imaginative stretch, be considered separate from her brothers," he wrote in the decision dated March 12, 1987. "She participated with her brothers in the arrangement and sought to gain the same benefit. Martha . . . shifted the entire risk to the Dealers by requiring the entire $15 million deposit to be non-refundable for any reason. This example was later followed by her brothers."[22] In upholding the OSC, Justice Reid stated: "The transaction is abusive in two ways. First, it is artificial. Second, it was contrived to circumvent the coattail, and thus frustrate the intention of its well-intentioned proponents, and confound the justifiable expectations, or, in Mr. Kierans' words, the 'reasonable assumptions' of investors and others in the marketplace."[23]

The dealers and the Billes Three sought leave to appeal the divisional court ruling. In April, without citing reasons, the Ontario Court of Appeal refused to hear the matter. "Whenever the Billeses emerged in the public eye, they starred in a Canadian version of Dogpatch," wrote Ian Brown in *Freewheeling*, his 1989 book about Canadian Tire. "The Billeses were a phenomenon: a family of great but recent fortune that did not understand its own wealth, or the consequences of it. They weren't used to having money, however much they enjoyed it. The Billes family, in other words, were a walking, talking, squabbling microcosm of the Canadian middle class."[24]

The dealers tried to put a brave face on their defeat. There was talk of another bid, backed by a $2 billion line of credit from Citibank Canada, to buy both voting and non-voting shares, though the dealers later denied that the plan was ever under active consideration. In a videotape sent by the bidding group to all employees, Paul Weber, a dealer in Windsor, Ont., explained why they had stayed quiet and

---

22 Supreme Court of Ontario, Divisional Court, *In the Matter of the Securities Act*, Reid J., 1816–17.
23 Supreme Court of Ontario, 1822.
24 Ian Brown, *Freewheeling: The Feuds, Broods, and Outrageous Fortunes of the Billes Family and Canada's Favourite Company* (Toronto: HarperCollins, 1990), 7–8.

been such poor communicators during the proceedings. "Dealers are retailers. We run stores and we run them well, but we don't have much experience in making multi-million-dollar stock offers."[25]

Behind the curtains on the main stage where the drama played out, Canadian Tire rolled on, oblivious to the actors' theatrics. In the same month that the OSC panel ruled, the company announced its financial results for 1986. Revenue was $2.3 billion, up from $2.1 billion the previous year. Profit had recovered to $89 million, a substantial turnaround after a loss of $108 million in 1985 during the last gasp of the Whites fiasco. "While the company has been surrounded by turmoil and some uncertainty, we have maintained our focus on running the business," chairman Hugh Macaulay told analysts.[26] "We finished the year with a flourish."[27]

So did Martha and her brothers. The February 1987 edition of *Financial Post Moneywise Magazine* estimated the family fortune at $140 million. Some people regard defeat as a blow to be borne, but Martha saw the loss as a way of advancing her own cause. She believed that a lifetime of living with her brothers and learning how to handle them would pay off. "I have a lot of faith in the human race, sometimes not all that well founded, but sometimes it proves out," said Martha in a recent interview. "I know my brothers extremely well. I created a plan. Guess who won?"

Martha's long-range view was lauded by board loyalist and close friend Maureen Sabia. "She was the link between her father and the future of this company," said Sabia. "She really did have his instincts and his savvy. It was hard for me to think that she might sell her interest. But I also knew Martha well enough to know that she understood the levers that had to be pulled in order to achieve the right result. Ultimately the right result was achieved. There was no sale.

---

25 *Globe and Mail*, February 14, 1987.
26 *Toronto Star*, February 17, 1987.
27 *Globe and Mail*, February 17, 1987.

She hoped and worked hard to keep the family connected with the corporation. Martha always wanted that to happen in her heart of hearts."

Martha had successfully tested a new strategy by forging an alliance, even with her enemies, when it suited her purposes to do so. The next step in her grand plan employed the same device with Stephen Jarislowsky, the investor who had fought so hard to beat her back. Martha had come to believe in accommodation, embracing other views, as a way of getting everyone on side. Reducing the number of enemies might not produce new friends, but it did clear the path of obstacles. For Martha, her plan included appointing a new member to the Canadian Tire board, one who would represent the non-voting shareholders who had felt so aggrieved.

In her search for such a person, Martha sought to defang Jarislowsky by seeking his counsel. "Martha called me very often," he said. "Much to the unhappiness of my wife, because sometimes she phoned at ten at night. She asked me for [names for] other nominations to the board. All that became quite pleasant after a while. The business meant a great deal to her." In 1987 Ron Oberlander, an executive vice-president at Abitibi-Price Inc., was designated as the first Tire director to represent non-voting shareholders. By taking charge of the negotiations to change the board in such a significant way, however, Martha had eclipsed Fred and David. "She spoke for them," said Jarislowsky. "They were totally uninfluential." Yet contentment was no more Martha's bedfellow than it ever had been. Said Jarislowsky, "I've always found her a pretty spirited if quite unhappy woman."

SEVEN

THE
WAITING GAME

*"It's what she wanted to do, and if you don't do
what she wants to do, then you're in trouble."*
— DENNIS GARDINER-BILLES

The TV commercial, which first aired in 1983, opened with a shot of some young boys on a frozen pond choosing sides for a game of pickup hockey. Two boys were designated as team captains, then each took turns selecting the best available player.

"I'll take Joe," said the first.

"I want Steve," said the other.

Tommy, Mike, and Patrick were named until, finally, there was just one lad left, a freckle-faced kid who looked like the youngest.

"I guess that leaves Albert," said one captain.

"Hey," says the other captain, "he's your kid brother. You take him."

The next scene showed the hockey equipment available in a Canadian Tire store, followed by a flash forward to a professional hockey game with fans lustily cheering "Albert, Albert, Albert." As Albert stepped onto the ice, the camera focused on the coach of the other team, who said, "I sure wish we had a guy like Albert."

So popular was the commercial that, when it ran on big screens in arenas during real games, spectators chanted Albert's name in unison. The message was clear. Equipment from Tire can make anyone an all-star. But there was an emotional subtext as well. The youngest can rise up, fight back, and become number one, to the detriment of others who failed to see that person's talent. Martha was about to prove that she was that kid who would go places.

On April 21, 1987, Martha activated the legal notice she had served the previous November and sued her brothers in the Supreme Court of Ontario. No one who knew the Billeses was surprised. Beyond their common interest in money, there had been little unity among the three siblings for years. Once the offer by the dealers had been scuttled, the real feelings held by Martha, Fred, and David towards each other bubbled to the surface like swamp gas. All second-generation inheritors of a family business need to feel legitimate; they worry that they will never match the accomplishment of a founding father. What they seek, instead, is respect by society in general, and the business community in particular, for their worthiness as stewards. With the Billeses, their actions had done little to command such a vote of confidence.

According to Martha, the boys had ganged up on their baby sister when they offered her the opportunity to buy their shares. Claimed Martha's suit: "The ability for Fred and David to combine their notices into one is not provided for in the agreement and creates significant economic hardship to Martha or deprives her of the right to purchase the shares from either only Fred or only David. The design and intent of the notice . . . is a breach of the fiduciary duty owed by Fred and David to Martha."[1] Martha's lawsuit asked that Fred and David sell their 1.4 million voting shares to her at $12.25 a

---

1   *Globe and Mail*, April 23, 1987.

share. She also asked for $2 million in damages. If the court agreed, Martha would have paid a relatively modest $17 million to acquire their 40.6 per cent and thereby gain control. Alternatively, Martha said she would accept $125 million in damages.

Dennis had advised Martha against taking such action, arguing that she was suing not only her brothers but also their children, because some of the shares had been put into family trusts. His words went unheeded. "I knew she did not have a firm foundation for the suit. I was just basically thrown out of [her lawyer] John Stransman's office because I was against it." Dennis felt Martha was so far in the wrong that he phoned Fred and David, offering to support them against her.

The marriage between Martha and Dennis had begun to unravel. His advice in opposition to her wishes only made matters worse. "It's what she wanted to do, and if you don't do what she wants to do, then you're in trouble," said Dennis.

Dennis filed for divorce. In an affidavit he referred specifically to the 1986 gathering at A.J.'s condo, complaining that he'd been subjected to "physical abuse." Dennis also said that, as a spouse, he had been little more than a lapdog who was expected to carry out Martha's every whim. He described himself as her aide-de-camp, escort, handyman, accountant, chauffeur for Owen, and official mucker-out of the horse stalls at Shanty Bay. "Once or twice a year I was responsible for loading up the respondent's household, including the dogs and the horses, and taking them to Barrie and/or Toronto and back."[2]

Dennis asked for $8,000 a month in alimony or a lump-sum payment of $4 million. Under the terms of their divorce settlement, dated December 21, 1988, Martha agreed to pay alimony of $4,000 a month, retroactive to October 1987, but stipulated that the payments would

---

2   *Saturday Night*, May 13, 2000, 53.

end if Dennis remarried or cohabited for more than ninety days. Dennis also got the 1981 Cadillac Seville as well as US$437,620 in a Credit Suisse bank account in Zurich. He renounced any interest in their Calgary condo at 35 Oakmount Court. Martha also demanded a halt in any legal action by Dennis against Fred and David "with respect to any alleged assaults by them or either of them" upon Dennis. The settlement got so specific that it included a request by Martha for Dennis to return a lithograph entitled *Sea Otters* and a tapestry called *The Musicians*.

The children of divorce can sometimes get lost in the shuffle. In this case, however, Owen couldn't have been happier. He was relieved to be rid of Dennis and to have him out of his life at last. "He had a nice, free ride for a long time," said Owen. "He didn't make anybody's life any easier. He lost, I won. I stayed, he went."

MARTHA WAS NOW ABLE to concentrate on her long-term ownership plan for Canadian Tire. Launching the lawsuit meant that she had effectively blocked Fred and David from selling their shares to anyone else. With Martha's lawsuit pending, no prospective buyer could be certain that either brother could actually deliver his shares.

David was shocked and hurt by her lawsuit. Despite their differences over the years, David recalled how close he'd felt to Martha when they were both at Forest Hill Collegiate. "So, all of sudden, now this person who had been my best friend is suing me for everything," he said. "Like, not suing me for ten dollars or a million dollars, suing me for everything. The part of it that's really bothered me the most [was] that she did not bother to phone up and have a one-to-one discussion. Because to me it was not critical to sell if something else could be done."

Ever the diplomat, David tried to settle the matter. He was motivated by the advice given to him by his lawyer, who said that any lawsuit had only a fifty-fifty chance of success because neither side could possibly know how a judge might rule. "No matter who won, or if the judge threw it out, what would we have gained? In my opinion, it was a no-win situation. It's a part of history I'd like to forget," said David. He talked separately to Martha and Fred, but got nowhere with either of them.

Any pretense that the three siblings could work together and agree on anything to do with Tire was gone forever. If one sibling sues another, the relationship can never be repaired. "You do absolutely everything possible first and then, if it's a matter that not suing will destroy you, then you might have to sue," said David. "But it's not the first step; it's the absolute last. From what I've seen, I mean I'm an amateur, I don't know anything about law, but I don't know how somebody gave her that advice. It is so antagonistic that it ruins your own life. For me, the period of time, which was over a year, that this lawsuit was outstanding was hell, emotionally. Back then when the lawsuit was on, [an employee of twenty years] was saying that he could tell if something had happened when I came in the next morning. I was all torn up. It was a real rotten time."

For all his declared angst, David did not surrender easily. On June 5, 1987, David and Fred countersued Martha for her 20 per cent of Tire plus $35 million, claiming that she was the one who broke the Aldamar agreement by striking a different pact from theirs with the dealers. "We were strictly defensive," said Fred. "As far as we were concerned, dear little Martha was just being her normal self. The rest of her life, and the kind of lawsuits and problems she's got herself into, speak volumes. If you can't get your way one way, you get your way another way. You get your way — that's the big thing, get your way. We never learned how to deal with her — nor did her first husband, nor her second husband, nor her various boyfriends, nor her son."

∞

BY THE TIME of the annual meeting in June 1987, Canadian Tire's management and directors were feeling under siege. The OSC rulings and the ongoing family feuds had been a double dose of negative publicity. "Canadian Tire has been in the news a lot recently — and not always for the reasons that we in management would like," Macaulay told the shareholders. "There's been a lot more speculation about the ownership interest than there has been coverage of the strength and growth of our business."[3] In an attempt to refocus the watching world on the storied past instead of the sullied present, A.J. was asked to stand and be recognized. On display were giant copies of catalogue covers, as if to assure shareholders of the church's one foundation.

Media attention was not easily diverted from ownership wrangles. "I believe the current status quo should be maintained," Martha told reporters. As for the trouble with her brothers, "All businesses that have family relations have their ebbs and flows," she said blithely. "I still have the option to buy. I always wanted to remain."[4] That statement, of course, did not mention the fact that the previous fall she'd put her block up for sale, but that did not seem to prevent her from revising history. "Any disappointment that I have came many months ago, when the brothers became determined on a course to sell. I was a little cog in that fiasco," she said. "I've been heartbroken ever since."[5]

A common enemy required to drive the family and the dealers back into each others' arms arrived in the form of a group representing nearly one-third of the 84 million non-voting shares. The group, calling itself the Class A Shareholders Action Committee, demanded more takeover protection for all shareholders. A special meeting required to vote on the takeover issue was set for July, but then

---

3 *Toronto Star*, July 5, 1987, F2.
4 *Toronto Star*, June 30, 1987, B1.
5 *Toronto Star*, October 17, 1987..

postponed to October. "Everyone had their own agenda," Martha said of the protracted negotiations over the summer. "It was like a Rubik's cube. I've been bending over backwards for many, many months, [but] my back's not quite broken."[6]

When the meeting was finally held in October, various possibilities were debated. One plan put forward would have allowed Fred and David to convert each of their voting shares to 2.75 non-voting shares, while Martha retained her shares and stayed on the board. Non-voting shareholders would also be allowed to convert their shares into voting shares and elect two-thirds of the board of directors. Of course, there was a wrinkle. The new voting shares wouldn't have the same strength as the voting shares already owned by Martha. Any takeover would require approval from both classes of voting shares in separate votes, thereby giving Martha and her holdings special status. The non-voting shareholders rejected that concept as unfair and defective. No new arrangements were approved.

That Halloween, public relations specialist Tom Reid offered an unusual treat at his home in Oakville, Ont. Along with candy, he gave the first one hundred children to his door one Canadian Tire Class A non-voting share, each worth about $12. The reason, he explained, was to encourage young people to invest in the stock market and learn about the free enterprise system. Martha, Fred, and David did not show up to collect.

FROM AN OWNERSHIP PERSPECTIVE, little had changed by May 1988, when the next annual meeting was held. There was, however, a shift in the momentum. Although there was no pre-arranged seating for the six hundred shareholders who gathered in the Bluma Appel Theatre at the St. Lawrence Centre in downtown Toronto, Martha sat

---

6 *Toronto Star*, October 17, 1987.

regally on one side of the auditorium, surrounded by fellow board members and senior members of management, looking for all the world like an heiress rampant with her courtiers paying homage. Fred and David, the dark princes, occupied a far corner of the kingdom. Despite their status as directors and the stature of their surname, the two brothers sat glowering alone together on the other side of the room, without the support of any such contingent of troops.

Shareholders were fed up with seeing Tire as a battle zone for sibling warfare. "When is all this infighting going to stop?" asked Ralph Haan of Scarborough, Ont., who had owned 2,000 shares since 1967. "I hope it's soon because it's costing shareholders money waiting for the stock to move up."

Fred had been preparing for his eventual exit since putting his house up for sale in 1985, asking $7.95 million for the 3,250-square-metre monster in the Bridle Path area of Toronto. In 1988 he sold his Yonge Street store to Ken Mann and began establishing residence in the Cayman Islands, a tax haven in the Caribbean. "I rolled through a lot of different things and I rolled out the end," said Fred. "I landed on my feet and kept running. Period. The time comes when you've got to move. You don't stay in the same rut. If you do, all it is is a grave with the ends kicked out."

Over the next two years Mann replaced the store and warehouses with a new outlet. (The store, which retained a portion of the original arched facade, went on to become one of best-performing dealerships, with $32 million in annual sales.) "Fred treated me like a gentleman," said Mann. "Each of us has our points we like to boast about and points that we don't want anyone to know about. I would not criticize Fred for anything. I think Fred had a very, very difficult situation with the Billes name and the whole mix of things that were going on at that time. Fred had a very heavy burden to carry. I think it would have been almost too heavy for any of us. I think Freddy just got burned out. He was in huge footsteps."

As for Martha, she had Fred on the run, heading for self-imposed exile. He began spending more time outside Canada, on Grand Cayman or in his other new residence just across the Canada-U.S. border in Alexandria Bay in the Thousand Islands region of the St. Lawrence River. In May 1989 he raised about $4.5 million by selling 200,000 non-voting shares on the open market, leaving him with one million non-voting shares worth $22 million as well as his 700,000 voting shares.

Both brothers were still on the board, but they might as well have been castrated eunuchs. As a result, Martha was able to put in motion another step in her plan to take over the empire. On October 30, 1989, Martha, Fred, David, and the dealers signed a new accord that extended portions of the Aldamar agreement of 1983 and set out new aspects of the relationship. Part of the understanding was that, as long as the combined interest of family members and the dealers was at least 50.1 per cent, there could be no new surprise owner. The four parties also agreed to mutual rights of first refusal, again to make certain that each participant would have an opportunity to buy out the other before a different potential acquisitor could even be approached. Martha made certain that no future purchase she made could provide a "coat-tail" for any other shareholder. She never again wanted to face the Ontario Securities Commission!

Going forward, each of the three siblings and the dealers would continue to appoint three directors to the board. Non-voting shareholders would be represented by three directors. The chief executive would be the sixteenth director. The pact would run for ten years. In retail, where planning what merchandise will sell next season was tough enough and three-year forecasts were just pie-in-the-sky, a ten-year contract was simply unheard of.

With peace, however, came a cost. The dealers agreed that the siblings could keep the $30 million deposits paid by the dealers in conjunction with their aborted 1986 purchase offer. Martha paid $2.5

million to both Fred and David, thereby redressing the original imbalance. With that adjustment, each of the three siblings received the same amount, $10 million. All lawsuits against each other were dropped. The dealers, owners of 17 per cent of the voting shares, agreed that they would not increase their holdings beyond 33 per cent. With that upper limit in place, they could never again take a run at control.

Martha was the biggest winner. She was best positioned to gain control of the company. The dealers were capped at 33 per cent. Fred and David could no longer trot their shares around, looking for the highest bidder, as they had set out to do in 1986. Any price she paid for control of the company was bound to be much lower than before because there could be no dealer group, no Imasco, no one else involved in a bidding war.

Fred and David also got what they wanted — a guaranteed exit when they decided to divest. When their shares were offered, the buyer had to purchase all of them, rather than buy some and leave the seller with a partial ownership. "That's why we had to have the final trap door, the final way out, a complete sale," said Fred. "You offer them all, and they can't take less than all."

Fred was not yet ready to sell. He even believed for a time that peace might prevail, but relations would never be the same. Fred did not bother to attend the signing of the 1989 agreement, sending a representative instead. The celebratory lunch was held at a restaurant on Toronto's Queen Street with a particularly relevant name: Fred's Not Here.

With her brothers boxed in, Martha next set out to impose her will on the other members of the board. "My sister wanted her electees to be very much 'yes men,'" said David. "My sister always said that she wanted somebody, when push came to shove, who would support her position. My opinion was that you had to have somebody who would always do what he thought was right for the company and, if you

Brothers J.W. (left) and A.J. wearing top hats and tails
for their sister's wedding in the mid-1920s (CANADIAN TIRE)

Store at Yonge and Isabella streets in downtown
Toronto in the early 1930s (CANADIAN TIRE)

Clerks wore roller skates in the Toronto store at Yonge and
Davenport from the 1930s to the 1950s (CANADIAN TIRE)

Martha, David, Fred, Muriel, and A.J. at their Shanty Bay cottage in the early 1950s (CANADIAN TIRE)

Martha (arrow, at right) with the Forest Hill Junior High choir c. 1954 (JOHN RUTHERFORD)

Gwen, John, and Dick, children of J.W. and Gladys, in the late 1930s (BETTY AND JOHN BILLES)

Jogwendi II, J.W.'s fifty-five-foot Ditchburn, with double-planked mahogany hull (BETTY AND JOHN BILLES)

Catalogue covers, including spring–summer 1940,
current at the time of Martha's birth (CANADIAN TIRE)

Gladys and J.W., A.J. and Muriel in the early 1950s (CANADIAN TIRE)

A.J. with spade, Gladys waving from earthmover, at sod-turning in 1956 (CANADIAN TIRE)

A.J. in 1963, grooming Fred (left rear) and David for roles in the business (*TORONTO SUN*)

Dean Muncaster, chief executive from 1966 to 1985, oversaw growth in
annual revenue from $100 million to $2 billion (*TORONTO SUN*)

(From left) Roger (Martha's first husband) and Martha, with A.J. and Muriel,
Barbara and Fred in the mid-1960s (CANADIAN TIRE)

The family in 1970: (back row from left) Alfred, Fred and Barbara, David and Donna,
Roger and Martha; (on settee) Heather, Owen with A.J., Garth with Muriel, Diana, and Alen;
(on floor) Maeve, Deirdre, and Princess (FRED SASAKI)

The family in 1983: (from left) A.J. and his second wife, Marjorie, Deirdre, Maeve, Garth,
Barbara, Fred, Dennis (Martha's second husband) and Martha,
Alfred with Liza, his wife, Sue, with Stephanie, and Heather (MARJORIE BILLES)

David during the Ontario
Securities Commission
Hearings in 1986 (*TORONTO
STAR* — F. LENNON)

Fred during the Ontario
Securities Commission
Hearings (*TORONTO
STAR* — F. LENNON)

A resolute Martha at the Ontario Securities Commission Hearings (*TORONTO STAR* — A. DUNLOP)

Dean Groussman, chief executive from 1986 to 1992, could never penetrate Martha's shell (*NATIONAL POST* — LYNN FARRELL)

A.J., TD bank chairman Dick Thomson, and Martha at the Canadian Business Hall of Fame in 1990 (*TORONTO SUN*)

Steve Bachand, chief executive from 1993 to 2000, had a prickly relationship with Martha (*NATIONAL POST* — PETER REDMAN)

Wayne Sales, named chief executive in 2000 (*NATIONAL POST* — GLENN LOWSON)

Martha in 1997 with bronze bust of A.J., copies of which exist at the head office, the distribution centre, and the Shanty Bay cottage (*NATIONAL POST* — LYNN FARRELL)

A triumphant Martha presents Fred with a photo album at his goodbye dinner in May 1998
(LISA SAKULENSK PHOTOGRAPHY)

Paul McAteer, Martha's lover and partner in Devoncroft Developments, outside a Calgary court in 2000 (CP PHOTO/*CALGARY SUN* — CARLOS AMAT)

Pamela Mason, whose marriage to McAteer ended when he met Martha
(CP PHOTO/*CALGARY SUN* — CARLOS AMAT)

In May 2001 Martha drove seven hours to North Battleford, Saskatchewan, to help the local Tire dealer distribute bottled water after the local water supply was infected by a parasite (*NATIONAL POST* — TODD KOROL)

were wrong, to tell you to your face, privately first, but if need be, vote against you at the board."

Martha had driven Fred out of the country; now circumstances were conspiring to push David off the board. His role was becoming increasingly time-consuming and less rewarding. Prior to every meeting, directors received an inch-thick package of documents. "It took me a couple of days to go through and prepare for a meeting, to read it all, and try and understand it," said David. "The financial stuff was above me, a lot of it. The logistics stuff, that was fine, the concepts. It was a lot of work, and not the type of work that I enjoyed."

In 1990 David decided that he no longer wanted to sit as a director. His continuing ownership position meant that he was still able to name three directors, including one who would replace him personally, but who? He had been watching Martha's influence on the board grow since the arrival in 1985 of Maureen Sabia. The two women made much of their independent views, but David could discern little difference between them. "The two of them were like two peas in a pod. They came with their agenda and one would support what the other one was saying," he said.

When David decided to step down and name a replacement director, a knowledgeable nominee was available. One of Martha's previous nominees had been Ted Medland, chairman and chief executive of Wood Gundy Inc., the Bay Street investment firm. David noticed that Medland's name did not appear on Martha's slate for the coming year. When he asked Martha why, she replied that Medland would not toe the line. Rather than look elsewhere for someone to take the seat he was about to vacate, David simply put Medland's name on his own list as his nominee. Martha, who had wanted to see the backside of Medland, could not stop David. No vetoes were possible.

In a recent interview, Martha denied dumping Medland for not kowtowing. "I expect the members of the board of directors to take a very, very even-handed view, to research and find out more about a subject if there's some question in people's minds. I expect them to stand for whatever it is that they stand for and not collapse, not just simply roll over because a group is pushing the other way." In Medland's case, she said she simply wanted a fresh face. "There's often need for change in chemistry in a boardroom. There should be change occasionally or when you see greater strength in someone else and you want to bring them in. I believed there was someone else that could benefit Canadian Tire at that particular time. I brought someone else on board."

Viewed from the outside, Medland's reappointment looked seamless. Viewed from within, it was anything but. Medland represented David and continued to serve on the Canadian Tire board for a further six years.

Such setbacks did not deter Martha. She began to monitor Dean Groussman closely. He provided her with plenty of ammunition. He even made the same mistake that Dean Muncaster had made by taking Canadian Tire into the United States, albeit on a much smaller scale. In 1991 the company opened three auto-service outlets in Indiana and Ohio under the banner Auto Source. Unlike stores in the Whites acquisition, each Auto Source outlet was new. Each featured twenty service bays and 25,000 square feet of warehouse-type retail space.

Groussman also pushed for changes in Tire's financial arrangements with the dealers, a relationship that Martha regarded as untouchable. In 1988, as a first step towards a new partnership, he gave them the security of five-year contracts, in place of the one-year agreements that had previously been in place. The contract also included a buyout if Tire was acquired by a new owner. That was the good news. In 1990 Groussman proposed the bad news: higher rents to help cover the increased costs of expansion.

Since time immemorial, rents had been charged on a sliding scale. The procedure was for a new dealer to start at a small store, then move to successively larger outlets. At each store the rent initially charged was 4 per cent. As the dealer increased annual sales, the rent paid to head office was reduced in stages until it reached 2 per cent, the minimum levy. Groussman wanted all dealers to pay a flat rate of 4 per cent, no matter what stage they were at in their careers.

The dealers, who would have had to pay more under Groussman's scheme, were appalled. "He didn't appreciate how the dealer network worked. He was making suggestions that caused a lot of ill will," recalled Steve Groch. Groch had started as a dealer in 1974 and spent five years working his way up through two small stores in Ontario to a larger one in Saskatoon. When Groussman told Groch about his idea, Groch cried foul and cited his own situation. He'd paid 4 per cent rent when he first moved to Saskatoon but, over time, the rent had been reduced and had reached 2.5 per cent of sales. Groch's annual sales were $10 million, so if Groussman jacked all rent payments to 4 per cent, the annual rent Groch paid would jump from $250,000 to $400,000. That additional $150,000 each year would come out of the money that had been going into Groch's pocket.

Groch urged Groussman to think instead about new marketing ideas that would help all stores increase their sales volumes. That way, rental collections by head office would increase in proportion to sales, but the proportion charged to dealers would stay the same. The rising tide would raise all boats. "I'm going to do both," replied Groussman. "We're going to increase sales volume *and* rent."

Groussman's method was similar to what he used in the States, where managers were employees. Canadian Tire was different; dealers wanted to be treated the same as the chief executive. The dealers came to dislike Groussman. They saw his jewellery background as useless in running a company that sold auto parts. He never got his hands dirty, they said with a sneer. "He didn't understand the culture," said Richard Hobbs, who had been in charge of dealers in the past. "It was a big bone of contention." Tire was being sidetracked into another battle that drained energy and poisoned relations. "When you're president and CEO of a company that is a dealer organization, you're CEO of a company that has four hundred CEOs," Groussman later recalled. "Anything that hurts their pocketbook, they're going to dig in. If I was in their shoes, I'd probably have the same attitude."

Fred had been instrumental in hiring Groussman and he continued to support him — with some reservations. "He wasn't a political guy and, with the dealers, you need to be a political guy," said Fred. Hugh Macaulay was also growing concerned about the conflict between Groussman and the dealers. "He had a little difficulty adjusting to Canada and the franchise system that we have in this country because American corporations have more regulatory control over their franchisees than Canadian corporations do," said Macaulay.

Martha saw Groussman's vulnerability. Her views mattered because she was increasingly regarded as the family member who would be around for the long haul. "Fred was one of the first to recognize that the dealer formula should change," said Groussman. "I don't think Martha would disagree with that, but Martha had many agendas. Never would I question that Martha didn't want the best for the company. Martha was probably more concerned about the negative attitude coming out of the dealers as a result of these protracted discussions than Fred was."

For Martha, the dealers were Tire's life force. Tampering with the relationship was taboo. The dealers had become so angry with Groussman and his plans that the Canadian Tire Dealers Association cancelled its participation in the annual convention held in September 1991. "Dean came at a time when the world was really starting to change around Tire and he had some hellish issues to address," said Martha. "These issues have not gone away. They've changed character, they've changed tenure, but life in the retail world is a constant, constant challenge. Dealers are out there on retail street, the corporation's inside here on the supply side, and Dean was not a 'people person' who could pull those two pieces of our culture together. He became the symbol of management and management domination. He wasn't the right man for that piece of the puzzle. They were very, very entrenched in their rights and he was very, very entrenched in what the corporation had to do."

Relations became so acrimonious that some dealers and others expressed anti-Semitic sentiments about Groussman — even though he is not Jewish. "The only people who know I'm not Jewish are Jews," said Groussman. "For some reason every Jew I meet knows I'm not Jewish and everyone else believes that I am. There's a good reason for it. My father was Jewish and I look Jewish and I probably talk a little Jewish, but I was raised in a Christian faith. I can't say I didn't have people discriminate against me as a result of the fact that they thought I was Jewish, but that's their prerogative."

Early in 1992 Groussman talked to a Tire director who put his tenuous situation as CEO at Tire into political terms. What if dealers were delegates to a political convention and Groussman was their elected leader: "How would you do with dealers on a referendum?" asked the director.

"Fifty-fifty," replied Groussman.

"If that's what you think, you're dead."

"He was out of his depth," said the director. "He was more a sales manager than a CEO. He was a nice guy, probably too nice. He saw the writing on the wall."

Ken Mann, the dealer who took over Fred's store and joined the board of directors in 1989, took a typically dim view. "As an individual, I liked Dean. It was just that he couldn't run the company. I thought the company was completely out of sync. It was going to rack and ruin. We had no clear-cut policies. We were not ready for the U.S. invasion [of Canada]. I'm not talking Dealerland; I'm talking the whole enterprise. It was frightening," said Mann.

Despite their discontent, Martha and the directors could not muster a consensus to dump Groussman. Such unanimity of purpose is rare on any board. Most directors don't like confrontation; that's why firing a chief executive is an unusual step at any company. For her part, Martha preferred not to be out in front on such an issue. While her nature may have been rebellious, she was unlikely to lead a revolt. As is the case with many savvy politicians, Martha would rather wait until momentum had become unstoppable before she'd position herself in front of the procession and appear to lead the parade.

As it turned out, no action by the board was necessary. Groussman was approached by his former employer, Zale Corp., to return to Dallas as chairman and CEO. In July 1992 he told the board of Canadian Tire he was leaving to replace Irving Gerstein, chairman of Peoples Jewellers Ltd., the Canadian retailer that had acquired Zale. Now Zale was floundering in the United States, just as Tire had with Whites. (When Zale emerged from bankruptcy protection in August 1993, Groussman quit. He returned to Canada and spent a fruitless three years as CEO of White Rose in a failed attempt to resuscitate the garden retailer. He now lives in Texas, invests in business ventures, and helps run them. He and his wife continue to spend five months a year at their cottage on Georgian Bay in Ontario.)

For all the infighting and instability, sales at Canadian Tire during the Groussman era rose 189 per cent to $3 billion, and net income per share was up 186 per cent. But a recession had arrived and, with the launch of the Canada-U.S. Free Trade Agreement in 1989, Canadian retailers appeared to be poorly prepared for the expected arrival of American banners. Tire seemed particularly vulnerable. Many stores were small and dingy. Staff was indifferent, the inventory control system wasn't working efficiently, and items advertised in the weekly flyer were often unavailable. Canadians gave their former favourite store a new name that was as insulting as it was descriptive: Crappy Tire.

DEAN GROUSSMAN WAS EASIER to get rid of than Dennis and those $4,000-a-month alimony cheques. Martha had become suspicious that Dennis was living with a woman. If she was right and he was cohabiting, alimony would end. In 1990 she hired a private detective, Martin Lafleur of the Calgary-based Elite Bureau of Investigation — an agency that snoops into a wide range of corporate, financial, and insurance matters using everything from electronic surveillance to old-fashioned tailing.

Elite discovered that Dennis did indeed have a girlfriend. When Dennis and Judy Hiscott began dating, he was fifty-nine and she was forty-three. Elite learned that the couple attended the theatre together, dined at a restaurant called Joey's Seafood, travelled to Halifax in July 1991 for three weeks, and spent the month of September 1992 in Britain. During a six-week period in February–March 1993 Elite sifted through Dennis's household trash half a dozen times, a technique known in the gumshoe world as garbology. Elite turned up such evidence as Christmas cards addressed jointly to Dennis and Judy. An invoice showing the purchase by Dennis of ladies' sleepwear for $21.99 was less incriminating because the gift could not be tied directly to Hiscott. Elite also took photographs of Hiscott through her apartment bedroom while she was naked and drying her hair.

Lafleur delivered a written report to Martha dated April 30, 1993. "It would appear that the subject is emotionally involved with Judy Hiscott," he said. "It would further appear that although they spent the week-ends together, they may not permanently live under the same roof." Lafleur also raised the possibility that Dennis might have a male roommate named Stan. "We must determine if your separation agreement specifies the nullification of spousal support if the subject lives with a male or a female."

Martha seized upon the report as providing sufficient proof that Dennis was not abiding by the terms of their divorce. She halted the monthly alimony payments and sued to have the agreement over-turned. In response, Dennis admitted having a relationship with Hiscott that meant he might stay overnight four times a month, but denied cohabiting with her. He also pointed out that Hiscott was not the only woman in his life. He saw Brenda Moore twice a week and had done so for the previous four years.

In his affidavit dated June 8, 1993, Dennis complained about the lengthy period of surveillance during which Elite had trespassed on his property as well as Hiscott's. At first he did not admit to Hiscott the specifics of Martha's action. "It's rather embarrassing to tell people that you're on alimony," Dennis said in a deposition. Two other women had dumped him as soon as they learned the source of his income. "As soon as they found out that I was receiving alimony, which basically means you can't get married if you wish, that termi-nated the association."

Dennis also took the opportunity presented by Martha's action against him to complain that she had not only withheld alimony pay-ments on occasion but had also nagged him for the return of specific items that he insisted he did not possess. "Your unreasonable letters each month do not merit an answer as you know full well that I would not take anything of yours, tablecloth, plant pot or dog leash," Dennis had written to Martha on January 12, 1991. "I thought I had demonstrated that when you forced me into a marriage and to protect your money I signed that marriage contract. I did these things for you, and demonstrated daily my honesty and integrity, but you choose to ignore this as you still do. I also have commitments, trying to rebuild my life after you, and a mortgage on, to use your expression, a 'little tacky box.' Why are you withholding my pay-ments? Are you in financial difficulties? P.S. Check the cleaners re your tablecloth; no doubt you have forgotten to collect it."

Martha's concern about such minor items seemed picayune, given her wealth and power, said Dennis in his 1993 affidavit. "The Applicant is an heiress to the Canadian Tire fortune and multi-millionairess. [D]uring our marriage, the Applicant and I maintained a very high standard of living and we travelled extensively and main-tained two or three different residences." In response, Martha denied that they had lived high off the hog. "We maintained a frugal lifestyle, did not travel extensively and I maintained a residence in Calgary and a summer cottage property. I will not inherit any money or property. This is well known by the Respondent, who acted as a Trustee in relation to my estate freeze."

In June 1993 the court ruled that there was insufficient evidence to support Martha's request to end the alimony payments. She appealed the ruling and lost again. Not satisfied, in 1998 she hired another investigator to dig up more dirt. Based on that report, she took the extraordinary step of suing Dennis and Hiscott for conspiracy to defraud. "I believe the plaintiff is using her position as Canadian Tire Corporation's director and majority shareholder and thus her superior resources to harass both Hiscott and myself without cause," said Dennis in his statement of defence.[7] The matter has not been set-tled and could yet end up in open court.

Through it all, Martha had the support of female friends such as Lahni Thompson of Fort McMurray, Alberta. Thompson found much about Martha to admire, such as her capacity to nurse a dog back to health or to do interior design. She could not, however, understand Martha's flawed judgment about male companions. "She has lousy taste in men and I've told her that. I've seen some of the men she's

---

7 *Saturday Night*, May 13, 2000, 54.

dated and I've seen the dollar signs in their eyes. Why doesn't she know any better? Beats the hell out of me."[8]

Even in those cases where a man had no interest in her money, Martha's relationships with men were difficult. In the fall of 1989 a friend of Martha's arranged a blind date with Stephen McLaughlin, an urban planner who had worked for three Toronto mayors, David Crombie, John Sewell, and Art Eggleton. From their first outing, Martha fretted constantly about her son. She told McLaughlin that Owen had attended all the best schools, but lacked ambition. She had bought him a new Audi, which he wrecked. She had given him her credit card to buy some pants, and he had made purchases totalling thousands of dollars. Like Martha, McLaughlin was twice divorced. Martha's tales of woe made him reluctant to get too close to her because she seemed so encumbered. As a single parent himself, one who was raising three daughters, he thought that Martha was handling Owen the wrong way. He told her to relax and be herself. "She really was concerned, but she had no inkling what to do about it," he said. "She always seemed to want to buy help." McLaughlin's contact with Owen was limited to seeing him at the downtown condominium he shared with his mother when she was visiting Toronto from her Calgary home. "Whenever I went to her place he was either asleep or lying in bed watching TV," said McLaughlin. "I don't think we had more than ten words together. He looked like a pretty sad guy. It was all a bunch of sadness."

For his part, Owen does not see himself as the spoiled brat portrayed by his mother. He had indeed crashed his Audi three months after getting it, but he'd been driving to his job at the Canadian Tire store in Barrie, hit black ice, and spun into the ditch. He was not injured, but the car was a writeoff. Owen did not take the incident lightly. "I was terrified of what would happen to me. Thank God

---

8   *Edmonton Journal*, May 27, 2000.

Dennis wasn't around at this point because there would have been a funeral or I would have had some prosthesis now. It's not 'Oops, I rolled it. Mummy, I need another one.' It's not like that at all. She's very frugal. Her idea of fun at the cottage is going out and mucking about in the woods, digging a ditch, or cutting a tree down." Owen admitted he ran amok with Martha's credit card, but he pleaded guilty with an explanation. At the time his clothing consisted solely of his school uniform. He owned no leisure wear, not even a pair of jeans. After being teased by friends for wearing grey flannels on the weekend, Owen asked Martha for her card, then went wild. After the statement arrived there were no more such blowouts. Said Owen, laughing: "I never got hold of that card again."

In addition to seeing McLaughlin, Martha had also been dating Bob Murray, the publisher of *Canadian Living* and *TV Guide*, but by 1990 they had concluded they should just be friends. She was equally open with Murray about her concerns regarding Owen. "There were some really tough times, but mother and son would make up and off they'd go to California and have a great holiday and they'd be just fine again," said Murray. "I think he found it difficult, Martha going here and there. You have to understand that one of the things that Martha does, and she may not know it, is that it's her way or no way. It's very difficult to be an independent person and have an ongoing, lasting relationship with Martha."

Martha also shared with Murray her unhappiness about how she was treated while growing up. "Martha is a very deep person who has been hurt terribly by her upbringing. She was the daughter who wasn't supposed to be any part of the business," he said. "She had more brains than the bunch of them combined. She was a woman driven. I don't know when the seed was planted, maybe at birth, [but] she planned to run that company. She knew every in and out, she knew what the directors were thinking, what the presidents were doing, she had papers there [at Shanty Bay] that she would go over.

Only a person who was really driven to run a company would be doing the kinds of things she was doing."

The possibility of love with Steve McLaughlin was as unlikely as it had been with Bob Murray, but she tried to fan the flames anyway. During the first half of 1990 Martha would call McLaughlin from Calgary when she was coming to Toronto and arrange to see him. In all, they dated about a dozen times. He thought he might at least be a friend because there were many aspects to her that he admired. "She was bright, she was strong, she was determined, and she attracted attention," he said. At times, however, Martha attracted the wrong sort of attention. McLaughlin was embarrassed by her bicycling get-up. "She was in an outfit that you couldn't believe. She looked like a bumblebee with brilliant red hair, purple glasses, a multi-coloured Lycra suit. There must have been twelve colours." McLaughlin led her onto the bike paths in Toronto's wooded ravine system where there was less likelihood that they would be seen together. "Fortunately, I didn't bump into anyone I knew."

While her clothing was bold, her attitude was bleak. Even a compliment by McLaughlin about her bike brought a snappish response. "It's a terrible bike," she said. "I asked the boys at Tire to get me this bike. They screwed up and got me the wrong bike." To McLaughlin, Martha was always the pessimist who saw the glass as half empty, not half full. "She's like one of those rough, prickly seashells with a delicate interior," he said. "Deep down, she's a nice person."

SEVERAL HUNDRED BUSINESS LEADERS and entrepreneurs gathered at the Metro Toronto Convention Centre on April 3, 1990, for the twelfth annual induction ceremony of the Canadian Business Hall of Fame. Lincoln Alexander, lieutenant governor of Ontario, graced the head table. Dick Thomson, chairman, president, and chief executive officer of Toronto Dominion Bank, was chairman of the black-tie event.

J.W. and A.J. Billes were to be inducted into the Hall of Fame, joining a list of dozens of other business tycoons including such famous retailers as Henry Birks, Sam Steinberg, and Timothy Eaton. J.W., of course, was long since dead, but A.J., still lively and alert at eighty-eight, was a happy head-table attendee accompanied by Martha.

The presentation began with a big-screen video outlining the history of Canadian Tire. Fred Davis, host of the CBC celebrity quiz show *Front Page Challenge*, supplied the voice-over. There were historic photos of the two honorees, tales of the early days, and a raft of pithy sayings coined by the founders, such as A.J.'s 1957 exhortation to employees about the profit-sharing plan: "Stick around and you'll be millionaires." J.W. was represented by his son Dick, who spoke of J.W.'s love of boating and described him as "intense, quiet, and reserved."

Next, the main participants, A.J. and Martha, made their way to the podium, where A.J. stood, stooped but smiling. The sustained applause washed up and over him like waves on a rocky promontory. His hearing was poor; he'd been listening to the proceedings using a giant set of earphones clamped on his head. His sight was also impaired; he peered at the audience through thick spectacles. A.J. appeared flustered, and the bright lights and the excitement made it difficult for him to read his speech notes.

There was, however, nothing wrong with his mind. A.J. began his remarks with some ad-libbed comments. "I think everything has been told," he said by way of mild complaint. "We've broken one of the greatest secrets we've ever had in our life, J.W. and I. Now we're going to get some competition." There was laughter all round. A.J. graciously acknowledged Dick, the nephew he drove off the premises in 1961, when he refused to give him power or responsibility. "I'm twice as old as he is and about half as good." Then A.J. turned to the matter at hand, the celebration of free enterprise and entrepreneurialism. "There's nothing like business. It's what makes the world go round.

We've seen what the opposite to free enterprise brings about in Russia. They're broke!" A.J. introduced Martha, and then he was helped back to his seat.

The Hall of Fame induction had turned into a ceremonial passing of the torch. A.J. was not accompanied by the ungrateful Fred, who had sought to sell his holdings. Nor was David, who had never cared about the business, on stage. The future was represented by Martha, A.J.'s little red-haired devil, the one who had so long been denied her rightful place. Passing the torch, be damned! At forty-nine Martha could have been the fiery torch itself with her pronounced cheekbones, sculpted nose, and long red hair that was piled up at the back and teased out on the right. Her two-piece outfit glittered in the spotlights. Throughout A.J.'s brief remarks, Martha stood beside him at the podium, but she could not remain still. She was in continual motion, her shoulders slowly swaying back and forth as if she were keeping time to some inner music that only she could hear. First the right shoulder was thrust slightly forward, then drawn back; then the left shoulder would come ahead and go back. Forward and back. Forward and back. If a woman could shimmy while she was supposed to be standing still, that's what Martha did. With that outfit, those sultry looks, and that sexy sashay, give her a song and she could have been Cher.

Martha was anxious about her speech. She wanted her words to be just right, so she had hired a speech writer to help draft her remarks and a speech coach to rehearse her delivery. "Canadian Tire, Canada's greatest retailer in the twentieth century, is a realization of a dream of two young men in their twenties," she began. "They had a unique and ever-evolving view of what they believed would make for a successful retail operation." After a quick survey of corporate history, she mentioned that A.J. liked to reminisce about the many heartfelt letters he'd received over the years from grateful customers. But rather than quote from the letters and keep the attention on A.J. and his accomplishments, Martha spoke of herself and her mother. "I also like to reminisce," she said. On an evening that was supposed to honour her father, Martha regaled the crowd with the story of how her mother had come up with the idea for Canadian Tire money and how she, Martha, had been present as a teenager when the idea was born.

As Martha wrapped up her remarks, she made the focus personal. "Thank you, Father, for the hard work, dedication, and the dream," she said. "Thank you for having shown a young woman that dreams are not only for poets, that dreams can be realized when they are supported by a strong will, hard work, and a dedication to a set of enduring values that hasn't wavered in all these years."

A.J. had shown her no such thing. Martha had completely revised and rewritten her own life story. Rather than be ignored by her father, it turned out that he had been advancing her cause all along. Rather than keep Martha out of the business for most of her adult life, he'd somehow helped her realize her goal. As for the role of her mother, no one else held the same view of Muriel's strong connection to the business that Martha did. "There was nothing in the dozen years I knew her that would ever even suggest to me she had involvement of that type," said Roger Henry of Muriel, his mother-in-law. "She was very proud of her husband and his business, but I think the ideas were all his, from the roller-skating to the gas bars, to the Canadian Tire money, to everything. Even his brother's ideas, those were his ideas."

Everyone in public life needs a schtick, a persona, a happy tap-dance that is theirs alone. Martha had created hers. According to Martha, she had been destined all along to inherit the family mantle, even though she had been kept off the board until 1980, had tried to unload her shares in 1986, and had sued her brothers the following year. As the self-anointed chosen successor, Martha was getting achingly closer to running the real thing.

EIGHT

GOOD MONEY AFTER BAD

"I told her my main issue, which it continues to be,
was the children. I thought, other than sleep with my husband,
she hadn't harmed me."
— PAMELA MASON

$\mathcal{A}$s had so often happened with Martha, other events conspired to distract her focus from her main goal: power. And, as had always been the case before, it was a man who put demands on her head, her heart, and her heritage. On January 5, 1990, Martha met with Michael Lavery, her long-time financial adviser, in the Calgary office of accounting firm Deloitte & Touche.[1]

Lavery had an investment idea for Martha: Devoncroft Developments Ltd. The real estate company owned Sunnybrook Courts, a thirty-two-unit apartment building in Red Deer, Alberta, as well as an interest in Kingswood Golf and Country Club, a nine-hole golf

---

1   Although official court transcripts and the 480 exhibits supplied most of the detailed information for this chapter, I am also indebted to published coverage by Carol Harrington, Bill Graveland, and Reg Curren of the Canadian Press; Ric Dolphin of the *Edmonton Journal*; Daryl Slade, Geoffrey Scotton, and Emma Poole of the *Calgary Herald*; Steven Chase of the *Globe and Mail*; and Ian McKinnon and Robert Remington of the *National Post*.

course and residential project with eighty-nine lots in La Salle, Manitoba, a village of four hundred inhabitants thirty minutes south of Winnipeg. Martha was interested, but only under certain circumstances. "Any investment I made, due to my limited time, had to be an automatic-pilot type of investment where there was management in place, and good management, and of course that there was a reasonable expectation of a reasonable return,"[2] she said.

Martha had always enjoyed risk-taking. Not for her the coupon-clipping life of the wealthy heiress who remained aloof from business. She liked to roll up her sleeves and see what she was getting into. Marty Godin, who lived in the same downtown Toronto condominium building as Martha, was both a boyfriend and a business adviser. He had steered her into a six-member investment group in the mid-1980s that supplied financial support to a pipeline contractor working north of Toronto for TransCanada PipeLines. After that, Godin had introduced her to a food services contractor supplying Quebec Hydro's James Bay project. In that case, Martha and James Slater, who had also been involved in the pipeline project, were the only backers. Slater knew the food business because he had owned a Toronto-based company that imported, roasted, and blended coffee for Dunkin' Donuts and McDonald's. Slater and Martha had travelled to James Bay to meet the contractor and inspect his operations.

The arrangement, known as factoring, was straightforward: Slater and Martha paid the supplier by buying his invoices to Quebec Hydro at a discount. The two got their money back, plus the discounted portion, forty days later when Quebec Hydro paid the amount that was owing. The process put money in the pocket of the contractor immediately; the investors made their profit on the spread. The risk taken by Martha and Slater was that Quebec Hydro might decide that the contractor was not living up to his commitments and would refuse to

---

2   Court of Queen's Bench of Alberta, Judicial District of Calgary, *Paul McAteer et al.*, Trial Transcript, 1577.

pay. As it turned out, Martha and Slater were always reimbursed. Over the eighteen months they were involved in the late eighties, each of them had put up about $100,000 a month.

Martha had done well with those two investments, so she was intrigued by Devoncroft. Lavery assured her that, as was the case with any real estate development, Devoncroft was speculative, but could be profitable. It had an excellent manager — a man named Paul McAteer — but he had run out of money, so was seeking a deep-pocket investor. Other possible partners who had turned him down included Dr. Charles Allard, an Edmonton-based cable TV magnate, and Earl Joudrie, a Calgary oil executive who was also a director of Canadian Tire. Martha agreed to meet McAteer.

When Lavery formally introduced them in his office two weeks later, McAteer presented his calling card, a busy little document that declared his full name, Paul Murray McAteer, announced his profession as a barrister and solicitor, and indicated he was an engineer, a lawyer, and a member of the bar in British Columbia, Alberta, and Manitoba. At six foot four and 240 pounds, McAteer was a big man with a salesman's winning way and the easy confidence of a gung-ho downhill skier. He was well dressed, well coifed, and, with his blue eyes and large moustache, had an expansive, happy face. He was forty-one, eight years younger than Martha. His fourteen-page curriculum vitae was impressive. He had graduated from the University of Ottawa in civil engineering in 1973, followed by law in 1976. He'd held jobs of increasing responsibility, beginning as corporate secretary at Qualico Developments Ltd. of Winnipeg. By 1984 he was senior vice-president at Carma Ltd., a Calgary-based developer, where he managed projects, arranged financings, and negotiated agreements. When McAteer lost his job owing to corporate downsizing, he decided to be his own boss. In 1987 he became involved in the ownership of a nine-hole golf course and later bought out his partner.

Martha did no in-depth investigation of McAteer or his scheme.

The only document she read was a marketing brochure that described the golf course in glowing terms. "Remarkable Kingswood!" declared the pamphlet. "In harmony with nature." While the concept of building houses around a golf course was common in the United States, and existed to a lesser degree in some Canadian cities, the idea of packaging lots with golf memberships was novel in Manitoba.

Martha instructed Lavery to investigate Devoncroft's finances, but did not ask for an independent third-party appraisal. Nor did she scrutinize the Devoncroft financial statements herself, relying instead on Lavery. She did visit the apartments in Red Deer, chauffeured by McAteer, who owned the building through a company with a cozy name, Home at Last.

At first, Lavery recommended that Martha invest $500,000 in Devoncroft, then he increased the amount to $750,000. On March 24, 1990, Martha agreed; the deal was set to close in April. For Martha the financials didn't matter as much as her personal instincts about McAteer, particularly the fact that he was going to remain involved in Devoncroft. As with past investments, she bet on the jockey as much as the horse. "I think that was about three-quarters of the reason that I was agreeable and amenable to both the purchase and the increased price, because I felt that Mr. McAteer was an extremely experienced executive in the real estate development business, which I knew nothing about, and that he was also an experienced corporate secretary," said Martha. "I bought an automatic-pilot corporation, and when I purchased the shares, I thought that the pilot was at the controls. I did not look to the assets; I did not look in any detail. I allowed that scope to be dealt with by my advisor."[3]

According to a later appraisal, Devoncroft was worth nothing like the $1.5 million represented by the $750,000 that Martha paid for her half. "From my conversations with Mrs. Billes I do not believe she

---

3 Trial Transcript, 1581, 1721.

was fully informed of the transactions that were occurring," said Jeffrey Cristall, a Manitoba-based business evaluator. "A prudent purchaser would have done more research of the value of the underlying assets. As of April 23, 1990, . . . the fair market value of the shares of Devoncroft Developments was $0."[4]

But value was whatever someone would pay, and Martha was a willing investor. "I had already done background work on golf courses, and people who had worked with Mr. McAteer spoke highly of him," said Lavery. "The project was speculative by nature. The golf course was only nine holes, not eighteen, and phase one of the development was dependent on lot sales. There was some chance of a downside. But I told her there was reasonable chance for profit, if developed properly." Others were not so convinced. "There were all sorts of people trying to warn her about Mr. McAteer," said Bob Murray, the publisher who was seeing Martha at the time. "He swept Martha right off her feet and pledged her his ever-lasting love."

For her $750,000, Martha was named a director and vice-president of Devoncroft, with McAteer as president and corporate secretary. He owned 10 per cent, his compensation was $5,000 a month, and his car expenses were reimbursed. His wife, Pamela, a freelance public relations and communications consultant, held the other 40 per cent in trust for their three children, Catherine Anne, thirteen, Sarah Elizabeth, eight, and Paul William Jr., five.

McAteer quickly insinuated himself into other aspects of Martha's business life, did some legal work for her, and eventually billed her $10,000 for his efforts.[5] "Mr. McAteer took great interest in assisting me," said Martha. "He told me that he was not only a partner, but he was a lawyer, and he wanted to help me and provide any assistance he could."[6]

---

4 *Edmonton Journal*, April 8, 2000.
5 Exhibit 40.
6 Trial Transcript, 1585.

As spring 1990 approached, the Canadian economy was slowing down. Unemployment and interest rates were rising, and consumer confidence was waning. Housing prices and stock markets were well below their peak. A recession that would last three long years had begun. Martha had bought into Devoncroft at the top of the real estate and economic cycle.

For a while, Devoncroft's future continued to look rosy because financial statements reflected the past, not where the company was headed. In May, McAteer faxed Martha a nine-page document, including a balance sheet, showing that, as of February 28, 1990, Devoncroft had assets of $1.8 million and earnings of $96,121. Sales projections for Kingswood were optimistic. To date, there had been revenues of $2.4 million. By 1996 the project was expected to produce a further $9 million in sales. The Red Deer apartment building, valued at $1.3 million on the books, generated revenue of $131,000 a year. McAteer believed he had found a kindred spirit in Martha. "I think the thing that fascinated me," he said, "was that I finally had somebody sharing the dream."[7]

MARTHA HAD BEEN SEEING both Steven McLaughlin and Bob Murray, but neither relationship was developing romantically, so Martha began looking at her new business partner, Paul McAteer, in a different light. In June Martha had visited Winnipeg three times to see McAteer and inspect Kingswood. She also met him several times during the summer to discuss the project. "We were becoming, I guess, friends and spent social time together," said McAteer. "We had no intimate relationship, but it was more than just business-related."

Every year Martha celebrated her birthday with a shindig at Shanty Bay, but September 7, 1990, was a special milestone. She was turning

---

7   *Saturday Night*, May 13, 2000, 58.

fifty. There were marquees on the lawn, plenty of filet mignon and drinks, as well as a band — in this case, The Good Brothers, a blue-grass group. Martha was at her social best, flitting about, making sure her friends and business associates were enjoying themselves. Love was in the air. Martha would later date one of the band members and was escorted that evening by Marty Godin. Paul McAteer was there and so was Bob Murray, but, by that point in their relationship, just as a friend. "She had a series of younger guys, forty or so years old, and I used to think 'Way to go, Martha.' I mean, guys are doing this all the time, having younger women," said Murray, who is now retired and living in Florida.

Three weeks later Martha stopped in Winnipeg on her way from Calgary to Toronto. McAteer picked her up at the airport and, on September 29, they dined at La Vieille Gare, a French restaurant in St. Boniface. After dinner, McAteer drove Martha to her hotel. She invited him up to her room for a drink, and, according to McAteer, Martha made the first move. They consummated their relationship.

Although the relationship between the two had reached a new level, McAteer continued with his plans to raise money through Martha. He hoped to expand the golf course from nine holes to eigh-teen, so he asked Martha for introductions to bankers. They visited the branch of the Canadian Imperial Bank of Commerce in Calgary that housed the Muriel G. Billes trust for Owen. They called on a branch of the Royal Bank in Calgary where Martha had dealings. Martha also asked executives at Tire for names at the Bank of Montreal in Winnipeg. Despite Martha's personal involvement, every institution turned McAteer down.

With commercial avenues closed, McAteer asked Martha for the money Devoncroft needed to expand the golf course. In November she decided that Owen's trust would invest $175,000 in return for a first mortgage. With family assets now involved, and their relation-ship spanning both boardroom and bedroom, Martha sought reassurance from McAteer that he loved her for who she was, not for her wealth. "I was a little bit worried about conflict with Devoncroft, his family, and any other aspects. He said not to worry, 'I will provide you with something that's absolutely ironclad,' and this is what he gave me," said Martha. "This was his expression of — in a legal way — of his intentions to look after and protect me."[8]

What McAteer offered Martha was a two-page letter dated October 7, 1990. The document was a sweeping guarantee that released Martha, her estate, and her heirs "from any act of negligence, be it gross or simple, direct or vicarious which occurs as a result of actions by yourself, agents, employees or any other person or corporation acting either with or without your knowledge, either individually or in concert with others. This release shall be applicable to all activities in which we participate together in either personal or professional capacities." As is often the case with such legal agreements, a token payment changed hands to seal the deal. Martha gave McAteer $100. In an accompanying note, McAteer made light of the exchange and referred to her prowess as a horsewoman: "The consideration is necessary and important, to ensure the contract and release is both binding and effective. I expect to spend it frivolously on presents or the cost of riding lessons."[9]

McAteer was now ready for his next move. On October 23, six days after his twentieth wedding anniversary, McAteer told his wife that he was having an affair with Martha. "I was surprised," said Pamela Mason. "I knew they enjoyed doing business together. When he told me, the marriage was over for me."[10] But McAteer, ever the salesman, wanted the two women to get along. "Paul told me she was distraught and very upset, that she was concerned about what I might do," said Mason. "I went to Mrs. Billes' house. She was crying. I was crying.

---

8   Trial Transcript, 1588–89.
9   Exhibit 22.
10 *Edmonton Journal*, March 14, 2000.

She didn't deny the relationship. I told her my main issue, which it continues to be, was the children. I thought, other than sleep with my husband, she hadn't harmed me."[11] The two women talked together as if they were old friends. Martha told Mason that she and McAteer should get a divorce. Mason agreed.

Three days later Martha visited McAteer's house. Martha and McAteer talked within earshot of Mason. "I heard her say, 'I accept your proposal,'" said Mason. "We briefly discussed what was going to happen and that the kids wouldn't be hurt by this." Mason wrote in her diary, "I do wonder if there's a wedding in the stars for them?"[12]

Martha later claimed that the marriage proposal was merely a cover story concocted by McAteer and Mason for the benefit of the three children. "They had come to some sort of an understanding between them as to how they would govern their affairs," said Martha. "Mr. McAteer expressed his desire not to have any negative repercussions with his children vis-à-vis his relationship, which had commenced three or four days before with me. The two of them together expressed their desire not to upset the children. Thus, the notional engagement to be married was to be the reason that Mr. McAteer was going to be assuming a different role and no longer living in that house but living in my house."[13]

The "notional engagement" did, however, include an engagement ring that Martha had designed in Toronto with a sizable stone that she proudly showed off to her friends. McAteer moved in with Martha, bringing with him some of his clothing and business files. He set himself up at the second desk in her home office, hammered a nail into the wall, hung his framed law degree from the University of Ottawa, and declared, "Now, I'm not only your partner, I'm your in-house legal counsel."

---

11 *Calgary Herald*, March 14, 2000.
12 *National Post*, March 15, 2000.
13 Trial Transcript, 1801.

Owen didn't believe the relationship would last. He'd met McAteer at Martha's fiftieth birthday party and didn't think the two were well matched. He recalled advice Martha had been given by her mother: "If you're going to marry someone, you bring them into your surroundings, and if they look uncomfortable and they don't seem to fit in, it's probably not going to work." Owen's concerns were confirmed when he saw McAteer's pathetic possessions. Martha owned antique furniture and oriental rugs; McAteer had primitive pieces that, to Owen, looked more like the ragtag belongings of a university student.

Pamela Mason seemed reconciled, even somehow relieved, with the new circumstances. She composed a Christmas letter to friends, dated November 30, 1990, that spelled out the new circumstances.

Greetings from Calgary,

This may not be your typical Holiday message, but when Pam's mother said to her on the telephone, "maybe you can write a letter and explain all this to me," it seemed like a good idea to do the same for all our close, personal friends.

"All this" refers to some major changes in the McAteer family. After twenty fairly wonderful years together as husband, wife, and the best of all possible friends, we're separating as man and wife, though planning to stay the best of all possible friends (and neighbours). "Why," you ask? The short answer is that Paul is going to marry Martha. "Who's Martha?" Well, she's a fine person, whom many of you in the East will no doubt get to meet in the near future as she and Paul will be spending quite a lot of time in Ontario. The rest of you will no doubt get to meet her closer to home, as they've bought a house just a few blocks away and will be spending the rest of their time in Calgary.

This will make it much easier for the children, who seem quite comfortable with the idea of having two homes, a new friend, and a mom and dad who still love them and one another.

A friend in our ski club lamented, "But you seemed like you really had your act together." Our reply, "We still do." "But you seemed to be so fond of one another." "We still are." We've never lived particularly conventional lives, so why worry about that now. (In all seriousness, when we look at the total picture, it seems not only right but somehow quite destined. In our minds there are no bad guys and no victims and we believe that all three of us will develop new and very positive relationships. In fact over the past few weeks, we've begun to do just that.)

The letter went on to talk about her house renovations, Paul's view of the economy, and the kids' schools, then was signed by "The McAteers: Pamela, Paul, Catherine, Sarah, Paul William, and the cat with no name (still)."[14]

It was a remarkable document by any standard: understanding in nature, mature in tone, and fully accepting of the marital rift. Either Mason was in total denial or she was a thoroughly modern woman — perhaps both. Her complete and utter acceptance of Martha was certainly unusual. Most women would not have been so accommodating when a husband was wooed away. Whatever Mason's motivations, Martha had captured McAteer with nary a peep from the only person in a position to put up a fight. Martha had found in Mason a bendable straw through which she was going to drink the love potion she needed: a new man in her life.

THE MONTH OF DECEMBER resembled giddy scenes from the popular 1970s TV sitcom *Three's Company*. Like John Ritter with Joyce DeWitt and Suzanne Somers, McAteer's two ladies got along famously. Martha invited Mason to lunch at the Westin Hotel. They discussed

---

14 Exhibit 27.

where and with whom the children would spend the holidays now that their parents were living apart. Martha and McAteer tootled around town together and took the children shopping. On occasion, Martha and McAteer picked up groceries at Costco for Mason, then dropped off the food and the children and proceeded on to other events. Martha, Mason, and McAteer all attended a school Christmas concert. On Christmas Eve, Mason delivered a tourtière to Martha.

Behind the social whirl of the holiday season, the legal separation of McAteer and Mason proceeded. Mason got the house and the Volvo; McAteer the GM van. The children would live with their mother and see their father on weekends. McAteer agreed to maintain a $300,000 life insurance policy, with Mason as the beneficiary. McAteer guaranteed dividends from Devoncroft for each child of at least $10,000 annually. As a freelancer, Mason's income was unpredictable. McAteer said he would cover any shortfall to ensure Mason an income of $2,000 a month.[15]

Martha and McAteer also came to an understanding. McAteer had already done some legal work for Martha, so he was learning about the extent of her wealth. He knew about the Muriel G. Billes Estate Trust for Owen G. Billes, but Martha also told him about other matters including the Martha Billes Family Trust (an estate freeze to minimize taxes at her death), Albikin Management (a holding company for Tire shares), and Marlore (her oil and gas interests).

Some of their assets were about to become intermingled. They had decided to buy a house together in the Mount Royal area of Calgary, so on December 23 Martha and McAteer signed a seventeen-page document known as a Matrimonial Property Act Acknowledgment that had the effect of keeping all of Martha's other assets beyond his grasp. They both agreed to be responsible for themselves as well as for the support and maintenance of their respective children. All

---

15 Exhibit 28.

property that either of them owned — even if acquired after the agreement was signed — was to remain separate.

The agreement between them was sweeping. One clause declared: "The parties realize that their respective financial circumstances may change in the future by reason of their health, the cost of living, their employment, and otherwise. No such change, no matter how radical or catastrophic, will give either party the right to claim support or interest support to the *Family Law Act*, *Domestic Relations Act*, or *Divorce Act* or any other legislation, from the other on separation or marriage breakdown." Another clause read: "Paul acknowledges that he may make contributions whether direct or indirect, to Martha's property. Notwithstanding this, no such contribution shall entitle him to make a claim for ownership of, division of or compensation by payment of an amount of money or by an award of a share of Martha's property ... even though such contribution may have increased the value of Martha's property."[16]

Martha believed she had taken sufficient steps. In fact, whenever her heart and her head became involved, no measures were enough. Legal aspects are easy to organize; love is impossible to impose.

MOUNT ROYAL WAS PROMOTED by the Canadian Pacific Railway as an exclusive Calgary neighbourhood right from its beginnings in the early years of the twentieth century. Named after the Montreal community where CPR president William Van Horne lived, the leafy enclave on a hill ten minutes from downtown Calgary became home to oil company presidents, bankers, and politicians. When Paul McAteer first moved there with Martha he must have thought he'd landed at the top of the social pecking order, dwelling as he now was among graceful homes with manicured lawns, alpine rockeries, and

---

16 Exhibit 21.

lush perennial borders. All the streets curved gracefully, as if laid out for genteel drivers who were never in a hurry. The sound of squealing tires might be music to the ears of a Tire dealer, but Mount Royal was a quiet place of refuge.

Their house sat nicely back from the street, across from a park where magpies stalked about, preening in their black-and-white clown suits. Steps led up to the front door past a two-car garage and a garden of pansies, poppies, and a crabapple tree. The 2,600-square-foot, two-storey, white stucco residence had a balanced look, with three large windows on each side of the front door — just the sort of place where you'd expect solid, respectable citizens to reside.

McAteer, the arriviste, could not deliver on his first promise. He'd agreed to split the $435,000 purchase price and was able to produce his half of the $35,000 deposit, but when the deal closed on December 28 he did not have the required $200,000. Martha provided all the funds. "He put the odd bit of cash into purchase of nails and glue and things like that," said Martha, "but cash monies against the purchase of the house, no." A month later, McAteer was no better off. "I can't come up with the $200,000," he said, handing her a promissory note from the company. "I'll secure my half of the house with this Devoncroft note. It's good, you know the company is good and solid, it's as good as cash."[17]

Like most dreamer-developers, McAteer cared little about the worries of today. The next big deal was always somewhere out there just beyond tomorrow. That transaction would not only solve all previous problems but also put him on easy street forever. But for now, money was tight at Devoncroft, even for ongoing operating expenses, let alone new construction. Since they already knew that the banks weren't interested in lending Devoncroft any money, Martha stepped in with two personal cheques, one for $7,500 and the other

---

17 Trial Transcript, 1647–48.

for $54,000. She also offered a $1.2 million loan from Owen's trust fund. Everything was done on a commercial basis. The $54,000 was written at 15 per cent interest, with one of the building lots as security. The $1.2 million loan was at 12.5 per cent, backed by a mortgage on the front nine holes. The financial infusion dramatically altered their relationship. Martha had been looking for an investment on automatic pilot. Nine months later she and the pilot were lovers. Trust funds that she helped manage were providing fuel for the flight into danger.

NO ONE CAN EVER completely escape the past. There are experiences to be savoured and mistakes to overcome, but, rather than learn from a faux pas, Martha Billes always seemed to make matters more complicated. She would circle back with the strength of all her resources to doggedly pursue those parties she believed had done her wrong. Victory was the only result she would accept.

Paul McAteer was not Martha's first real estate partner. Before him there had been Ed Wenzel, who had grown up near Camrose, Alta., the son of German Canadian farmers. After his Pontiac-Buick dealership had failed, he turned in the 1980s to real estate development in Calgary and Victoria. Wenzel met Martha through a mutual friend, and she became his financial backer in a subdivision development called Land's End near Sidney, BC, on Vancouver Island. The business relationship soured, and Martha launched a civil action claiming that Wenzel had stolen $537,614 from her.

Wenzel paid back the money, but the Victoria RCMP laid criminal charges against him. Two days before his trial was set to start on February 18, 1991, Wenzel visited his brother, Willy, in Camrose, then set out to inspect some oil leases he said he might buy. The sun was shining, the view was unobstructed, and the visibility was excellent when Wenzel brought his rented Pontiac 6000 to a stop on a gravel road where it crossed Highway 13, three miles west of Camrose. He then proceeded into the intersection, with an oil transport truck bearing down on him. Driver Randy Taylor hit the brakes, his rig jack-knifed, and he crashed into the Pontiac. Wenzel was killed instantly.

The investigating officer suspected suicide. "I was in highway patrol for 17 years," said Russell Olansky. "I've picked up more bodies than anyone should have to, and this one always bothered me."[18] There was also the questionable matter of a $5 million insurance policy that Wenzel had recently taken out on his own life naming, as beneficiaries, his ex-wife and their three children. Yet before the accident Ed was in good spirits, according to Willy, and had just taken up with a new, young girlfriend, so he seemed to have every reason to continue living. An investigation by the life insurance company was inconclusive. A settlement was later reached for less than the policy's face amount.

Martha was scheduled to appear as a witness at Wenzel's trial. Despite her common-law relationship with McAteer, it was Marty Godin who accompanied her to Victoria. On Sunday, Godin was in the hotel room with Martha when the telephone call came from the crown prosecutor: the trial scheduled for the following day would not be going ahead because Wenzel was dead.

When Martha later described her relations with Wenzel and his sudden demise, she was cold and clinical. "The final piece of the puzzle fell into place the second week of February 1991," was how she put it.[19] "Martha was not unhappy," said her friend Ruth Reimer. "She didn't like him very much. He'd stolen her money."[20]

---

18 *Edmonton Journal*, May 27, 2000, H1.
19 Trial Transcript, 1586.
20 *Edmonton Journal*, May 27, 2000.

IN MARTHA'S MIND the potential existed for every man to be such a thief. Wenzel was dead, but the memory of what he had done lived on. Martha now found herself in a similar situation at Devoncroft and she was becoming nervous about the growing sums of money she had at stake. She wanted to enlarge the circle of involvement, so she told McAteer they should keep Mason informed because of her status as the third Devoncroft shareholder. McAteer was a regular visitor at Mason's, hanging wallpaper and varnishing doors in his former wife's house, so the three had tea at the end of March to tell Mason about the loans. Martha had asked for Mason's signature on documents involving the $54,000 loan. Mason felt that Martha's request showed she did not trust her and requested that she never again be asked for her signature.

In addition to worries about the money, other aspects of McAteer's life were beginning to irk Martha. She resented the time McAteer spent away from her with his children, particularly family ski weekends at Sunshine Village in Banff National Park. "That drove her crazy. She couldn't understand that. Martha is used to having her way," said McAteer.[21] When Martha was with McAteer and his children, they were just too rambunctious and far too attached to him. Martha and Owen had a different relationship; they were not accustomed to such overt demonstrations of affection. "His kids obviously loved him lots and lots and lots," said Owen. "They were all over him, and I'm not like that. Give me my space and stay away." To make matters worse, the children did not follow Martha's rules and were unresponsive to her demands that they help with the chores.

McAteer was causing her grief, too. She worried about whom he might be seeing when he was in Winnipeg on business. In this case, there was good reason. Martha was angry when she heard that he'd been squiring around a thirty-six-year-old aerobics instructor.

---

21 *Canadian Business*, May 1, 2000, 45.

McAteer assured her that the relationship was platonic — just company for him on the Winnipeg cocktail circuit.

Over lunch on April 23 at The Dock, a bistro near Glenmore Landing in Calgary, Martha told Mason that she was growing increasingly worried. "She and her children and Mr. McAteer and I were shareholders of Devoncroft," recalled Martha. "My son Owen had loaned the money on the mortgage in November, and now here my dead mother was joining us in financing the golf course. We also discussed the fact that the bank loan had been paid — was to have been paid down, and I believed that it had — down to the $300,000 limit or below, but that no sooner does the coffer get filled [but] the money seems to be pre-spent with the golf course construction going on."[22] In her diary that night Mason described the lunch as "pleasant enough," but also noted that Martha made the "usual criticisms of the kids [and] Paul's preoccupation" with them.

The bad feelings were mutual. McAteer and his children were at Shanty Bay a few weeks later when he read in his daughter Catherine's diary that Martha treated his children badly when he wasn't around. "At that point I realized it just could never be a marriage," said McAteer. "She was very nasty to my children and they are my first love and I dedicated my life to them. That's what killed it."[23]

Martha had sent out invitations for a June soirée at Shanty Bay. As with her birthday gathering the previous September, The Good Brothers were on hand to provide the music. Rain fell briefly as early arrivals gathered, but the skies cleared and the evening turned beautiful. There was widespread anticipation among the guests that this event was intended to celebrate the engagement, perhaps even to announce a wedding date. After all, Martha had been looking at churches in Toronto where the ceremony might be held. "Between the invitations going out and the actual day in June, the whole thing

22 Trial Transcript, 1608.
23 *Saturday Night*, May 13, 2000, 58.

fell apart," said Bob Murray. "I'll never forget Martha standing up in the middle of this tent with maybe two hundred of her friends, employees and whatnot, dog in her hand, just welcoming everybody and not being able to say anything about Paul one way or the other. It was a very traumatic time." McAteer was on hand, but when some friends he had invited arrived in a yacht and tied up at Martha's dock, he made himself scarce.

As the personal relationship faded, the business was beginning to flounder. On September 5, 1991, Paul sent Martha a plaintive ten-page handwritten letter blaming hard-nosed bankers, thick-headed accountants, indecisive home buyers, everyone but himself for Devoncroft's financial troubles. "I have never experienced at one time such a series of broken promises, incompetence and failures to perform. When I look at it in hindsite [sic] it seems almost too unreal to believe this would be happening."[24] Still, McAteer held out hope. He said he could see the day when Devoncroft would be worth $8 million and be earning up to $1.5 million more in revenue than it would be paying out in expenses — a sizable and positive cash flow the company had never previously enjoyed.

But to get to such a point, Devoncroft needed to spend more money, and that money could only be raised by taking out yet another loan to pay for McAteer's next big idea — a golf dome that would generate year-round business. Household Trust was prepared to lend $700,000 (and perhaps as much as $500,000 more), but it wanted Martha's personal guarantee that the sum would be repaid if the project went sour.

Martha was unwilling to provide Household with any such personal guarantees. By now, she had more than $2.3 million invested in Devoncroft. There was her original $750,000 purchase price, a $175,000 mortgage, and a $1.2 million loan from Owen's trust, plus

---

24 Exhibit 52.

$200,000 that had been advanced over recent months from her hold-
ing company, Albikin Management.

Martha and McAteer had scheduled a week-long bicycle holiday
together in the Loire Valley later that month. McAteer saw the trip
as their last such time together, a chance to withdraw from the personal relationship but to keep the business partnership going. "With
everything converging upon me at one time I know that this trip was
a God send and is there for the right reason," McAteer wrote to
Martha on September 5. "I desperately needed help and understanding both personally and in the business sense. This is why strong
financial/operating partnerships survive. Overcoming adversity
together brings people together. My theories of positive and negative
energies are again coming home to me. The stress, pain and hurt of
the last six months is coming out like the after effects of poison ivy.
Please help us both back to the right side of the energy and all will
unfold as it should. France will provide us with an opportunity for
new beginnings in the relationship which was meant to be."[25]

Martha did not like weak men. Yet if there were powerful warriors
about, they never made themselves known to her.

MARTHA AND MCATEER WERE AMONG sixteen holiday cyclists who
gathered on September 9 near Tours, southwest of Paris. The Loire
Valley is flat and the road runs beside the river, so there are no heart-
pumping hills to climb. As a result, the trip was ranked "easy," but
the group was high-powered, boasting a sports agent, a biochemist,
and two lawyers. Most of the participants were Americans, but there
were also some Europeans and other Canadians in addition to Martha
and McAteer.

Each morning began with breakfast, followed by a briefing from

---

25 Exhibit 52.

the two guides about the day's highlights. The cyclists then headed out at their own pace, armed with maps, to cover the thirty-five-to-seventy-kilometre distance to that night's hotel. A van transported their luggage and, during the day, sought out individual cyclists en route to offer water or a snack.

Martha was among the most athletic and would often zip directly to the next hotel, then double back to admire the many turreted chateaux dating from the sixteenth century. Among the fabled sites they saw were Chenonceau, once occupied by Catherine de' Medici; Villandry with its geometrically designed gardens; and Chambord, rising like a confectioner's creation out of the royal game forest.

Martha seemed aloof and preoccupied. She didn't participate freely in the camaraderie among the strangers, who bonded as they enjoyed the same sights and ate the same food. "She was a bit more reserved and serious a person," recalled one tour participant. "She didn't get any more relaxed as the trip wore on." In contrast, McAteer was an ebullient boy on two wheels, often show-boating past his fellow cyclists, then roaring back to see how they were doing in his wake. At the end of the day he'd arrive at the designated hotel with his water bottle filled with wine that he'd bought at the roadside. "They have the best gas stations I've ever seen," McAteer said, as he shared his bounty with the others before they freshened up for dinner.

Martha and McAteer became such a closely watched couple that some members of the group were aware, one day in particular, when McAteer was in the doghouse as far as Martha was concerned. To cheer him up, they bought him a drink at the end of the day.

AFTER THE BICYCLE TOUR was over and everyone was home again, McAteer knew for certain that his love affair with Martha was finished. "I once again apologize for my insensitivity," he wrote on September 18. "It seems to be so illogical that I cannot sense were [sic] I am falling down and where not. It is a lifelong problem that I have carried and continue to. Take care and please call if you wish to speak to me. I won't call unless it is important as I sense that you would prefer that I didn't."[26]

But the ever unpredictable Martha had changed her mind. Her money would keep them together. She was now prepared to advance Devoncroft additional funds — but there was a catch. In a fax sent September 22, Martha said: "Paul, provided that you are prepared to recommit 100% of your efforts to realizing the dream as originally agreed when we became partners, I am prepared to have the funding provided to see the dream realized." There was a second demand: Martha wanted control of Devoncroft. "I believe that it is the normal commercial practice for a lender to provide for, or in fact take, voting control to safeguard its rights and interests in respect of a potentially high risk loan, where there is little equity support, until such time as the loan is repaid," said Martha. After the hammer came the honey. "Paul, I do not want to assume or run the business or to have someone else do it. I want you to nurture the business and to work hard to ensure its success, to our mutual benefit and that of all the children."[27]

The next day Martha and Michael Lavery travelled to Winnipeg. McAteer picked them up at the airport and the three of them spent six hours discussing the financing and looking at possible sites for the proposed dome. McAteer provided a two-page document containing talking points about the dome and how it would attract business, revenue, and more buyers for Kingswood. Martha agreed to pour in new money, but concluded that her family-related companies had invested enough. This time, funds would come from Newmat Drilling.

When Martha arrived home that night, two faxed documents from McAteer awaited her. One was a copy of his talking points; the other was a thank-you card. On the front of the card was sketched a bird and some flowers with the words, "Thank you, you really didn't have

---

26 Exhibit 53.
27 Exhibit 55.

to . . . " Inside, the printed message continued, saying, ". . . but I sure am glad you did!" In his own hand McAteer wrote: "Thank you. I will try to be in Wed[nesday] evening or Thursday early a.m." The card was signed, "Love Paul."[28]

Martha was well aware of the potential conflict of interest in the deal. She was lending money from one company in which she was a partner, Newmat, to another company in which she was a partner, Devoncroft, so she did not participate in the arrangements. "I, in the biblical sense, washed my hands of the deal," she said. "I let the people involved on each side negotiate the deal."[29] McAteer acted for Devoncroft; Lavery and lawyers acted for Newmat.

The loan, originally intended to be $1.9 million, was bumped to $2.1 million to take account of the $200,000 that Paul still owed Martha for his share of the house. Newmat borrowed the funds from Alberta Treasury Branches, then reloaned the money to Devoncroft at an interest rate one percentage point higher than Newmat paid. The loan was secured by a mortgage on the golf dome property. McAteer agreed to live in Winnipeg full time so he could manage the golf course and the dome on a daily basis.

Martha and McAteer had barely made it past their first anniversary. On October 26, 1991, McAteer agreed to sign a further document on top of the previous understandings that released Martha from any claim by him against her. Initially, Martha and McAteer were scheduled to meet in the office of Michael Robison, a lawyer in the Calgary office of McCarthy Tétrault, but the papers arrived at Martha's house when McAteer happened to be there. Martha's assistant, Ruth Reimer, was also present, so McAteer decided he might as well get the matter over with. "Let's just sign this thing now," he said. "Ruth, you witness it."[30] Reimer was happy that Martha's relationship with McAteer

---

28 Exhibit 317.
29 Trial Transcript, 1642.
30 Exhibit 70.

appeared to be on the wane. She had never liked him. "I'm always kind of put off by charming men," she said. "They want to look into your eyes to see their own reflection."[31]

McAteer had mixed feelings about the two Marthas he had come to know. "We really did enjoy each other's company," he said. "She's a very pleasant person when she's not mad at you."[32]

For her part, Martha tried to look at the bright side. While the personal aspect might be crumbling, she bravely believed that the dream of commercial success was still possible. In fact, the nightmare had only just begun.

---

31 *Edmonton Journal*, May 27, 2000, H1.
32 *Canadian Business*, May 1, 2000, 45.

NINE

HOPE
AGAINST HOPE

*"You used an expression once about the elephant dancing amongst
the chickens. I wonder if she realized why she had red feet after?"*
— Paul McAteer

When the recession of the early 1990s began to bite, every business in Canada suffered, but real estate projects were among the first to feel the effects of the slowing economy. The golf dome was supposed to produce new revenue for Devoncroft. Instead, there were cost overruns before the facility finally opened on December 20, 1991. Early in 1992 McAteer hired George Harms as chief financial officer in an attempt to bring some order to the financial chaos. Martha also sent Owen to work in Winnipeg. He had spent a year after high school studying political science at the University of Marseilles in France, and, on his return, took some courses at a community college in Barrie. He wanted to work at Canadian Tire head office in Toronto, but Martha thought he should try something else first. As far as she was concerned, it wouldn't hurt to have another pair of eyes and ears on site in Winnipeg.

Harms quickly identified Devoncroft's problem. "Paul really shuffled money between the different entities, depending on where it was needed and which particular creditor was causing the most frustration,"[1] he said. McAteer was blasé about the sorry situation. "His comment to me was not to worry, that he would pull a rabbit out of his hat," said Harms. "Much to my shock he said to me one time, 'When we really need money, all I have to do is sleep with Martha.'"[2]

The time came when such sexual services were not enough. In March, McAteer asked Martha to reduce the interest rate on the loan held by Owen's estate. Martha refused his request, but offered to forgo interest payments until July. She also gave McAteer a pep talk. "We are both aware of the tremendously difficult business climate in the country," she said. "In particular real estate is a disaster. I have every faith that if anyone can sell lots in La Salle and make the other things happen which are necessary for our corporate success it is you."[3]

Martha expressed a sudden enthusiasm for golf domes. She suggested that maybe they could build one in Toronto. "I believe the *Star* or *Globe* ran an article sometime in the past few weeks about domes in that area," she wrote to McAteer on March 27, 1992. "Thus the time is ripe and we must act quickly and prudently to enter that market early enough so a [sic] to be a leader both in product and in quality. We have an excellent team and a fine record in Winnipeg. We can all be very proud of the [Devoncroft]/Kingswood success!"[4]

Pamela Mason met with Paul and could see the growing strain. "Sounds like [Paul's] work is disintegrating again. There are problems with Martha," Mason wrote in her diary on March 20. "He cried a bit before he left. I think he's in pretty bad shape."[5] In May, Martha visited Winnipeg to investigate the company's health first-hand.

1   *Canadian Business*, May 1, 2000, 45.
2   *National Post*, April 5, 2000.
3   Court of Queen's Bench of Alberta, Judicial District of Calgary, *Paul McAteer et al.*, Exhibit 87.
4   Exhibit 89.
5   *National Post*, March 15, 2000.

McAteer tried to shock her into realizing the depths to which matters had sunk. "I never cry wolf unless the wolf is through the front door and in the bedroom," he wrote to Martha later that month. "Well, the wolf is here!"[6]

By June the situation had not improved. The back nine was completed and the golf course had finally become a regulation eighteen holes, but McAteer phoned Martha in Toronto to say that he needed $60,000 just to cover bills and pay expenses over the next eight to ten weeks. Martha agreed, but stipulated that none of the newly borrowed money could go to paying off loans already owed to her. On June 5 Martha stopped in Winnipeg to give McAteer a cheque from Albikin for Devoncroft for $60,000.[7] Later that month McAteer sent Martha a two-page memo saying that the golf course had been profitable in its first twenty days of operation, but staffing remained problematic, trees had died as a result of damage by animals, plans to pave the parking lot had been delayed by rain, membership sales were slow, and the bank was testy. "The Royal bounced our credit," said McAteer, "and I had to dance for them one more time."

Ken Mann, the Tire dealer and trustee on Owen's estate, raised an alarm about her investment, but Martha appeared oblivious. "I just felt it was all pie-in-the-sky," said Mann. "Yet Martha, up until the last five or six months, maybe longer than that, a year, would say, 'People are coming in, it's starting to pay off.' 'I'm not seeing black-and-white figures,' Mann would tell her. 'All I'm hearing is that everything's going to be good. It's like having an empty bowl. The soup's coming, the soup's coming, but I've never seen the soup.' She felt that the dome and the golf course would work. I thought the dome had a hope, but I thought the golf course didn't have a hope in hell. I could get nothing out of [McAteer]."

---

6   Exhibit 274, 2.
7   Exhibit 99.

In June and July, McAteer gave Martha cheques to cover amounts due and payable, but asked her to wait a few days before cashing them. In at least one case he never did give her the go-ahead. On July 8 McAteer turned to Owen for help, asking him to see if the interest rate on the $175,000 loan from his trust fund could be reduced from 15 per cent to 10 per cent. McAteer made it sound as though Owen owed him a favour. "I hope through the past 9 months you can understand that I have tried to make an environment for you which has helped you grow outside the umbrella of your family and heritage," he wrote. "I can understand how difficult it has been for you and expect that we will, as in the case of [golf course managers] Gary and Wayne, be able to yell and kick behind closed doors and come out friends working together. You have come through trial by fire well and I wish to congratulate you. I sincerely hope that we can somehow complete the Toronto Dome as I think you will enjoy the experience, profit by the venture and move through another big step in your personal development."[8] Owen, who had no control over the trust fund, took no action.

McAteer, who was nothing if not brash, asked Martha to double his monthly salary to $10,000, retroactive to April 1. He pointed out that his annual income of $60,000 from Devoncroft was only one-quarter of the money he'd earned in the 1980s. He did not ask that the higher compensation actually be paid; he just wanted the money to accumulate and be turned over to him eventually. Martha rejected that request too.

IF PAUL MCATEER had ever harboured any real feelings for Martha, they were gone by July 13, when he sent a two-page fax to her at Shanty Bay. And, if typos could pass for tears, his message was heartfelt.

---

8 Exhibit 441

"Your brief visit last week reminded my how alike we are in many ways and how dramatically different in others," he wrote. "We both have the intense need to be part of a couple with another to share our trials and dreams with. Maybe that is why I still feel such a strong bond of friendship after we have been through so much personal turmoil. Who knows what the future holds for us individually and what roll each will play in the others."

"Since this letter is personal," he continued, "I will not bring in anything which is business and cloud the nature of the letter. I can only say that while the company is operating as it is the two must remain separate and distinct. Your May trip to Winnipeg made it so clear that they cannot be combined at this juncture. If we are to survive in any type of relationship we both must let go, let the business run it's cycle and see where the future carries us. I am certain that you have felt the change in me since that time. When the economy turns and the cash issues are resolved, stresses of my personal and business relationship with you will be reduced."

At that point, halfway down the first of two pages, Martha must have drawn a deep breath. "I expect that within the next year I will know if I will be working for us, myself or a large corporation for the longer term." McAteer then outlined the precarious nature of his own financial situation, saying that, although the long term might be bright, the near term was bleak. "The cutting of the dividends last year, the purchase of this house and starting over in Winnipeg have ensured that as each month passes I am closer to the edge," he said. "I have been here before. The big difference was that before I always had control of my assets and had never allowed them to be wrapped up together. What is the old chestnut? Never put all your eggs in one basket." As for himself, he'd learned a lesson. His children had adjusted to the divorce, but "the winter did bring me to the realization that I cannot in the long term substitute children for a spouse." With that self-knowledge, apparently, had come the further realization that Martha was not the person with whom McAteer wanted to spend the rest of his life, although he was quick to say that he had not found anyone else just yet. "I have not ventured to far from home. You are aware that I did see someone on a purely platonic bases over the winter. It was better than staying at home alone but certainly not what was needed. It did give you and I the time to sort through our relationship a bit more without the complexities another person would have added. Only since your trip in May, have I made the emotional break to be free to spend clear time with anyone."

Emotionally free: McAteer was about to flit away like a butterfly with its fill of the flower's nectar. "I really am quite fine and will carry on. I do think about you often and expect that our lives will be intertwined for a long term most for our mutual benefits." If ever there was a kissoff letter from a man to a woman, this was it.[9]

Martha was devastated. "The mixing of personal and business matters seems to be never-ending," she wrote in response two days later. "My having allowed a personal relationship to enter into a business partnership was indeed a terrible mistake for me. You say that you are now emotionally free to spend time with someone. That is great for you. Congratulations! My situation is different; I am still hurting badly. Enough said."[10]

Martha later claimed that her personal relationship with McAteer had ended in March 1991 and that she was referring to someone else, not McAteer, when she made the "hurting" comment in her response to McAteer dated July 15, 1992. "'My situation' that I was referring to was that in September, 1990, I was in a long-term relationship and had been with Mr. Martin Godin. That relationship was abruptly brought to an end in late October, 1990, by Mr. McAteer involving himself with me. By the time July 1992 had rolled around, I had mended some of the fences with Mr. Godin, but by that time Mr. Godin had a

---

9 Exhibit 309.
10 Exhibit 107.

different lady friend, was buying a house with her. I had lost very badly."[11] With Marty Godin and Paul McAteer both gone, Martha was lovelorn twice over.

LOVE BETWEEN TWO PEOPLE is difficult enough to nurture at the best of times. When business pressures are also involved, every problem is compounded. Martha was faced with a growing series of dilemmas that included debt, a deteriorating economy, and a continuing demand for funds in what was supposed to have been an automatic pilot investment. "I was being fed a bill of goods by management. I had been told to keep my nose out of the business and yet I was being asked again and again to supply funds." For a time Martha continued to be a believer. "Hope against hope, good money after bad," she said. "I was listening to only the good parts, the potential, the future. I wasn't paying sufficient attention to how poorly my dead mother's estate and my partners at Newmat were being treated."

Martha encouraged McAteer to look for another job so he could continue running Devoncroft without being a drain on the company's resources. "I had been asking him to please find a way to support [himself] during this recessionary period," she said. "I had been begging him to let me know what was going on. He would not." Owen had proved to be no help as an informant. In fact, Martha disparaged his role. "My son was a gofer at the dome. He did not have financial information."[12]

Other attempts to pull back the veil and find out what was happening proved equally unsuccessful. Martha and Michael Lavery talked with the Royal Bank in Winnipeg about the bank's loan to Devoncroft. When McAteer found out, he was angry. "I received verbal abuse from Mr. McAteer," said Martha. "He told me that I had

---

11   Trial Transcript, 1984–85.
12   Trial Transcript, 1766–69.

no status; that I had no right as a director of Devoncroft contacting the bank that held the bank account for Kingswood; that I had no business interfering in Kingswood or Kingswood's financial dealings with the bank; that, in fact, at law I was committing a breach. I was in shock."[13]

The business relationship had come unhinged. In her "hurting" letter, Martha said that Albikin could no longer be a crutch for Devoncroft because Kingswood lot sales were lagging and the banks were jittery. She issued a stern warning: "Paul, you must accept the reality of the Devoncroft situation and adjust your affairs accordingly. You, of all people, are not short any cards, but the companies are short funds. The present [economic] situation may indeed be a cycle but perhaps one unlike any other we have known. Precipitous actions would not be prudent." Martha set a deadline of October 15, by which time she wanted to see improved circumstances. "If there is no major upswing in [Devoncroft's] financial situation by that time, the best course of action for the company's survival would be that you find other employment."[14]

McAteer tried to be reassuring. "I remain genuinely fond of you," he said. "We 'both' made a terrible mistake entering into the personal relationship and mixing it with the business. But the clock cannot be turned back and the memories eliminated. I suppose what I said was misunderstood, like so many discussions of the past. You are not the only one who hurts. I am very aware of your feelings but cannot fix the problem at this time."

McAteer proposed three options. First, they could continue as partners for five years. Second, they could close the business, with McAteer departing. Third, they could keep operating, but allow McAteer to work elsewhere on a part-time basis. McAteer favoured the first choice, preserving the status quo while doing a workout that

13 Trial Transcript, 1666.
14 Exhibit 107.

would restore corporate health. Cost-cutting measures could be insti-
gated that would include firing Harms. Even after paying for
replacement accounting help, McAteer estimated that the company
would save $40,000 annually.

MCATEER COMPLAINED that Martha had ruined his life. "Since I became
emotionally involved with you, I have lost a wife after 20 years of
marriage, my children have lost their father and I have lost them,
even our relationship has been destroyed by your suspicions and jeal-
ousies. You used an expression once about the elephant dancing
amongst the chickens. I wonder if she realized why she had red feet
after? You have only two areas where you can inflict further damage.
Take my company from me and bankrupt me in the process. If you
really are trying to get even, I will go down fighting like I have never
fought before."[15]

On August 2 McAteer wrote to Harms, claiming he had been
discussing confidential Kingswood matters with unnamed people in
Winnipeg. McAteer wanted such discussions to stop, and he said he
wanted to be informed or involved any time Harms talked to Michael
Lavery, Larry Newel, Owen, or Martha. The following day McAteer
fired Harms, telling him his services would no longer be needed once
year-end financial statements had been prepared.[16]

Martha was astounded by McAteer's pre-emptive strike against
Harms. "I trusted George," she said. "George communicated with me
often. Paul would have George call me to explain things to me that
weren't quite right or, in one instance, to ask for a $5,000 or $7,000
personal loan to the company for a short period of time. George was
a voice of reason. George told the truth."

⬳

15 Exhibit 109.
16 Exhibit 112.

AT LAST MARTHA seemed to comprehend the peril of her predicament. "I was left with nowhere to turn," she said. "I had by this time realized that what Mr. McAteer was doing with the Devoncroft assets was just a black hole. Monies would go in, monies would disappear and I just put 200,000 bucks in. I was shocked, I was devastated. I didn't know what to do."[17] Lavery had also given up on McAteer. "I was not happy with the management and if the management could not be changed, then the [Billes] trust should take steps to protect the assets," Lavery said.[18]

McAteer tried to explain the inexplicable in a letter to Martha on August 7. "George is not what he seems to be. I want to see the fences mended and move on. Please let us sit down and talk. If there are any disagreements only you and I can resolve them. My only objective now is to regain your trust and move forward and put the business on track. More importantly, I want to remain your friend and put some fun back into the relationship for both of us."[19]

Fun! How likely was that? Martha now had about $4 million invested in Devoncroft projects, none of which had any immediate prospects of producing a profit. Martha asked McAteer to step aside and let someone else take over, to see if operations could be salvaged.

In response, McAteer escalated the war. On August 9 he wrote to Martha saying that she had no real estate experience and did not live in Winnipeg, so she could not possibly understand what had happened. He informed her that he planned to continue running Devoncroft and drawing his monthly salary of $5,000 for the next two-and-a-half years, until March 1995. "Let us go back to square 1 and see if we can make this work. There are millions at risk and a bright future when we come out of the recession." If Martha disagreed, he

---

17 Trial Transcript, 1668–69.
18 *National Post*, March 29, 2000.
19 Exhibit 114.

said, she'd have to propose some severance payment to get rid of him.[20]

With McAteer girding for battle, Martha armed herself. She retained Len Sali, a lawyer with the Calgary law firm of Bennett Jones Verchere, and told McAteer that he should be prepared to meet with Sali in Winnipeg on August 13. "It is unfortunate when competing fiduciary duties put business partners at odds but I suppose that is where we are," McAteer replied the same day. "We are all liable for what we are found at law to be liable for, so to accept that which exists is only to state that which is obvious."[21]

At the meeting, Sali told McAteer's lawyer, D'Arcy McCaffrey of the Winnipeg firm Taylor McCaffrey, that Martha felt "excluded from the decision-making process and somewhat stone-walled by McAteer." In response, McCaffrey told Sali that McAteer had no money. He was not in a position to buy out Martha; the parties had to find another solution. Sali advised McAteer that he had until September 15 to come up with a business plan. If Martha was not satisfied with McAteer's recommendations, McAteer had an option until October 31 to buy her out for $500,000. If he did not choose to exercise that option, then Martha had a month in which to buy him out for the same amount.

McAteer formally replied, through his lawyer, on September 23, saying that he wanted an extension until the end of December to assemble the money required. If that was unacceptable, he proposed splitting the assets. McAteer would get the golf course, Martha the dome. Meanwhile, he would list for sale the Red Deer apartments.

Correspondence between Martha and McAteer continued while she considered his proposal. In a letter McAteer wrote on September 10, 1992, he commiserated with Martha's problems at Canadian Tire, one of the rare times the family business came up in their many

---

20 Exhibit 116.
21 Exhibit 118.

exchanges. Dean Groussman, president since 1986, had announced his departure in July. "I expect the changes with Grossman [sic] leaving have kept you very busy. A mixed blessing, I suppose as he was never your favourite. I wish you good luck with that one as it must be very stressful for you."

Those niceties done with, it was back to McAteer's usual complaints about poor weather plaguing the golf course and promises of eventual profitability. "Please let us start to communicate," McAteer implored. "I would encourage you to join with me in the effort, as I am certain that if we can move beyond the recent emotional issues all other matters could be worked out."[22] In fact, matters were becoming much worse. For the financial year ended September 30, 1992, Devoncroft lost $767,000 on top of the previous year's loss of $535,000.

A shareholders' meeting was set for October 9 in Sali's Calgary law office for Martha, McAteer, and Mason. Five days before the gathering, McAteer wrote Martha a ten-page letter that had all the earmarks of a "cover your ass" memo — the kind that bureaucrats compose to put their version of events on the record when they know such correspondence will become public in future proceedings. He began the letter with one last attempt to explain his July "emotionally free" letter. "I was trying to openly respond to your direct inquiry and say to you that I was through one of the most difficult points in my life," he wrote. "It was not meant to be insensitive to your own feelings of hurt, anger or suspicion." McAteer said he had hoped personal issues could be set aside in order to fix the business relationship.

IN A MEMO TO MARTHA later filed in court, McAteer tried to win Martha back by telling her tales about George Harms. The allegations were

22 Exhibit 124.

never proven. "I have been told that George, in large audiences made bar room humor out of your evening after the four of you were out in Calgary during his spring visit. This was superceded by constant jokes about 'you being off with some big stud in Mexico.' I still find it hard to believe, that an Officer of a corporation would say such things about one of the Directors of the parent company, but it is one example of his approach. If such graphic descriptions existed of that situation, I can imagine what other sexually demeaning comments were made in more candid situations about you, me and Owen."

McAteer dished out more dirt. "Are you aware that, apparently, George approached Owen on a number of occasions to become his personal advisor and manage his business and investments? Are you aware that he was exposing us to sexual harassment actions from the younger female employees? Two incidents which were reported to me are as follows: He, on one occasion looked down one of the Golf Course staff's blouse and while leering said, 'What sexy lingerie are you wearing today?' On another occasion, he commented to another employee, 'Why don't you go out with a real man like me.' I expect that these teenage employees were very upset and afraid of George." McAteer then moved on to speak his mind about Owen. "I've had George, [and golf course partners] Gary, Harry, and Wayne say to me more than once how much Owen dislikes ('HATES') me and how sarcastic his comments are about me. This undermined authority and severely effected the moral and stability of the organization. Martha, I can assure you that I have no ill feeling toward Owen. It is fair to say, however, that his presence cost us dearly with reduced moral, extra unproductive costs and instability in the business. My only hope is that he learned something in the process."[23]

Martha was unmoved by McAteer's allegations. When Martha, McAteer, and Mason met in Sali's office on October 9 for the share-

---

23 Exhibit 135.

holders' meeting, Sali observed "an obvious tension" between Martha and McAteer. McAteer spent much of the morning going over financial statements and talking about his plans to build two more golf domes, one in Regina and another in Toronto. He wanted Martha to forgo interest payments until January, by which time he hoped either to have more cash flow from the business or to have secured replacement financing. "I was adrift," said Martha. "I had no handle on what was happening, so I wasn't interested in hearing about future dreams. I wanted to know the facts. I got no facts that I can remember in the morning."

MASON SEEMED TOTALLY UNAWARE of the financial problems that had been plaguing Devoncroft. As the meeting broke for lunch, Martha handed Mason a copy of the loan agreement and said: "Here, read these and you will understand why I'm so upset."[24] Mason was not surprised by Martha's demeanour, but she was taken aback by what she regarded as an "aggressive and hostile" Len Sali. "I expected Mrs. Billes's strident behaviour but quite frankly was surprised and greatly concerned by Mr. Sali's tone, particularly as I had been told this was to be a conciliatory meeting to share information among the shareholders."[25]

After lunch, Sali tried to direct discussions away from the dreams of the future to the dilemmas of the present, given the fact that Devoncroft had fallen far behind on interest payments owing to Newmat and to Owen's estate. At one point Sali lost his patience, grabbed a sheaf of papers from the conference table, and waved them at McAteer, saying: "If you want her and her people to extend to you many, many, many months then my response to you is that you have to guarantee that there are no problems with anything. We need

24 Trial Transcript, 1777–78.
25 Exhibit 137.

financials, we need to know exactly where we are at, we need to know exactly where we're going and that every detail is covered."[26]

The trio was making no progress. "I had lost faith in Mr. McAteer," Martha later recalled. "He would not come to grips with real issues during that meeting. I admonished myself for having allowed things to have gone as far as they did, but I could get no cooperation."[27]

Finally, Mason brought the shareholders' meeting to the point of decision by asking Martha, point blank: "Do you want to do business with Paul?"

"No," replied Martha.

Mason then turned to McAteer and asked: "Do you want to do business with Martha?"

His answer was an equally unequivocal no.[28]

The meeting was over. After McAteer and Mason had left, Martha and Sali discussed ways of removing McAteer from Devoncroft management, but could find none. "It seemed that they were all dead-ended because of his control of the corporate structures," said Martha. "We couldn't manoeuvre in the mine field. We couldn't figure out how, and they were adamantly against us proceeding. It was extremely difficult to deal with Mr. and Mrs. McAteer. They worked in tandem, and we couldn't talk sense to Mr. McAteer. He was at that time talking of suing."[29]

In a follow-up letter to McAteer's lawyer, Sali fired his own salvo. "I would also ask that Mr. McAteer refrain from making comments describing Martha as his financial partner, being in default of her promises, express or implied, warning Martha not to involve herself in the business affairs of Devoncroft and suggesting that she is or may be in breach of a fiduciary duty. If he wishes to engage in that sort of

---

26 Trial Transcript, 1782.
27 Trial Transcript, 1681, 1992.
28 Trial Transcript, 1780.
29 Trial Transcript, 1988–90.

dialogue, presumably for reasons best suited to his own interests, he will have to understand that it will not be tolerated any longer."[30]

Mason feared for the worst. "All I heard about was Mrs. Billes' concern as a lender that her interest payments were in arrears," she said in a letter to McAteer. "I had no indication during the eight hours we met that she had any interest in or was prepared to accept responsibility for her part in the decision making that brought the company to this position. It remains to be seen whether Martha Billes will uphold the statements she made to me two years ago when she agreed that no matter what transpired between the three of us, the children would not suffer. If she is sincere that all she wants is her loans repaid and a fair return on her investment, this present situation will be resolved. However, if this is about vindication for perceived personal injury, we'd better all prepare ourselves for more than financial disclosure."[31]

Mason supported McAteer's plan for him to continue running Devoncroft for two years, but she expected that litigation was unavoidable. "I was suspicious that Billes, although she owed a fiduciary duty to myself and my children as a director of the company in which we held shares, was using her position of controlling the secured creditors in order to exact some revenge against McAteer for these personal matters," she said.[32]

On November 17 Newmat turned up the heat on McAteer by demanding immediate payment of $104,277.66 owing in back interest. Six days later, Murray Froese of the Winnipeg firm Pitblado & Hoskin sent letters to McAteer formally calling the loans held by Owen's estate and Newmat. That demand was for repayment within four days of the principal amounts and the interest. The estate was owed $1.2 million, plus $78,571.27 in unpaid interest. For Newmat, the

---

30 Exhibit 138.
31 Exhibit 137.
32 Exhibit 270, 5.

amount was $1,950,000, plus interest of $104,423.36. (In the six days since the first demand, the interest owed had grown.)

McAteer, of course, did not have sufficient funds to comply. Such letters are formalities to establish the position of the person owed the debt, in this case Martha, to move in and seize assets. Martha did just that on November 27, 1992, when she exercised her right as the major creditor to appoint a receiver to manage Devoncroft. "The estate trust needed to find out whether Devoncroft was or was not a viable business," said Martha. "We had given breathing space by not demanding our interest payments from April, 1992 forward. This was one of the saddest days or the saddest things that I have ever done in my life."[33]

War had been declared. McAteer returned fire by suing Martha in February 1993 for $10 million in general damages and a further $1 million in aggravated or punitive damages, alleging that she had broken a shareholder's agreement and improperly taken control of the company and partnership. McAteer claimed that Martha failed to disclose her interest in Newmat, the company that had lent Devoncroft $2.1 million.

The firm that was appointed as receiver, Sill Streuber Fiske Inc., found that Devoncroft's financial condition was far worse than anyone realized. In addition to the $4 million Martha had invested (through Newmat, the estate, and Albikin), plus the interest owed, a further $800,000 to $1 million was needed to pay Devoncroft's bills. "There are no effective management or accounting controls in place," said a report completed by the receiver in March 1993. "The result is that current and reliable accounting information has not been available to management, shareholders or investors. The accounting records have not been kept current or accurate. This fact undoubtedly contributed to the loss of confidence which Martha G. Billes

---

33 Trial Transcript, 1862.

now has in the management and control exercised by Paul McAteer. Mr. McAteer delegated very little authority to others and did not consistently communicate information regarding events, decisions and transactions initiated by him. Mr. McAteer was often away from the Golf Dome location in Winnipeg where control of the accounting and financial authority is centered. It would appear that Mr. McAteer's strengths and interests may lie more in his creative abilities to develop and promote business opportunities than in his ability to manage existing projects."[34]

Martha was amazed at the mess in which she found herself. "I was shocked to find out that somehow $800,000 to $1 million would be required to pay the payables, without even looking for principal repayments on the long-term debt. I was shocked to find out that there were no proper financial controls in that company. I was shocked to find out that management had been headstrong and had been misleading me."[35]

The report included a few bright spots. The golf dome had broken even in its first year of operation. The golf club had been profitable to the end of April 1992. Fifty-six of the eighty-nine lots had been sold in the first phase of the La Salle residential project, but only two lots had been sold in the previous seven months. Until more sales occurred, there could be no activity in the development's second phase of eighty-three lots. The receiver concluded that until disputes between Martha and McAteer were resolved, "the current state of disruption experienced by the Kingswood companies will undoubtedly continue."

The receiver was optimistic that, under the right circumstances, the companies could do well. "Current operations of the companies indicate that profits are below or near 'break-even' level. There is, however, potential for significant future profit and cash flow inherent

34 Exhibit 186, 4, 12–13.
35 Trial Transcript, 1870.

in the operations of the Golf Dome and the Kingswood Golf Club provided effective management is in place."[36]

Martha was no longer willing to wait. The receiver's report convinced her that Devoncroft could not survive without reorganization, so she asked the receiver to sell assets and thereby realize whatever value existed. A prime buyer for the assets was Martha herself. She got the apartments in Red Deer, the golf dome, and the unsold Kingswood lots.

In a letter that was later filed in court, McAteer wrote to Mason on January 25, 1994: "What we have to accept is that they will continue to lie and cheat their way to success if allowed to. I am more convinced than ever that the necessary evidence is there to prove your case and win compensation for the injustices placed upon you and the children. I will continue as a thorn in their side every step they take to force them to the table."[37]

McAteer's personal situation deteriorated. In 1994 his unemployment insurance payments ran out and he had to borrow $2,000 from Mason. In 1999 he was joined in his lawsuit against Martha by Mason, who had by then moved to Ottawa, where she worked as manager of fundraising and development for the Juvenile Diabetes Foundation. Mason also sued Martha for $11 million, claiming that Martha grew "bitter and vengeful" and purposely set out to destroy the company. In return, Martha countersued both McAteer and Mason for $5.1 million.

While Martha focused on Paul McAteer, fighting broke out on a second front. The weak economy that was affecting Devoncroft was having an impact on Canadian Tire as well. Martha's heart and heritage were both under siege.

After Dean Groussman resigned, Martha and the board recruited Stephen Bachand, the second American in a row to be president

---

36 Trial Transcript, 1870–71.
37 Exhibit 319.

and CEO of Canadian Tire. At fifty-four, he had been executive vice-president and chief operating office of Hechinger Co. of Landover, Maryland, a family-owned home-improvement retailer. Born in Massachusetts, Bachand (rhymes with fashioned) had grown up working summers and weekends in a hardware store and had obtained his MBA from the University of Virginia. In his final five years at Hechinger he had taken the company's warehouse division, Home Quarters, from six stores doing US$100 million in sales to forty-five stores and sales of US$1 billion.

When Bachand arrived in 1993, Canadian Tire was in poor shape. Sales had been stuck at $3 billion for three years, while net profit had fallen by 43 per cent. Dominion Bond Rating Service Ltd. had issued a warning about the company's long-term debt. Share price had responded to the continuing bad news by sinking from $20 to $13 in a year. "This place was on its way out, in my opinion, if nothing had happened quickly and substantively," said Bachand. "The challenges were an obsolete plant, a poor working relationship between the corporation and the dealers, and an enormous change in the retail environment. The dealers saw what was coming, they saw the difficulty, and there didn't appear to be a joint effort to take it on. When you're not doing well, everybody seems to have a shortened fuse. And if your livelihood is threatened, it's even shorter than that."

Disgruntled shareholders were promised better performance. "Business as usual will no longer be the business of Canadian Tire," Bachand said at his first annual meeting in 1994. "This is not a time for complacency. This is not a time for polite retailing in Canada. Canadian Tire can no longer afford to be tentative in its thinking or actions. There's a fire at the Tire."

Martha and the dealers welcomed Bachand's no-nonsense savvy. "The dealers and the corporation had drifted quite far apart," said Adam Bucci of Montreal, then president of the dealers' association. "He was honest and convincing; that's all we needed. There was no immediate change. He just said, 'We're in this together, how can we get the job done?'"[38] Bachand's chairman was equally impressed. "I've yet to meet the dealer worth his salt who didn't think he could do the job a helluva lot better than whoever was president of Canadian Tire," said Hugh Macaulay. "It's the kind of abrasive interface which has led to what Canadian Tire is today. If it's kept within reasonable bounds, it's a helluva lot better to have people arguing with each other than agreeing with each other. Out of those differences of opinion emerge the right decisions. Dean Muncaster was a master of that. Steve Bachand was not only a master of that, he could walk into a store and have people following him around wanting to hear what he had to say. That's respect."

Bachand wisely realized that most customers saw shopping at Tire the same way they enjoyed sitting down to a hot meal of comfort food. Shoppers might be open to new products, but they want the old standbys, too, such as tires and batteries. "The brand equity was pretty substantial and we had the financial resources to do something," Bachand said. "People like this place and they don't like it when it's not successful. Sometimes family businesses fail because somebody in the family wants to run it. Canadian Tire has had a number of non-family executives and the controlling family hasn't been averse to doing that. That has served them well. The company has historically demanded good performance, so it hasn't been willing to get itself into the position that Eaton's found itself. The department store business went through a revolution in the U.S., which should have been an obvious indicator of what needed to be done. Canadian Tire almost got itself in that position."

Martha and the board admired Bachand's self-confidence. "There were occasions in some of the early board meetings where he took a very strong position where his point of view ultimately prevailed,"

---

36 *Financial Post*, February 17, 1996.

said Macaulay. "He was forcefully making some points which caused people to back up a little bit and realize he was right." With Martha's consent and support, Bachand began by setting out to change the very nature of Tire. Head office had always viewed itself as a wholesaler, with the dealers responsible for generating retail sales. "Historically, we bought product, told [dealers] what we had, and said, if you want some, let us know. Store size, layout, fixture selection, what customers are telling us, that was not front and centre. It took a lot of time to refocus and retrain our people," said Bachand.

Initially, Bachand decided against the big-box concept of building new stand-alone stores, choosing instead to stick with locations that Tire already occupied. In 1994 Tire tried eight "new format" stores, called "class of" because they were seen as a learning experience. That business model, a combination of updating old stores and building new ones, was adopted. Under Bachand's plan, these stores would come in four sizes, depending on the local market. Bachand focused on three core businesses, using highly visible colours in the stores: red for automotive, blue for home products, and green for sports and leisure. The number of items available was increased from 65,000 to 78,000. The 3,000 suppliers became linked directly with Tire through a computer network. A no-hassle returns policy was instituted, and Canadian Tire money was introduced in western Canada.

Tire's second attempt at U.S. expansion was performing poorly, so Bachand froze expansion of the ten-outlet Auto Source chain. In 1994 he closed the chain after losses of $109 million. Unlike Muncaster, who ran afoul of Martha by letting Whites bleed for far too long, Bachand took decisive action as soon as he could. Of course, Auto Source had been Groussman's idea, so Bachand could readily kill it. Even better, the mother ship was already turning around when he took the job. Revenue in 1993 rose 8 per cent and earnings were up 13 per cent, the first such increase since 1989.

Bachand had just nicely settled in when the real enemy arrived. In January 1994 Wal-Mart Stores Inc. bought 122 Woolco outlets in Canada. In March, Home Depot bought Aikenhead's. Such acquisitions meant that both Wal-Mart and Home Depot had immediate access to Canada — they weren't building just one location at a time.

Within five years Wal-Mart had captured 36 per cent of the market share among department stores in Canada. Home Depot struck such fear into the heart of Robert Dutton, president of Rona Inc., that he predicted Home Depot would top Rona as the leading hardware dealer in Quebec — even before his competition had opened any stores in that province. "They are merciless and show unparalleled aggressivity," said Dutton. "So let's be realistic. No one will be able to dislodge them."[39]

Bachand was able not only to keep pace with the newly lethal competition but to become Canada's most successful retailer of the 1990s. Revenue at Canadian Tire grew from $3.4 billion in 1993 to $4.7 billion in 1999. During the first five years of Bachand's tenure, share price rose from $10 to $45, a 35 per cent annual increase. "When the U.S. retailers came to Canada they thought Canadian Tire would roll over and play dead and we didn't. Steve was the man we needed at the time he came in," said Maureen Sabia. "He was an excellent communicator and he was able to bring the dealers on side. He also presented an exciting vision of the future. That turns most of those people on." Bachand was aided by a new period of peace in the Billes family, the first protracted time of corporate calm that Tire had enjoyed in years. "From a management point of view, the family relationships, the history of agreement or disagreement, were never a part of our life," said Bachand. "Nor did any of us, including me, have any special knowledge about what was going on. We weren't players in that arena."

Such relative tranquillity did not mean that the Billeses had changed

---

39 Montreal *Gazette*, April 19, 2000.

their spots. Fred respected Bachand's optimism, but did not fully agree with his strategy. "They built too many big boxes in too many places," said Fred. "It would have been as effective to build three-quarters of a box and, if indeed there was the business there, they could add the other one-quarter. Bigger stores often had an initial increase in sales, then fell back to previous levels. You can sell more in a big store, but not many of them do."

Bachand shrugged off Fred's opposing views as part of his provocative style. "Fred felt there was value in controversy and getting a dialogue going [about] which someone would think, 'My God, this is so off-the-wall, it's disruptive, we're wasting our time.' Everybody has their own personality, their own style. Fred had his — not to say it's not an unique one," said Bachand.

But Bachand also stood his ground against criticism. "Fred was suspicious about e-commerce and how transactions would get lost on the cyberworld," said a director. "At one discussion, Steve basically cut him off, saying 'This is the way it's going.'"

Martha was a tougher sell. "When she gets into a debate on any issue at the board she came across as somebody who likes to win," said the director. "It's her manner. She would get quite emotional. More often than not she was sticking a stake in the sand, but if she got outvoted, she got outvoted."

Of course, financial success of the sort that Bachand achieved was sure to make an owner more amenable, even admiring. If Paul McAteer had been even half as successful as Steve Bachand, he likely would have continued to command Martha's full support, maybe even keep her love. But as much as the loss of McAteer mattered at the time to Martha, it was minor compared with another loss — one that would clear the path for her final push towards control of Canadian Tire.

TEN

TIRE
'N' ME

"I'm glad I'm out because it certainly simplified my life.
This is just one more reason why there hasn't been a relationship
redevelop [with Martha] because I never know what to expect."
— DAVID BILLES

lfred Jackson Billes died on April 3, 1995, in North York General
Hospital. He was ninety-two. The obituary published in the
Toronto Star quoted A.J. as once telling a reporter, "If you want something badly enough and you don't care how much time you spend on
it, you can't lose." It was a motto that Martha had adopted as her own.
One successful concept, Canadian Tire money, was by itself enough
to establish A.J.'s legacy as a retailer. Tire money was more than just
a customer loyalty program, wrote Wayne Grady in *Saturday Night*.
"Canadian Tire money is a metaphysical construct. It keeps you
going back to Canadian Tire, since, theoretically at least, that's the
only place you can spend it. Yet the more Canadian Tire money you
spend, the more you get back. It sticks to you like fly paper. Canadian
Tire likes the program because it compels us to spend like Santa but
save like Scrooge. Canadians like Canadian Tire money, however,

because we can thwart the cycle; we can turn the money to our own use. It's become our unofficial second currency. We've all heard the one about the guy who paid an unsuspecting cab driver in Mexico with Canadian Tire money."[1] Beyond these apocryphal tales the coupons have actually been accepted as payment in such diverse enterprises as Rosa's Cantina, a Halifax night club; Diane's, a Toronto corner store; and Joe Kool's in London, Ont., where restaurant owner Mike Smith took in about $50 a week in Tire money despite the company's warning letter against such activity, a framed copy of which hung on the wall.

A.J. and his brother J.W. had created a great Canadian institution. A.J.'s ideas about profit-sharing and share ownership gave Tire employees the chance to become wealthy, an opportunity most employers do not offer. Canadians flocked to the stores in droves. But A.J. was more successful as an entrepreneur than as a father. All his children had let him down. "I know he was disappointed that David didn't take too much interest in the business," said Fred Sasaki, A.J.'s loyal friend and long-time confidant. As for Fred, well, there was no chance for close ties with his elder son because, as Sasaki put it, "their personalities were so different." A.J.'s concerns about Martha ranged from worrying about the different men she brought with her when she came visiting her father to what she might do after he was gone. "I looked after A.J.'s personal finances for a long time until he died," said Sasaki. "I saw him once a week and he told me a lot of things. She wanted to have the control in the Billes family, but on her own terms."

A.J. had decided to leave all his personal wealth to his second wife, Marjorie. He told Sasaki, who was his executor, that he worried Martha might contest the will. "He knew that Martha didn't respect Marjorie," said Sasaki. Martha and her brothers were not mentioned

---

1 *Saturday Night*, July–August 1999, 22.

in the will, not even by way of a small remembrance. "I think she'd be hurt that she wasn't mentioned. I assume she'd be quite upset."

After A.J. died, Martha approached Sasaki at the R.S. Kane Funeral Home on Yonge Street during the visitation. She asked him to send her a copy of her father's will. "I thought, this is the wrong place to ask," said Sasaki. He complied with Martha's request, but he also enclosed a copy of A.J.'s signed declaration that he was of sound mind when the will was drawn up. Sasaki was relieved when she took no legal action.

Sasaki had been sitting in his suburban Toronto living room recalling the past and wrestling with what to make of the changes that had taken place in Martha over the years. He could not reconcile the Martha of today, the doting daughter who speaks so glowingly of her father and the tradition of Tire, with the Martha of 1986, who was eager to sell the company against her father's wishes. "She's changed, you know. It baffles me. Maybe she wanted to repair her image. She certainly wasn't that way at the time of the crisis." If her new posture and interest in preserving the family ownership of Tire was supposed to please her father, it did not work. "He was quite disappointed." Sasaki rose abruptly from his chair, walked to the dining room, and returned with a Billes family photograph taken in 1970. In it, A.J. and Muriel were beside each other on a settee at Fred and Barbara's. A.J. held Owen, Martha's adopted son, and Muriel dandled Garth, Fred and Barbara's youngest. Five more grandchildren were arrayed around them. In a row behind stood Alfred William, with his parents Fred and Barbara, along with David and Donna, Martha and Roger. Even Princess, the ever-present West Highland White, seemed to grin behind the whiskers. "It shows you the happier times," said Sasaki. "It's the early, early days when Martha was still with her first husband. It's a very happy family. I like that."

⚮

IN MAY 1996 there was a changing of the guard at Canadian Tire. Gil Bennett, a lawyer who had been a director on such companies as Consumers Gas, Eldorado Nuclear, and Algoma Steel, replaced Earl Joudrie, who had been chairman of the board since 1944. Fifteen months earlier Joudrie had been shot six times by his wife, Dorothy, with her .25 calibre Beretta in the garage of their Calgary home. He survived the shooting and Dorothy was charged with attempted murder. Evidence at the trial showed that Joudrie began beating his wife two years after they were married and drove her to alcoholism. The jury found her not criminally responsible after her lawyer argued that she was in a robotic state due to years of domestic abuse. The day after the verdict was announced, Earl Joudrie stepped down as Tire's chairman.

Martha remained loyal to her chairman throughout. On May 11, 1996, the *Edmonton Journal* published a 4,600-word feature on the Joudries and how their marriage had turned murderous. Writer Rick Mofina interviewed Martha as well as numerous friends, business colleagues, and politicians. Martha's contribution was to vehemently denounce the view that Dorothy Joudrie was a Calgary socialite. "As far as I'm concerned, and you can quote me, she is not," said Martha. "I met her at a formal dinner in Calgary in 1986 and she snubbed me. We were introduced by a mutual acquaintance and she looked right through me and that was my one encounter with the majestic Dorothy."[2] "The majestic Dorothy." Here was a woman who had just been through hell, but she had snubbed Martha ten years earlier, so she had been forever stricken from the ranks of acceptability.

Other personal slights in Martha's life were about to be rectified as the dealers met in Halifax in September 1996. With A.J. dead for more than a year, Martha was ready to flex her muscles by declaring herself as the custodian of the corporate and familial past. Martha used her

---

2 *Calgary Herald*, May 11, 1996, F1.

keynote speech to establish her growing influence. "Good afternoon," she began, "my name is Martha Billes, and I like making waves." As if she knew that the Tire dealers attending the Halifax gathering would cringe and worry what craziness Martha had in mind, she quickly added, "You can relax, I mean only the best waves, positive waves. Canadian Tire is my family and all of you are part of my family, so it's nice to be home again with you."

Family was an ironic theme for a woman who had graduated in home management from the Macdonald Institute, but had been unable to oversee her own household successfully: two divorces, a runaway son, and litigation against a lover as well as her brothers. In fact, beyond her adored dogs, the closest thing Martha ever had to a real family was Tire, an eclectic collection of management, dealers, and products as ever-changing as the sea itself. For Martha, the relentless search for self-esteem and her place in the world could only be accomplished through Tire.

The theme of that dealer meeting, "making waves," appeared on a sign behind her. During her thirteen-minute speech Martha used the word "waves," or a variation of it, a total of twenty-seven times, a repetition that might have made some listeners seasick. Accompanying her on the textual voyage was her usual crew of ghosts from the past. Many corporations are proud of their history, but few owners spend as much time in public retrospection as Martha. "I like to make waves. How could it be otherwise? I come from a heritage of wave-makers. My father A.J. and his brother made waves. Don't you think profit-sharing, when A.J. introduced it, was considered making waves? And what about our cash discount coupons? Our Canadian Tire money with the look and feel of real money. Unique in all the world. Isn't that another example of how to make waves? We would do well today to reflect on A.J.'s vision of our corporate, dealer, employee partnership, unique in its time."

Such recollections were crucial to Martha's wielding power because such specific memories provided a place for her in the continuum. Her theme was almost biblical: As it was in the beginning, is now, and ever shall be. "My mother, too, made corporate waves. Remember our roller-skated employees? Her idea. Quite revolutionary in its time. My brothers Fred and David" — and here Martha paused ever so slightly and altered the timbre of her voice to emphasize the next two words, "and I," then returned to the previous tone and cadence — "made waves when we purchased control in 1983."

Having established her connections with the past and her affinities with the dealers, she came to the conclusion, that stirring part of a speech where mutual commitments are made between a speaker and an audience, a leader and her followers. "Let it be said of each and every one of us that we honoured the memory of our founders and secured our future by making waves. Let's resolve to go out there together, dealers, management, employees, Billeses, and the board, and let's make waves."

Following Martha at the podium was Tire's new chairman, Gil Bennett. He began on a light note. "My remarks will be brief. Actually, I had intended to speak at length, but Martha and I were allotted a total of fifteen minutes. Steve [Bachand] suggested that Martha and I should get together and negotiate a fair sharing of the fifteen minutes, which we did, with the result that Martha took thirteen-and-a-half and I have one-and-a-half." Concluded Bennett, after the laughter had subsided: "Negotiating with Martha is very hard on one's self-respect."

BY THE SPRING OF 1997 Fred's patience as a major shareholder of Tire had come to an end. He wanted to get out — once and for all. David, who would have preferred no change in the ownership, made a last-ditch attempt at reconciliation. "The best thing would have been if the three of us agreed on a concept, we would put it forward. If one had an idea and the others thought it was not appropriate, then it wouldn't [go forward]," said David.

Fred was adamant and David could not change his mind. But rather than side with Fred in selling, as he had done in 1986, David told Martha he would join with her to buy Fred's shares. This was not what Martha had in mind; she wanted to see the backside of both her brothers. David was unaware of Martha's goal, so he spent his time focusing on ways to accomplish their buyout of Fred at the lowest possible cost.

Any purchase-and-sale agreement among the three Billeses had to be done adroitly. Based on the 1987 OSC ruling, Martha and David couldn't pay Fred more than 15 per cent over the voting share price on the open market or they would trigger the coat-tail provision. Then they would have to acquire and pay for all the non-voting shares as well, adding hundreds of millions of dollars to the cost of their transaction.

David didn't want to borrow the money he needed. Rather, he wanted to raise the funds necessary to pay for his half of Fred's shares by selling some of his non-voting shares. Martha and David would have to sell the equivalent of 1.15 of each of their non-voting shares to raise the money they would use to pay for each of Fred's voting shares. But that would trigger substantial capital gains taxes and increase their out-of-pocket costs, so David devised a proposal that would not only reduce those costs to both Martha and him but also keep the regulators happy.

The value of the voting and non-voting shares had been closely tracking each other. There was a provision in the company bylaws that allowed any shareholder to convert voting shares to non-voting shares. David's idea, which he proposed to Fred and Martha, was for Fred to convert his voting shares to non-voting (which Fred could readily sell on the open market), following which Martha and David would pay Fred a top-up amount that was the equivalent of 15 per cent of that realized value. Under this scheme, Fred would effectively receive a premium for his voting shares, but David and Martha would not have to sell as many of their non-voting shares to complete the deal. "My brother agreed to it; he didn't like it, because it was a little more complicated, but he could see the point," said David. Because Fred was a resident on the Cayman Islands, he would pay no capital gains taxes, so David's proposal had no impact on his final proceeds. Fred was intrigued, but he knew Martha would not agree. "It did depend upon Martha's cooperation, which I didn't expect. Anything that we could propose, Martha would be against — it wouldn't matter what it was," said Fred.

Martha tried to dissuade David by telling him that his scheme gave all the other common shareholders an unfair advantage. After the transaction, the value of all common shares would rise because there would be fewer such shares in existence. David suggested that he and Martha ask the dealers to join them in buying Fred out, thereby sharing the cost. "She said, 'Well, even if they did, there's the other private individuals. They'd be getting a free ride,'" recalled David. Even though Martha's voting shares would also increase in value, she did not want the other holders of voting shares to enjoy a similar uplift — that was the "free ride" she opposed. "She would be paying my brother her share of the 15 per cent, I'd be paying, but nobody else would be," said David. "And these other people would all be getting a 'free ride' — and she couldn't accept that. It was at her expense, and my expense, and not at their expense. This is the whole concept of share buybacks by companies."

Other scenarios were discussed, but David continued to see his share-swap idea as the best solution. He mistakenly believed that Martha was giving serious consideration to his preferred route. He naively expected papers to arrive from her lawyers that would, when signed, put his plan into motion. But when July came, David had heard nothing, so he asked Martha: "Well, what's happening? How's it coming along? Do you have your money ready?"

"What do you mean?" she inquired.

"We're going to buy Fred out. We were talking about having him convert—"

"No, I'm not doing that," Martha cut him off.

Stunned that Martha had not only rejected his idea but hadn't even bothered to advise him, David decided his next step on the spot. "Fine," he said, "you're buying us both out."

Martha had achieved her life-long dream at last. David's impulsive decision was the perfect ending to her perfect plan launched in 1986. Both her brothers now wanted to sell; under the terms of their 1989 agreement, she was first in line to buy their shares. The boys were about to be forever dumped from the rumble seat of A.J.'s Buick coupe. Martha was at the wheel. Control of Canadian Tire on her terms was now assured, in much the same manner she had taken possession of the property at Shanty Bay. Fred couldn't possibly proceed in concert with Martha; David had dithered and backed down. In the end, Martha was left as the sole owner.

David hardly knew what hit him. "Like, the rationale, the logic behind it? I don't understand it. You talk about erratic decisions. As it happens, I'm glad I'm out because it certainly simplified my life. It is not a position I coveted, being a controlling shareholder. This is just one more reason why there hasn't been a relationship redevelop [with Martha] because I never know what to expect." Fred was not so naive. As far as he was concerned, Martha in control was the only possible outcome, given her personality and perseverance. "She wanted me gone when she was five years old," said Fred. "There's been no change in the girl's personality, and she hasn't learned anything from life."

In pursuing her goal, Martha was doing what came naturally to her. "She's a Billes," said Dick, the cousin who was cut out in 1983. "She's got tremendous drive. She's very bright. I guess the Billeses will do things . . ." and here Dick's voice trailed off as he searched for a word until he came up with "stubborn, maybe? They get hold of something like a bulldog. It would be smart to let go and they don't. It has a certain meaning to the personalities of the stronger people in the Billes family. [Elizabeth Ann] my daughter's got a little bit of that. She'll hang on to things and she just won't let them go."

So there are Billeses and then there are Billeses. There are those like Martha, who have an iron will. There's Fred, who gave up along the way, and David, who preferred an impossible peace. And there's Dick, who claimed to be serene about Martha's triumph. "It was out of our hands. It was our father [J.W.] that set it in motion. He gave the shares to A.J. in the first place. A.J. didn't buy them; they were given to him. My father must have wanted it that way. I can't get myself upset over something I can't control. I had to make my own life and do the things I wanted to do, which I did." Dick sold his store in 1992. "It was a lot of fun running the store. There wasn't a day that I didn't want to get up and go to work, except for the last year. It's a young man's game."

Now the whole company was a woman's game. Once David decided to sell, the agreement was drawn up and signed on August 1, 1997. Martha paid Fred and David a total of $45.3 million for their 1.4 million voting shares, thereby giving her sole control of 60.9 per cent of the voting shares. She paid $32.38 a share, a price that was less than 15 per cent above the market price, so no coat-tail was triggered.

Martha's manoeuvring to achieve this victory demonstrated a self-assurance she did not possess in 1986 when she turned down the chance to buy out her brothers. "We all evolve over time. We all acquire, as we get older and more experienced, more self-confidence," said Maureen Sabia. "The Martha that you see today is a much more confident Martha than may have been the case in those days. Remember, she joined this board quite late, in 1980. In the lives of all people, there are moments of less confidence and more confidence. The events [of 1986–87] hardened her resolve. She is icily determined or she would never have stepped up and bought her brothers' shares. That determination has grown and grown and grown over the time that I have known her."

The plan Martha launched in 1986, coupled with her lawsuit against her brothers the following year, took a decade to bear fruit, but her persistence paid off. In 1986 the dealers were willing to pay $160 for each voting share. If Martha had matched that demented price, buying out her brothers would have cost $224 million. Even at $99.95 per share, the price Fred and David set in 1986 when she declined to buy, Martha would have paid $140 million. By closing off the avenues of sale by her brothers to other parties, then simply waiting, Martha paid a relative pittance — $45.3 million — to gain control of a company with $4 billion in annual revenue.[3] "Sometimes," said Martha, "I absolutely startle myself and dumbfound myself with what I am capable of accomplishing."

The ousted David felt dispossessed and driven from his boyhood home by Martha. "It's a real major change because Canadian Tire has been a part of my life since I was a little kid." He was upset that none of his three children or Fred's five could ever inherit shares in the family business. "I'm a little disappointed,"[4] said David.

Fred was relieved to sell out at $32.38, even though the price of the voting shares rose to $55 over the next two years. "If I'd held on I could have increased my profitability, but I wasn't selling out necessarily for a profit. I was selling out to get clear. I didn't like the way it was running and I didn't like it more and more as the years went by," said Fred.

---

3 The dealers owned 20.4 per cent and the employees' profit-sharing plan, 12.2 per cent. As a result, about 94 per cent of the voting shares were now in the hands of a tight little circle consisting of Martha, the dealers, and the employees. The rest are publicly held.

4 *Calgary Herald*, July 22, 1997, A1.

David had been off the board since 1990. Martha wanted Fred to vanish and be quick about it. "Martha insisted that I leave the board when the sale was made and not continue through to the next annual meeting, which would have been normal. I don't think that was very pleasant," said Fred. "A director has a certain amount of residual responsibility and it would have been nice to know what was going on during that period of time." When Martha was involved, there were no such niceties. No one was allowed to save face.

MAYBE THE PHRASE "family business" is an oxymoron, a pair of words that don't belong together, like jumbo shrimp or military intelligence. The Canadian landscape is littered with siblings who have fought publicly over ownership or direction of their family businesses, but few wrangles have been as bitter or have lasted as long as the fights among Martha, Fred, and David. About 70 per cent of family businesses in Canada have not selected a successor, and 66 per cent don't even have a process in place to get things started. That's a major reason why only 30 per cent of family businesses get to the second generation; a mere 10 per cent make it into the third. In addition to the brawling Billeses, there have been fights among the French-fry McCains, the grocery Steinbergs, the meat-packing Mitchells, and the pulp-and-paper Krugers. Measured against these other clans, Martha was the she-lion who persevered.

Martha saw herself in a new light and suddenly had a new role to play. "You always think this kind of thing is in never-never land, then all of a sudden there it was," she told Zena Olijnyk of the *Financial Post*. "The best-qualified person should do whatever the job is — one role is to be a symbol of the founding family."[5]

As the newly crowned head of the household, Martha sought to

---

5   *Financial Post*, October 7, 1997.

reassure the various members of her extended family — share-holders, dealers, and employees. "It's going to be business as usual. I'm very interested in the ongoing development of the stores. We'll be looking at line reviews — why we should sell something and what else we should be selling." As for the threat posed by big-box retailers such as Home Depot, Martha saw this competition as a help, not a hindrance. "We know who we are now, for sure, and where we're going."[6]

With her control position secured, Martha set out to take her message public and present herself as the only Billes who mattered. In November 1997 she made her first public foray beyond the friendly confines of the dealer meetings with a speech to the Canadian Club of Toronto entitled "Reflections of My Father's Daughter." She described herself as her parents' only daughter, an unusual, self-absorbed description for a woman with three siblings, one of whom was called Tire. After all, she told the audience, Tire was "the company I regarded, growing up, as another sibling, because Canadian Tire was always my father's first-born child and ever the centre of our family's life."

If, as Barbara, Fred's wife, has said, Martha resented not being number one, that resentment was aimed not just at Fred, as the eldest, but also at Tire itself. Owning Tire was not just about beating two brothers, but about controlling the third sibling as well. Martha's victory provided no balm for her old wounds. She remained angry about past slights and perceived slurs. "Would it surprise you to learn that there was no place for me at Canadian Tire until 1980?" she asked her audience. "It was not until 1980 that I joined the company's board of directors, on which my two brothers had sat since the early 1960s. My father made a place for me by giving up his own seat. For me it

---

6   *Calgary Herald*, September 16, 1997, E1.

was both a victory and a sadness that only through the generosity of my father was I permitted a seat at the table." The fight had made Martha who she was. "My brothers had always been considered by everyone as 'heirs apparent' simply because they were male. Fighting the stubborn notions, whether of society or family, as to where — if at all — women fit in the corporate world has been, for me, a way of life. And perhaps I am better for the fight. I know I am stronger because of it and icy firm in my resolve."

Icy firm. Maureen Sabia called Martha "icily determined." It was as if Martha were a frozen lake and no one was allowed to plumb her depths. Even among kindred spirits, Martha was guarded and unwilling to warm up. At the annual Women of Influence series sponsored by *Chatelaine* magazine, she was the featured speaker in Calgary in November 1999. After she had delivered a message similar to the Canadian Club speech, the floor was opened up for questions. Someone asked: "Who are your female role models?" The very title of the luncheon series should have alerted Martha that the question might come up, but she seemed flummoxed, as if she had never given the matter a moment's thought. "She's not quick on her feet," said someone who attended the event. "She thinks before she answers. Thirty seconds is a long time for the audience to wait. The silence went on for so long I was getting itchy, as someone who knew her. She finally came out with Laura Sabia, whom I guess Martha knew quite well. Then she also said Maureen [Sabia] and said how she admired Maureen's work. I was surprised when she had no answer. I would have said Madam Gandhi or someone." Or her mother and the roller skates. Or her grandmother Moore, who instilled the love of reading.

THE NAME SAID IT ALL. When Martha incorporated a new company to hold the 1,400,767 voting shares she bought from Fred and David, she called the company Tire 'N' Me Pty. Ltd. and named herself president. Not Tire 'N' Us; just Tire 'N' Me. Her business card says controlling shareholder. At last Martha had arrived on the private planet for which she had yearned in high school so long ago. (Martha's other Canadian Tire shares are also held in companies she controls: Albikin Management Inc. and Albikin II Holdings Inc.)

Chairman Gil Bennett assumed that Martha would want to name herself chairman of Canadian Tire, so he offered to step aside. He was surprised when she declined. "I feel it's better to work as a shareholder and as a member of the board rather than holding the office of chairman of the board," Martha explained in an interview. "I think I can accomplish an awful lot more of my vision and my desires by not being in the chairman's office. That is a current feeling. It may or may not last, one never knows, but that's the way I was then and that's the way I am now."

Martha used her power in a different way. As controlling shareholder, she was able to choose nine of the sixteen members of the board. At the 1998 annual meeting, she replaced five directors with others who were more to her liking. They included John Stransman of Stikeman Elliott, her long-time lawyer and adviser; Gordon Cheesbrough, president of Altamira Investment Services Inc., a mutual fund company; James Fisher, an adjunct professor at the University of Toronto's Rotman School of Business; and Rémi Marcoux, CEO of GTC Transcontinental Group Ltd.

Martha named herself to the management resources and compensation committee, the group that focuses on executive remuneration and succession. She also appointed herself chairman of the governance committee, the powerful board committee that recommends committee chairmen, sets directors' remuneration, and assesses the performance of the chairman of the full board. The governance committee also recommends the three directors who represent those shareholders who own non-voting shares of Canadian Tire. Under

Martha, two of the three have been replaced. The new directors are Frank Potter, chairman of Toronto-based consulting firm Emerging Market Advisors Inc., and Roy MacLaren, a former minister of international trade in the government of Jean Chrétien and, from 1996 to 2000, high commissioner to the United Kingdom. (The dealers also name three directors, and the CEO is automatically on the board.)

Beyond those specific steps, Martha attends all meetings of the other two board committees, the audit committee and the social responsibility committee. In recent years, committee work on most corporate boards has become a time-consuming affair even for a director who sits on only one committee. The hours Martha spends preparing for and attending so many meetings are substantial. In 2000, for example, there were twenty-three meetings of the four board committees and seventeen meetings of the full board, a total of forty lengthy sessions in all. Meetings of the full board begin at 8:30 a.m. and often last for six hours.

On the one hand, such activism indicates that Martha cares deeply about Tire and wants complete knowledge of everything that happens. On the other hand, her constant presence must make other directors feel as though they are working for an owner who keeps a close watch. The message transmitted by Martha must surely be: Don't take any action without listening to my advice and receiving my consent, unstated or otherwise.

Tire directors are well paid. They receive a stipend of $20,000 a year, almost twice the average fee paid by Canadian corporations. They also receive $1,250 for each meeting they attend and are reimbursed for all associated travel costs. Directors also receive a special discount of 21.4 per cent off all items purchased at Tire under $200 and 10 per cent off items worth more than $200. (Gasoline is not included in the plan.) The discount is not taken at the cash register; it must be claimed later. For all her personal wealth, Martha makes certain she receives every possible benefit. In 1993, for example, she filed receipts for fifteen different purchases at stores in Barrie and Calgary totalling $458.92 and requested her director's discount of $98.21.[7]

OF ALL THE DIRECTORS at Canadian Tire, none is closer or more important to Martha than Maureen Sabia. The relationship goes well beyond work to being best friends. Martha calls Sabia "Mother" because Sabia offers her so much advice. Sabia stiffens Martha's backbone when needed, helps write Martha's speeches, and speaks for Martha at board meetings in the full knowledge that she can raise an objection or put forward a proposition that Martha may not want to state. This arrangement allows Martha to be one step removed, observe how others react, and have deniability if the need arises.

In 1995 Martha travelled to Asia with Sabia, who had been invited to give a series of trade-related speeches in her capacity as former chairman of the Export Development Corp. They visited the Philippines, Malaysia, Thailand, Hong Kong, Singapore, and Indonesia, where Martha participated in official lunches and evening receptions for local business leaders hosted by Canadian diplomats and trade officials. "Martha is a shy individual, but handles herself well socially," said Sabia. "Everyone knew Canadian Tire over there. As soon as they understood Martha's relationship, there was a huge interest in her and in Canadian Tire in Southeast Asia." Martha was not just a tag-along tourist. "She was very interested in how cars got serviced in Bangkok, for example," said Sabia. "The thing that struck us both was that you'd see these very small garages with a naked light bulb and a 500 [series] Mercedes being serviced in this very small and unscientific space. She was fascinated by people's buying habits and how they might change if they had something different. She was constantly interested in how things worked."

---

7 University of Western Ontario, Canadian Tire Archives, J.J. Talman Collection, box CTP0872.

The two women also did some personal shopping. Martha bought jewellery, Jim Thompson Thai Silk, and a sculpted stone horse that she had shipped to the cottage at Shanty Bay. "She's not the consummate shopper I am," said Sabia. "She's quite focused. She likes to buy jewellery. You can't be too rich or too thin. And you can't have too much jewellery."

On some topics, they might as well be twins. For example, Sabia has been a key source for Martha's views on female directors. "It disappoints and even angers me that talented and qualified women are still, to a large extent, invisible to business leaders," Martha told the Canadian Club in 1997. "It disappoints and angers me that so many believe women are not qualified, that many companies aren't looking for women for their boards, or, most lamely of all, that so many say they don't know where to look."

But Martha also knew from personal experience how men felt about female directors. "Men aren't comfortable with the thought of women on their boards," she said. "We look different. We sound different. I happen to think we view the world differently and I know we are more independent. Women are good for business."[8] Martha did not, however, position herself as a militant feminist. "I don't believe men are our enemies or our oppressors. No, I don't believe that women are victims. In fact, when women reject once and for all the victim mentality so fervently thrust upon them by the professional feminists, women will do much better in their progression toward equal status in both reality and perception."[9]

Martha follows the teachings of Sabia and her mother, Laura, that there should be neither quotas nor targets, just equal opportunity. "Martha does not play the numbers game," said Sabia. "Equality of opportunity is what my mother fought for all of her life. Equality of results is something very different from equality of opportunity. That's

8   Empire Club of Toronto, Speech, February 8, 2001.
9   Canadian Club of Toronto, Speech, November 1997.

why Martha and I say we are traditional feminists. I believe men and women are equal in the sense that women can do any job a man can do just as well if she has the experience, training, education, smarts, all the same things that men would have to have to do a job well. You guys have had two thousand years of experience. We've just started."

Martha does not, however, believe that men and women are equally gifted. She sees positive attributes in women that are not possessed by men. "I would like to find more women [as directors], not because they're women *per se*, but I find women are a little more tenacious and tend to keep on top of something over many weeks and many months," said Martha. "Memories are different. The female brain works quite differently than the male brain. To have a nice balance would really, really help the functioning in the boardroom. I'd really like to get another lady or two on our board. Maybe it'll happen in the next few years."

For all Martha's preoccupation with the issue, the number of women on the Tire board — three — is the same today as it was fifteen years ago. In 1996 Martha added Lilia Clemente, CEO of Clemente Capital Inc. of New York. Women in management at Tire have fared little better than they have at other retailers. Only about one-third of Tire management is female. Only eleven of the four hundred dealers are women.

There is nothing naive about either Maureen Sabia or Martha Billes. "She doesn't trust easily," said Sabia, "and neither do I." If there was a single important thread that ran throughout Martha's life, that was it. Her incapacity to trust has been both a distressing fact and a driving force.

THAT LACK OF TRUST extended to Martha's view of management. Once she got the board looking and sounding the way she wanted,

Martha focused next on her other competitor for control of Tire, Steve Bachand. Their relationship was prickly at best. Analyst George Hartman arranged a small dinner meeting in Calgary so institutional investors could meet Bachand and hear his story. Martha attended, but Bachand barely acknowledged her presence. "He spoke as if she wasn't there. He attempted to keep Martha away as much as he could. Because she believed the hype that he was doing well, she tolerated it," said Hartman.

At board meetings, the relationship was little better. He was defensive; she was suspicious. If Martha asked a question with a hint of innuendo, a thin-skinned Bachand might all too easily rise to the bait. Alternatively, he sometimes thought Martha was trying to push him around, even though she may have been doing no such thing. "They weren't at each other's throats," said Bennett. "Steve's personality conflicted with quite a few people, not just Martha." Martha was well aware how tricky her situation was. "The relationship between board and management is a highly delicate balancing act," she said. "It takes great independence, healthy confidence and more than a bit of courage both on the part of management and the board to successfully navigate through its intricacies and pitfalls. Having said this, I did feel that having discussions with the chairman and the CEO in advance of formal board meetings could only facilitate our decision-making process as it would encourage our alignment."[10]

Those cozy meetings were something she had tried unsuccessfully to put in place during the previous regimes of Muncaster and Groussman. Bachand was no happier to hold such sessions. "A controlling shareholder can be a very intimidating world," said Bachand. "If the board didn't want me to continue on as CEO, they've got the right to fire me. I don't mean to be cavalier about it, but I

---

10 Empire Club of Toronto, Speech, February 8, 2001.

wasn't worried. I had a certain style and I had certain things I wanted to get done." Bachand wanted everyone to know that his "alignment" with Martha was not automatic. His independence was demonstrated when, in front of new directors attending their first board meeting in 1998, he tore a strip off chairman Gil Bennett. At another board gathering he castigated Maureen Sabia, who stood her ground.

As time went by, Martha's relationship with Bachand improved. "I thought Steve was becoming more comfortable with the fact that he didn't have to prove to himself and maybe to his management team on a daily basis that he was the boss," said Bennett. "His ego didn't get any smaller, but he was able to allow his accomplishments to speak for themselves."

When Bachand's five-year employment contract expired in 1998 and he negotiated a new deal, he was careful to request a clause that permitted departure with one year's notice. Speaking to the directors who were involved in the discussions, Bachand insisted he had no particular retirement plans. "I'm just going to wake up one morning and feel like I don't want to do this any more," he told them. "I don't know when that day is going to be, but I think that's what's going to happen."

That day soon arrived. In late 1999 Martha and the board concluded that Tire needed a new corporate vision. Bachand disagreed and told them Tire should continue to focus on improving the core business through his well-established renovate-and-rebuild plan. Not satisfied, Martha and the board asked him to think about where Tire would go from there and to commit himself to seeing the strategy through to its conclusion. Bachand decided that he didn't have the stomach to devise a new business plan and to spend the three or four years required to put it in place. In January 2000 he told Martha and the board that he was exercising his "one year and out" clause. "There is no such thing as indentured service," said Bachand. "I could have said, 'Hell, yeah,

I'll give you five' and left in two, but I'm just not that kind of guy. I did not want to do this for five more years. If you're CEO of Canadian Tire, you better like what the hell you're doing or you're a nut."

Some of Bachand's close associates were caught off guard. In December Bachand and John Rankin, senior vice-president, dealer relations, had a long and wide-ranging conversation about Tire. Rankin felt so secure about his future at Canadian Tire that he bought shares at $34 and leased a new car. "I came back from vacation and my world fell apart because he announced he was leaving," said Rankin. "It really was one of those 'Trudeau in the snow' kind of things. Steve was a very quiet, introspective guy. He was an only child and very self-sufficient."

Personal considerations also played a part in Bachand's decision. He and his wife, Phyllis, were both American; their grandchildren and his aging father lived in the United States. At sixty-one, he was running out of steam. "It requires high energy," said Bachand. "This is a place that has to be driven and at some point all that stuff goes into the bowl, gets stirred around, and you say, 'I don't want to do this any more.'" The money made the decision possible. Bachand had earned $15.5 million by cashing stock options in November 1999. A retirement allowance of $7 million brought his total compensation for the year to $27 million.

Moreover, Bachand was tired of dealing with Martha. In private he complained about having to put up with her. "He wasn't having fun any more," said someone who had listened to Bachand's lamentations. "He described her in a way you would describe almost any heiress who had a chip on her shoulder about the professional managers, with a bit of a reverse sexist tone. He just got fed up." Martha's unpredictable nature had worn him down, Bachand confided to friends. "You would have thought that a woman of her age was past those moods," Bachand said ruefully.

Bachand says his difficult relationship with Martha was not material to his decision. "To me, it was less a family question than it was a board question. Family members, three going to one during my tenure, were very supportive of what we were trying to do. They were very knowledgeable of the strategy. The family never had any interest beyond [saying], 'We want this to be a growing successful company with an untarnished reputation in the marketplace.' If things are going well, things go well in your boardroom. When things aren't going well, there are a helluva lot of things that you're told to do or not do."

Fred was among those who firmly believed the tension between Martha and Bachand did help to precipitate his decision. "I know he had a lot of trouble with Martha. Bachand left for a reason and it wasn't rheumatism, arthritis, or age. I don't think he had any red-hot place to go." Indeed, Bachand took on no new full-time role. He and his wife split their time between houses in Maine and in Florida.

Bachand must have known that six good years were about to come to an abrupt end. George Hartman, an analyst with Dundee Securities who had been watching Canadian Tire since 1969, heard rumblings about poor earnings, but was unable to corroborate the rumours. That spring, management had been optimistic; in November they quietly spread the word to analysts that earnings wouldn't be as good as previously thought, but they provided no details. This kind of information matters to analysts such as Hartman. They base their recommendations on what they hear, and what he was hearing behind the scenes was worse than the official word. In December, out of frustration, he phoned Martha to find out what she knew. Like everyone else, she seemed to be unaware of any major problem brewing. Bachand "shut her out, he kept her away, but she allowed it because the numbers seemed to be OK. Something about him bothered her but she never took any action," said Hartman. When he couldn't unearth any proof there was a problem, Hartman continued to recommend that investors buy shares in Canadian Tire.

For Bachand and for Gerald Kishner, the chief financial officer, their timing was fortuitous. They both exercised their stock options in November. In February 2000, a month after Bachand announced his retirement, Tire declared that the company was taking a $58.5 million write-down. (Kishner retired four months later.) Those losses, which were much higher than expected, were attributed to costs in launching the on-line site, preparations for Y2K as the millennium ended, and Bachand's retirement allowance. When Bachand exercised his stock options in November 1999, the share price was $34. By early January it had fallen to $29, then tumbled $10 on the day the write-down was announced. Within weeks, share price hit $15, its lowest level in three years, before recovering to the low $20s a year later. All Bachand's hard-won improvements in the 1990s began to look less lustrous. Annual revenue had increased from $3.1 billion in 1990 to $5.2 billion in 2000, but profit had remained flat, $144 million in 2000 versus $148 million in 1990. During the 1990s the TSE 300 doubled in value; Tire shares ended that same period virtually unchanged. "That's not a good record, not if you're at the same share price, because the dividend yield is insignificant," admitted Bachand.

Martha was among those injured when the roof caved in. The value of her share holdings in Canadian Tire, which had peaked at $150 million in 1999, were knocked down by one-third to $100 million. "I certainly have been disappointed by the share price," she said. "The market is a cruel place. Our management team is aligned, they're bright, and they are determined to re-establish our company in the minds of the analysts. They know it'll take a few quarters, a number of quarters with good, clear, precise, concise reporting, a lot more disclosure. It's a good strong company; it's seen itself through some difficult times."

Hartman believes Tire's problems are not yet behind them. A year later, when results were announced in February 2001, earnings had not improved. If the write-down was really just a one-time wonder, why didn't results bounce back? Increased revenue did not lead to higher profits.

As an owner, Martha was learning that, in retailing, it takes a lot of running just to stay in the same place.

ELEVEN

ADVENTURES AS
A CAPITALIST

*"She's very tough and I think a lot of guys don't want to take it.
There's still that old school of the female ruling the male.
I don't think they like that."*
— MARLENE SMITH

At the intersection of Second Street and Sixth Avenue in downtown Calgary stand two ten-foot-tall statues, one yellow, the other red, by sculptor Sorel Etrog. Called *Sadko and Kabuki*, the creations look as if they were assembled from spare parts out of a giant's tool box. According to the plaque: "The design of the sculpture of *Sadko and Kabuki*, which is a Japanese theatre ritual of dance, music, and drama, was inspired by Sorel Etrog's fascination with nuts and bolts in a Canadian Tire store."

In March 2000, at the Court of Queen's Bench two blocks away, the love feud between Martha Billes and Paul McAteer was also displayed for anyone who cared to take a look. For six weeks Justice John Rooke presided in Courtroom 503, a dreary place with a dated orange carpet, harsh lighting, dull wood panelling, and motley ceiling tile.

In contrast to the drab surroundings, Martha's style each day verged on the flamboyant. She favoured wool suits with skirts fashionably above the knee, swathed herself in capes, and wore black leather gloves. Her honey-blonde hair was flowing or pulled back in a French roll. The dark glasses she sometimes wore were a strange touch, hardly necessary in a Calgary March. They made her look like one of those faded movie stars who don't want anyone to recognize her, but was upset when no one paid attention.

Martha usually sported her diamond-encrusted gold Canadian Tire lapel pin. For Martha, that triangular emblem, familiar on street-scapes across the country, was more meaningful than any Order of Canada some lesser mortal might wear. Such awards were a dime a dozen, given out by the handful twice a year. The Tire escutcheon was different: she'd won this honour in the field of family battle.

Preparations and preliminaries for the trial had taken more than seven years since McAteer had filed his lawsuit. The flurry of black-robed lawyers who gathered at fees of $350 an hour and higher included Patrick Lannan, a sole practitioner with offices in Turner Valley, representing Paul McAteer, and Brian Davison of the Calgary firm Davison, Worden, acting for Pamela Mason. For Martha there were three lawyers, including Bill Code, one of Alberta's top litigators. Because there were also issues involving professional advice, counsel represented accounting firm Deloitte & Touche as well as law firms Bennett Jones of Calgary and Taylor McCaffrey of Winnipeg. Martha likely spent more than all the other participants combined to defend herself. The paperwork was voluminous. There were 480 exhibits and 10,000 pages of documents. More than a year later, in July 2001, the judge still has not ruled on the case.

On the first of her five days of testimony, Martha was accompanied by her friend of ten years Judy Romanchuk, an investment dealer in the Calgary office of Loewen, Ondaatje, McCutcheon. Romanchuk had that morning spotted a front-page story in the *National Post* with the headline: "Love, lust and money take centre stage at trial." The story was not about Martha; it described a New York court case involving a Canadian porn star who allegedly profited from Wall Street insider tips. Presiding over that trial was Kimba Wood, dubbed the "love judge" because her past included a high-profile divorce case in which she had been named co-respondent. She had also been a Playboy bunny in the 1960s. Romanchuk pulled the article out of her handbag, handed it to Martha in court, and said: "At least you haven't been a Playboy bunny." Martha read the story and laughed.

Among those who accompanied Martha to court was her current beau, Mark Sanderson, a Calgary divorcee in his mid-forties with three children. On two of the hearing days a curious Dennis Gardiner-Billes showed up to watch the proceedings. Martha and her ex-husband did not speak to each other.

Unlike most witnesses, who show up only to testify, Martha sat in the courtroom most days, taking copious notes. She revealed emotion only once, when George Harms, once Devoncroft's chief financial officer, repeated McAteer's boast, "When we really need money, all I have to do is sleep with Martha." On hearing that statement, Martha looked up from her notes, stunned. "You should have seen her face," said the court clerk. "My God!"[1]

Martha and her libido became national news. Her testimony and photo appeared in newspapers. Footage of her walking into court was aired on television newscasts. She was featured on the cover of *Canadian Business* and in *Saturday Night*. In 1986, when the Ontario Securities Commission hearings opened, Martha had such a low profile that Barbara, Fred's wife, was erroneously identified as Martha and the wrong photo was sent out to newspapers across the country. Because of Courtroom 503, Martha suddenly went from anonymous to notorious. She even became fodder for *Frank*, the muckraking scandal sheet. In a cover story about wealthy women called "Cash

---

1 *National Post*, April 6, 2000.

Cows," Martha placed eighth on the "Rich Babes" list. Toronto dealer Ken Mann, who testified at the trial because he was a trustee for Owen's estate, watched and listened in amazement as Calgary taxi drivers gave their thumbs-up approval and shouted at her, "Way to go, Martha." Martha was chagrined. "I hate people knowing," she said to Mann. "I'd just prefer they don't know who I am." Said Mann, "She likes to go home, mop her own floors, wash her own windows, and dig her own ditches. She was much better known than she'd ever hoped to be."

The public interest said as much about a prurient society as it did about her. If Martha had been a man who'd gone through a couple of wives and several lovers, and then appeared in court to battle one of them, few people would have paid such rapt attention. As a woman, she was judged more harshly. For all its supposed advances, society still has a different measure for men and women, employing the double standard that Martha has fought all her life. Women were more sympathetic to her plight because they, too, had suffered similarly unfair treatment in a male-dominated world.

Martha hid her face from photographers on the street and, at times during her testimony, closed her eyes as if to transport herself to some happier place — anywhere but Courtroom 503. On several occasions Martha seemed vague and confused, or she wept and dabbed at her eyes with tissues. Twice Judge Rooke admonished her for trying to introduce hearsay evidence from conversations in which she was not a participant. "I apologize," she said, by way of explanation. "Perhaps this has gotten to my head."

But the many other moods of Martha also made cameo appearances. She could adopt a winning way, acting almost girlish as she tried to make a convincing case about some matter that had been raised. She could be brittle and loathing. When that happened, those who had caused these proceedings had no doubt where they stood. At one point Brian Davison, who represented Pamela Mason, whispered to Patrick Lannan, Paul McAteer's lawyer, "What do you see when you're examining her?"

"I see hate in her eyes," replied Lannan.

"Really!" said Davison, who then watched with particular care the next time Lannan led Martha through a series of recollections. When Lannan returned to his seat, Davison whispered, "You're right. She hates you."

Martha's own view of herself as a businesswoman seemed remarkably inconsistent. Before the trial, during the examination for discovery on January 13, 1998, this exchange occurred between Martha and the lawyer who was interrogating her.

Q What is your employment experience? Did you work as a teacher?

A Yes.

Q How long did you do that for?

A About five years.

Q After you taught, what did you do?

A I've been a venture capitalist. I have worked as a research scientist briefly. Always been a venture capitalist.[2]

At the trial, when Davison read into the record that testimony, given under oath, Martha claimed she couldn't remember drawing that self-portrait. Of course, sounding so knowledgeable about business deals didn't suit her now that the McAteer matter had reached open court. She preferred to describe herself as someone who relied on others for financial advice. When pressed further by Davison about the description "venture capitalist," Martha adroitly altered the phrase to say that she had "enjoyed adventure as a capitalist."

Martha then listed some of those adventures. "I would have been

_____

2 Court of Queen's Bench of Alberta, Judicial District of Calgary, *Paul McAteer et al.*, Trial Transcript, 1859.

making reference to joint venturing in the oil and gas field with a number of companies since the mid-'70s. I would have been referring to helping out daughters of a friend of mine in a bagel enterprise in 1998. I would have been referring to going with some other people in a joint venture to rebuild sections of the TransCanada Pipelines. I would have been talking about doing factoring for a company called Domco, who supplied services, food services, and food to the building of the Quebec Hydro dams on Baie James, James Bay. Those are the kind of things that I was referring to, joint ventures."[3]

Patrick Lannan raised the topic of her business acumen, suggesting that Martha must be knowledgeable about business. After all, she had been a member of the Canadian Tire board since 1980. Martha did not agree. She admitted that she had been a director on three corporate boards, positions that gave her experience "at the senior highest level of stewardship." Such stewardship, however, did not, in her mind, translate into business experience.

Asked Lannan: "And did you consider yourself in 1990 [an] experienced business person at the highest level?"

"No, sir," replied Martha. "A work in progress."

"Not to be trite, is that work still in progress, Madam?"

"Oh, yes, sir," she said.[4]

Off the stand, Martha was more adept. In particular, she attempted to massage media coverage. She spoke several times with Ric Dolphin, who covered the proceedings for the *Edmonton Journal*. When he asked whom among her friends he could interview, she supplied several names. Martha also encouraged other friends to phone him and feed him quotes.

Saturday Night commissioned Dolphin to write a story for the issue of May 13, 2000, the magazine's first edition as a weekly. Martha declined to pose for photographs, but she did get a friend to provide

---

5   Trial Transcript, 1860.
4   Trial Transcript, 1714–15.

several pictures of her riding a show-jumping horse, as well as photos of her holding one of her Lakeland Terriers. Because of deadline pressures, Dolphin drove the pictures to the Calgary airport for speedy shipment to Toronto.

On the return trip from the airport, his cell phone rang. It was Martha, now prepared to be helpful personally with more photos. "Do you want black-and-white or colour?" she asked. Dolphin allowed that the magazine would probably like both, to give the editors more choice. She said she'd drop off a selection that evening at the Palliser Hotel, where Dolphin was staying in Calgary.

As Dolphin waited in front of the hotel at the appointed hour, Mark Sanderson appeared at Dolphin's side with an envelope and asked Dolphin if he'd like to talk to Martha in her car. They walked to her Lexus, parked on 9th Ave. SW, just east of the hotel. Sanderson climbed into the back seat and held one of Martha's dogs. Dolphin got in the front passenger seat, with Martha behind the wheel. As songs from *Phantom of the Opera* played on the sound system, Martha flipped open a photo album and showed Dolphin pictures of the Winnipeg golf dome under construction. Included were scenes of Martha standing on the dome's fabric as it lay on the ground and another photo of her pretending to tee off. At the back of the album were coupons from a local Canadian Tire store for use at the dome.

"She starts pointing at these coupons with this long lacquered fingernail," said Dolphin, "and I don't really know what she's getting at so I said, 'Well, what's all this about?'"

"This was our most successful promotion in Winnipeg ever," Martha replied. "Mr. McAteer struck a deal with Husky Oil."

Dolphin realized that arriving at such an arrangement with a Canadian Tire competitor would be unacceptable to Martha. "So," he asked, "was that the straw that broke the camel's back?"

Martha's answer was unspoken but graphic. She looked Dolphin in the eye, put her clenched hand over her heart, and rotated her fist as if she were turning a screw into her bosom, all the while making a grinding sound with her mouth. Once her devastation had been so dramatically displayed, the interview was suddenly over.

On reflection, Dolphin sympathized with Martha. "She always seemed to be trying to find a guy like her dad. Martha could never really find men her own age with the same amount of money because they usually had trophy wives or they were after young model-type women. And when she was disappointed, she had the wherewithal to go after them."

David doesn't believe that Martha sought a man in her father's mould. "She wouldn't have been happy with a person identical to my father because he was far too demanding and would not have allowed her to make the kind of decision she would want to make. He kept control even though he did it very nicely behind the scenes, and that's not what she wanted. I don't think she could take it for a period of time having somebody trying to control her."

Perhaps the type of man Martha has looked for has mattered less than the ones she ended up with. She was Cinderella, waiting for the right man to come along, solve her problems, and make her happy.

MARTHA'S "ADVENTURES AS A CAPITALIST" outside Canadian Tire have indeed included investments across a wide range of sectors, some more successful than others. In several instances the go-between was Marty Godin, who was both her lover and, when he was in the Toronto office of accounting firm KPMG, the general partner on deals involving Premier Pipelines Ltd. and Domco Site Services Ltd.

Those two investments made money, but the bakery business did not. In 1997 the two daughters of James Slater, a fellow investor with Martha in Premier Pipelines and Domco, decided to expand their successful Toronto bakery into a franchise called Bagelworks. Slater and Martha both became backers. "We didn't put enough money into it," said Slater. "We should have put more money into it and covered the waterfront, but at that point the bagel business was fading and it really looked like a business that we shouldn't be in." Bagelworks was sold in 1999.

As a partner, Slater respected Martha's business judgment, with one caveat. "She's absolutely a hands-on investor and is able to remember from prior meetings the number that doesn't exactly compute with a number that's given at a present meeting," he said. "She's a very smart woman, but every now and then your emotions take you where you don't want them to go. I think that's what that very unpleasant business in Calgary was." That's not to say Martha became blinded by love. "There are people who say, 'Well, I'll give him a lot of slack because of a personal involvement,'" said Slater. "She doesn't. She says one is personal; one is business. It isn't mixing business with pleasure [where] you say, 'I made an agreement, I like him, and I'll let it go.' Martha is good at compartmentalizing."

In addition to her losses on bagels, Martha poured money into a musical based on the life of Napoleon. In the mid-1980s Martha met Marlene Smith, a Toronto theatre impresario. As a result of that connection, she became an investor in the Toronto production of *Cats*. "She really likes showbiz," said Smith. "It's wonderful that there's somebody out there who likes being an angel because, God knows, they're hard to find." *Cats* was popular with both audiences and critics. Investors earned a profit. "*Cats* wasn't the toughest thing to finance because everybody knew what it was," said Smith. "*Napoleon* was a different story, but she's always had a lot of faith in it and she genuinely liked the show."

Martha's involvement in *Napoleon* began with a trip in 1991 to Shanty Bay by Smith's partner, Ernie Rubenstein, and the show's lyricist, Andrew Sabiston. They brought with them a cassette tape of music from the show, but the cottage was undergoing renovations and Martha's stereo was not available. Then she remembered a cassette player in her car, so the threesome sat in her vehicle to hear the music while Rubenstein made his pitch.

Rubenstein was seeking money for a workshop that would allow cast members to run through the entire production, get a feel for the show, and identify problems. Before playing the tape for Martha, Sabiston set the scene. "It's not just about staging a historical event," he said. "It's about getting inside the minds and hearts of these characters. It's a rise-and-fall story with tragic consequences."

The tape was no big production number: it was just Sabiston and composer Timothy Williams singing their songs to the accompaniment of a piano. "The boys" — as they are universally known — had grown up in Victoria and had been working on the project since they were teenagers. Sabiston told Martha she'd have to use her imagination. Martha pointed out the car window to a tarpaulined portion of her cottage and said, "You see over there? I'm imagining that one day there's going to be a greenhouse there because that's what the builders are telling me that they're going to build. If I can imagine that, I won't have any trouble with this." No one could figure out how to operate the reverse or fast-forward features of the cassette player, so they listened to the entire forty-five minutes straight through. After chatting for a few more minutes, Sabiston and Rubenstein departed, leaving the tape and a script behind.

Back in Calgary, Martha played the tape for her old high school acquaintance Roger Perkins, who had been involved in theatre productions at the Canmore Opera House in Calgary's Heritage Park. Perkins, who has also been music director at the Shaw Festival at Niagara-on-the-Lake, was not impressed. "I don't like musicals," he said, "but I told her it was very much the story, scope, and music, the sweeping stuff that people like. Her tastes lie to popular entertainment. She likes to get away from the concerns of her work and her daily life. My sense is that she's not committed strongly to the arts."

Martha decided to finance the entire workshop herself. "She

responded to the human drama of ambition and the love story," said Sabiston. "She saw that it had some potential. Her support for *Napoleon* has been monumental." After the workshop, when the decision was taken to proceed with a full production, Martha was among two dozen investors who contributed $4.5 million for costumes, salaries, set construction, and rehearsal hall rentals.

Investors knew enough not to expect a return on their money. "The process is not a business process at all," said Geoff Smith, Marlene's son and one of the rights holders of *Napoleon*. "For 90 per cent of the investors, it's purely a labour of love. There is the hope that they will do well, and you have a success, and if that happens that's great. But it's not something that you would invest your last dollar in. Out of all the investors that I've come across, she is one of the most practical and knowledgeable. She's very insightful. She does a tremendous amount of homework."

Investors were treated as insiders, with access to the glamour and the glory. "She did appreciate the material and the music that had been written by the boys. She had a chance to see it, literally, as the notes were going on the page," said Geoff Smith.

Napoleon opened in 1994 at Toronto's Elgin Theatre to mixed reviews. Some critics were negative, others positive, but their overall tone did not generate good word of mouth. Ticket sales were poor and the show closed after only three months. Everyone agreed that there were numerous problems, particularly in the book, or story line. Characters appeared and disappeared without sufficient introduction.

Rather than abandon the project, Sabiston and Williams decided to focus the play as more of a love story between Josephine and Napoleon, then reopen in London's West End. For the next two years Martha was the only financial backer. Eventually, there were six Canadian and ten European investors. Total costs prior to the opening in 2000 were £4.5 million ($10 million), of which Martha contributed about $1 million. Throughout, Martha was no silent partner. She sat in on workshops and attended creative meetings run by director Francesca Zambello at the American Church in London. "She was very tuned in to the story line, the subject matter, and how the audience would feel," said Geoff Smith. "She was always careful not to say a whole lot, but when she said something, it was meaningful."

Martha was also an assiduous reader of paperwork and contracts. "She'd go over the documentation with a fine-toothed comb and almost always have intelligent comments on things no one else caught," said Geoff Smith. "If I wanted something reviewed, I'd give it to Martha. I've chuckled sometimes, when I get a fax from her with a circle around it. 'Did you see that? Did the lawyer see that? No. I didn't see that.' But she saw that." Such careful readings must have been difficult for Martha because she has problems with her eyes. During the 1980s she wore both glasses and hard contact lenses at the same time and she left the lenses in place even while she slept. In the 1990s she underwent laser surgery to correct her vision. The procedure was successful in the right eye, but not the left. Three more procedures on the left eye brought no improvement. As a result, she no longer reads much for pleasure.

After previews that began in September 2000, the vastly revised *Napoleon* opened the following month at the Shaftesbury in London's West End. Martha was optimistic. "I've been with the boys since 1991," she told Martin Knelman of the *Toronto Star*, "and we're still going strong. We can see what went wrong the first time, and we can see what's going right this time. This time we have the right people doing the right thing. Of course, when you deal with the whims of the public it's always a huge risk, but I think we have the product this time. It's a winner."[5]

Martha attended the opening gala. Some of the lyrics could

---

5   *Toronto Star*, October 11, 2000.

have been about her own life. On the eve of battle, Napoleon steeled himself by singing:

We have a dream within us, a will to improve our lot
In your heart you're a general, don't believe you're not.

The relationship between Napoleon and Josephine also offered parallels to Martha and her family relationships:

Affairs of state outweigh the heart
The needs of France tear us apart.

The reviews were savage. In *The Times*, Benedict Nightingale said the show had music that "often went tum-tum, lyrics that regularly went plonk-plonk and rhymes that sometimes left me wishing no such thing as rhyme had been invented." For Paul Taylor in *The Independent*, the score was "talentless" and the lyrics "dire." Nicholas de Jongh in the *Evening Standard* described the songs as "unmemorable and unhummable."

Napoleon had support from some of the greats in modern musicals. Andrew Lloyd Webber (*Phantom of the Opera*) and Alain Boublil (*Les Misérables*) loved it, but the critics killed it again. *Napoleon* closed on February 3, 2001, after a four-month run. Martha lost her $1 million. "She may well be at heart a romantic, maybe because she hasn't found the 'right man' of her dreams," said Marlene Smith. "I don't think she has a lot of luck with men. She would be very difficult to live with. I don't know that she always means to be demanding, but she is. Not a lot of bullshit goes down with Martha. I don't know how well loved she is in the boardroom. I think she's very tough and I think a lot of guys don't want to take it. There's still that old school of the female ruling the male. I don't think they like that."

⚮

MARTHA SAT IN THE FRONT ROW at the annual meeting of Canadian Tire in the Metro Toronto Convention Centre in May 2000. Unlike her Calgary courtroom appearance the previous month, this time the ruler was fully in charge. Her votes were sufficient to approve or reject any matter that came up for consideration.

Martha wore electric blue, as though she were a hand-painted ornament placed among less valuable bric-a-brac. She might be dressed to attract attention, but her demeanour suggested she couldn't make up her mind whether she wanted to be a public figure or a private person. She would slouch as though to make herself smaller, then suddenly sit up straight as if to reassert herself in her surroundings, before hunching into attempted invisibility again. Most of the 150 shareholders had not seen Martha since she had appeared in those newspaper photographs six weeks earlier, scuttling along the side-walk to the courtroom. Photographers were again on hand, one crouched so close to Martha that the controlling shareholder's black pumps almost touched the photographer's rear end.

Meanwhile, there was business to be conducted. Martha had a role and she was ready to play it: she would not be dissuaded from her duty by anyone. On several occasions chairman Gil Bennett called for a vote, even though such a show of hands was just a formality. Martha raised her right hand in a manner so tentative that, when viewed from behind, her fingertips barely showed above her shoulder. No matter, it was only Bennett who had to see how she voted. A raised eyebrow would have sufficed.

When the formalities were concluded and the meeting adjourned, Martha rose from her chair and turned to chat with her fellow direc-tors. The informal moment suddenly became an opportunity for a public memento. Four photographers circled like wolves coming down on the fold. Flashes from the cameras lit her fair skin. Martha was horror-struck. Such shenanigans were not just unexpected but unacceptable, even unspeakable. Martha whirled and burst past the photographers, beetled at top speed for the safety of a side entrance, and disappeared down a dark hallway, leaving the predators behind, their bellies still empty, staring at the empty space where their quarry had been.

With Martha so much in the public eye, the process to replace Steve Bachand moved forward in private. When Bachand was hired, there had been three owners; now there was one. The dual-share structure of Tire, with both voting and non-voting shares that allowed such control, was not permitted to any company listed on the New York Stock Exchange. Any candidate for CEO would be forgiven for wondering who would really be in charge. Martha likes to describe herself as someone who prods management into action rather than issuing orders, but she is well aware of the power she wields. "It's hard for me to call myself a dictator, but I expect that's what I would be defined as," she said.

Still, any such concerns did not disrupt the process. Martha was on the search committee chaired by Bennett, and every one of the twenty individuals the committee approached was interested enough to participate in a first interview. "Most of them asked what sort of relationship Martha had with Steve and expected to have with the new CEO and she told them," said Bennett. "Martha said, 'I want to be a director and I want to exert my influence, such as it is around this place, in the boardroom.' There's no question when it comes to votes she's going to nominate and elect a majority of directors."

The top-ranked internal candidate was Wayne Sales, executive vice-president, retail. The Virginia-born Sales had joined Tire in 1992 from Kmart Corp., where he had run the sporting, leisure, and automotive departments. Among others, the short list also included Andy Giancamilli, then president and chief operating office of Kmart Corp. of Troy, Michigan. (He resigned from that post in March 2001.)

In August 2000, following six months of scrutiny, Martha and the other members of the search committee recommended for president and chief executive officer the man they already knew, fifty-year-old Wayne Sales. It wasn't because he had a particular vision; he didn't present one. The board was just looking for someone to run the company. For Martha, the main predicament faced by Sales was the same one that had preoccupied Dean Groussman and Steve Bachand: relations with dealers. "I think our current president is going to be faced with a lot of those same problems. I think he is a people person and I think he's going to have his battles, but I think he's going to get alignment," said Martha.

Tension between management and the dealers is not only acceptable but essential. "I always call it a tug of war," said Martha. "But if that knot crosses the line, either way, it's the wrong side. It goes a little bit this way and a little bit that way, but there's only a very, very fine tolerance. That's the marketplace." Still, Sales knew Martha; Martha knew Sales. Surprises, everyone hoped, would be kept to a minimum.

FOR MARTHA AND SALES, the way ahead for Tire is uncertain. When Bachand arrived, every Tire store was a different size and offered a different layout; each dealer decided on product selection. Bachand's response was to renovate old stores and build new ones in one of five sizes, ranging from 53,000 square feet to 17,000 square feet. Layout, colour, signage, and product availability were all homogenized in a process that has, so far, affected about 275 outlets at a cost of $1.25 billion.

In two years, that strategy will have run its course. There will be 480 Tire stores in Canada, and the company will have no more room to grow. When that happens, any retailer stagnates, withers, and dies. Increased revenue from other sources in any large amount seems unlikely. E-commerce sales were launched in 2000, but future success from the 12,000 items available on-line is difficult to predict.

PartSource, a chain of stand-alone stores selling auto parts to heavy users, now has twenty-eight outlets. Wayne Sales has put a pause on Bachand's plan of two hundred stores in four years, preferring instead to spend the money on a new distribution centre in Calgary. (PartSource outlets are different from Tire outlets. Only three are run by local Tire dealers, and the other twenty-five are franchise operations.)

The thought process Tire is going through is reminiscent of 1977, when Dean Muncaster began talking about running out of room in Canada. In 1979 Tire expanded to Australia, followed by British Columbia and Texas. That kind of institutional memory makes Martha less likely to believe those who say Canada will be "stored out" any time soon. "It's an ever-evolving business," she said. "I'm not worried about being 'stored out.' I don't think we will be. 'Stored-out' is a very finite way of looking at an animal that is ever-changing and growing and it's my hope there will be something quite different going on into the future. Larger, smaller stores I don't know, different businesses, different aspects. There will be another face on Tire that will take us off into the ether and then another one after that."

The future could include a third attempt to break into the U.S. market. "It's always there and we're always here, and if something comes along that makes sense in whatever guise, then it'll be investigated," said Martha. "It's not that we haven't been looking at things over the past number of years; it's just that they didn't make sense."

One aspect is certain. Competition in Canada has become intense. In the last five years, 120 "big-box" stores have been built in Canada by Home Depot, Wal-Mart, Revy Home Centres, and the rest. Canada saw proportionately as much big-box growth in those five years as the United States did in fifteen. At some point, perhaps even now, Canada will have too many retail outlets fighting for too few consumer dollars.

Wayne Sales will complete the Bachand building program, but he intends to take Tire in a new direction, one that permits less individuality among the dealers. To make his point, Sales cites his travels in China, where he quickly tires of local food and yearns for the familiarity of a Big Mac. That has become his template for Tire; Sales wants every Tire outlet to be as predictable as a McDonald's. "Consumers were confused about what Canadian Tire represented," said Sales. "We must deliver a constant shopping experience in format, pricing, and product." Some dealers have been reluctant to cede their autonomy. "They do have a tendency to slow down the process, but in the end, they help you get it right, they help prevent costly mistakes," said Sales. "Customers will choose to shop where they feel they have personal relationships."

Martha concurs with the lookalike approach. "There's always room for the entrepreneur, but there have to be constraints around what a Canadian Tire store is and represents to the public," she said. "You go in a store in Halifax and you go in a store in Vancouver, and the fact of the matter is that they have been extremely different over the last twenty years. Continuity and cooperation with data and with the creation of the stores has been, on both sides, a give-and-take, a healthy dynamic. The tug-of-war that I see is in committee — it's part of the evolution of new processes and the new formats. It still exists, and the fact that we know more about each other makes it easier to go ahead with an appropriate business model. We've had good reaction to our stores; people love the new format. For everyone not to attempt to emulate that model across the chain doesn't make sense. We are Canadian Tire; we should be as one."

Such unity means less individuality for dealers. "They're beginning to use the 'm' word, mandatory," Sales said. "We're trying to seek the right balance." The next two steps Martha and Sales plan to include in any strategy seem basic. First, make sure that products, particularly those items heavily promoted in advertising, are actually in stock when customers come to buy. Second, improve customer service, specifically by having cheerful employees who know where items are located and can provide product information. To achieve that goal, Canadian Tire has increased staff training. Fifty thirty-minute self-teaching courses are already available via the Internet to employees; within eighteen months, there will be 250 such programs.

With Martha's consent, Sales also replaced some members of the executive team. Within six months of taking over, Ralph Trott, senior vice-president, business development, and John Rankin, senior vice-president, dealer relations, a Bachand appointment who had been at Tire for five years, took early retirement. "If there is a weakness in our strategy, it's uniform, consistent customer experience, store after store," said Rankin. "We've got the same look, we've got the same product, but there still is a variation in customer experience and part of that is the dealer's commitment. Some of them are very committed; others are less so. That's the opportunity [Sales] is talking about. If we had a whole chain like the top half or the top quartile [of the stores], there wouldn't have been much to worry about. It's getting the guys on the lower end up to the same level as the guys on the higher end."

Dealers are certainly well rewarded. The average dealer makes $500,000 a year, before tax. That means dealers, in total, earn about $200 million a year, about the same as the company earns in profits and seven times what shareholders are paid in dividends. Dealers who are performing below par will be told to improve. In particular, Sales has targeted the worst forty performers. "If you can't make the trip, you have to exit the organization," they have been told. "I have a stewardship of this triangle that I take very seriously, and how Canadians think about Canadian Tire. The strength of this is limited to the weakest link that we have in the organization," said Sales.

All dealers have not yet bought in to his vision. "I believe he's a hard-working, capable individual," said Steve Groch, who runs a Tire outlet in Calgary and is president of the dealers' association. "Time will tell how he makes out as top dog. He knows retail, but I'm not sure how comfortable he'll be dealing with finance, the Internet, and global issues."

One area of immediate improvement from the Bachand era is a better relationship between the CEO and Martha. "I think it's more open," said Sales. "I have a lot of respect for her. I have not found her intrusive in the business. I have not found her anything outside of trying to be helpful and trying to understand what's going on in the company, and I'm not intimidated by that at all." "The meetings with Wayne are more relaxed than they were with Steve," agreed Bennett. "Steve's very intense. When he came to a board meeting with something he wanted to do, his style was to bring that intensity into the board meeting. Wayne is much more easy-going. While he's every bit as determined as Steve was, his style leaves everyone less on the edge of his or her seat. Wayne is more open to the uninformed question. When someone asks a question that, to an experienced retailer, would have a very obvious answer, Wayne takes the time to give the answer. Steve, with his intensity, might have been a little less inclined to answer with the same patience."

Sales saw the consolidation of ownership under Martha as a positive development. "It's easier for the board, it's easier for the organization to understand how she may be feeling about things," he said. "If she's saying one thing and there's two other people that are saying something else, it creates confusion." Martha meets with Sales and Bennett for an hour before each board meeting, just as she did with Bachand.

Going forward, Martha, Sales, and the other directors are scheduled to approve a new strategy for Canadian Tire by the fall of 2001. When the planning sessions began six months earlier in March, any direction was possible, including expansion to the United States, the Far East, or South America. Martha has a particular interest in Chile. In 1999 she was named honorary consul for southern Alberta by the

Chilean government. She also has her eye on China and visited that country twice in 1999. "What she has said is that everything's on the table; there nothing's that's ruled out by reason of past experience," said Bennett. "She's not closed-minded about going to the States or going anywhere else simply because the company hasn't done very well in the past." This was the wide-ranging discussion Steve Bachand did not want to have in the fall of 1999.

It had taken Martha almost two years to get where she wanted to go with her new man, Wayne Sales. For Martha, who had spent her entire life achieving control of Tire, the pace of change was irrelevant. Viewed from the throne, slow motion was just fine with her, as long as her will was done.

TWELVE

THE REIGNING
QUEEN

*"She was very naive in the early stages of the
problems she had in Calgary.
I'm not saying it hurt the company, but it certainly didn't help."*
— ARCH BROWN, RETIRED DEALER

f all the places in the world, Martha has always felt the most at
ease at Shanty Bay. The cottage has been her retreat and her reward.
As she walks through her woodlot or works in her garden, she
escapes theatre critics, journalists, television cameras, all those petty
people who have peered into her private life.

Martha is no social butterfly. Not for her the phony life of the
see-and-be-seen fundraiser events. At cocktail parties she has never
moved easily among the preening participants. Rather than sweep
in, greet people, then become another flower in a conversational
bouquet, Martha prefers to linger on the periphery, as if angling for
the moment when she can slip away without being missed.

She shares Shanty Bay only with those she chooses. In 1997 she
invited Tony van Straubenzee and his wife, Mary, for dinner and an
overnight stay. She instructed van Straubenzee, managing director of

the recruiting firm Russell Reynolds Associates, to look for her in the garden if she wasn't at the cottage when they arrived. Sure enough, no one answered when the couple knocked on the door. The only activity visible was a backhoe digging a ditch in the distance. They walked over to ask the operator Martha's whereabouts and were surprised to find her at the controls, wearing a shirt, pants, and boots.

Among other recent changes, Martha has created terraces on the land sloping to the water to improve the view of the lake. She has equipped an office on the second floor with all the necessary accoutrements for modern-day business communications. There is a bronze bust of A.J. on a pedestal, the same as the one at head office and at the distribution centre. If Martha could use that backhoe to dig a moat around her personal space, she probably would. The world is angry and dangerous, and Martha wants a protected place to share with her dogs, her constant companions.

A recent real estate transaction showed the lengths to which she will go to preserve her environment. In 2000 Martha decided to sell a cottage she owned on the eastern edge of her property. Buyer Brian Ablett paid $600,000 for the building, six acres of land, and 150 feet of lake frontage. According to Ablett, who has bought and sold many houses, he's never dealt with anyone so interested in the details. Martha's devotion to matters seemed particularly unusual given that the cottage in question wasn't even visible from her place. It's not as though there would be any recurrent intrusions. "What strikes me as odd is that it gets down to the very fine print. She has clearly spent a great deal of her personal time looking at the financing, the purchasing, the lot lines, the ongoing responsibility of who manages a ditch that runs between the two properties, those kind of things," said Ablett. "She's clearly an eccentric individual. It's odd that someone with the wealth and power that she has would be so interested in the minutiae of what I thought would almost be incidental to the rest of her life."

Martha's constant companions at Shanty Bay have been her Lakeland Terriers. She has imported British Lakelands to help improve
Canadian bloodlines and has had success in the show ring, including
top Lakeland in Canada with more than one dog. Lakelands look similar to the Scotties she grew up with, but stand taller on longer legs.
"Same sentiment, same little characters," said Martha. "They always
want to be there with you. They want to figure out where you're going
and be there first with the greatest enthusiasm. They are pretty smart
— not smart like the police dog, but smart enough to know that
they're people and they're the most important people in the house.
When it's their dinnertime hour, our dinnertime, they're the most
important ones. I've always loved dogs and had dogs. I usually have
two or three dogs underfoot in the house all the time. Last year I had
six dogs in my house. I'm down to three now. They all have a place
in my heart."

Martha's long-time favourite was Monkey, a fifteen-year-old terrier
that she had to have put down in the summer of 2000. Monkey was
such an integral member of the household that she had a series of
hats. One, worn for birthday celebrations, consisted of bows. During
the Christmas season, Monkey wore a pair of reindeer antlers held on
with a chinstrap. Six months after Monkey's death, Martha still carried a photograph of the dog in her purse. "Although everybody in
the litter was born the same size, she just didn't have the gumption to
nurse very well," Martha said. "By the second day I thought she was
fading, so I had to tube-feed her to get her started again and then
tube-feed her brothers and her sister to give this one a chance at the
milk bar. When all the pups were sold, Owen insisted that I keep
Monkey. I kept her for Owen and she turned into my right-hand
man." (Tube-feeding is an intricate life-saving procedure using a
pliable catheter and syringe. The owner must be careful that the tube
does not damage the stomach wall or cause aspiration pneumonia.

The whelp also has to be burped, just like a baby.)

Martha breeds her dogs, to have a flow of younger animals for herself and also to sell or give away. One pup's esophagus had a genetic defect, so Martha found it a home with a family where one of the daughters suffered from a similar condition. "You meet a lot of neat people," said Martha. "I get stories of my dogs and what they've accomplished and what they've done. There were people who bought a dog when Owen was at school out in B.C. He used to go spend weekends at their home. I've made a lot of friends through dogs."

Martha may love her dogs more than anything else. Her face goes soft when she talks about them; no other topic brings her such apparent serenity. Perhaps the explanation is as simple as it is sad. The dogs give her something that no human ever could: unconditional love.

SINCE MARTHA BOUGHT OUT her brothers in 1997, her friends have noticed a personality change for the better. Martha's current Calgary boyfriend, Mark Sanderson, has played a part in making her newly happy. Until the purchase, her life had been focused on beating her brothers and owning Tire. "I don't know that she would tick if she didn't have a challenge," said Marlene Smith. "She absolutely adores winning. You have to have that fight in you and always believe that what you're going to do is right. She seems to be taking more trips and enjoying life a little more. She is the top person and she's got some rhyme and reason in her life. Everything is running a little smoother, so she's relaxing a little bit."

Martha herself has sensed the difference, but refuses to relax completely. She remains on guard, ever watchful, always on the alert. "I feel quite different than I did five and ten years ago. They probably see a peace because a lot of things have been settled and we have moved forward from where we were. The pleasure of getting on with something that has been denied for a long time, I guess that creates a lot of inner peace, but it also creates a lot of worry and turmoil. It's a big responsibility."

With her life more safely under control, Martha has begun to warm to those she used to snub. In 1998 her Macdonald Institute classmates held their thirty-fifth anniversary reunion. Martha had planned to attend the festivities in Guelph, but at the last minute changed her mind and stayed home. One of her dogs was due to give birth to a litter of pups and she wanted to be on hand to help. About two dozen alumnae attended the events on campus during the day, then half of the group dined together at the Bookshelf Café. Martha sent a large bouquet of flowers to the restaurant in downtown Guelph, telephoned during the proceedings, and spoke to each attendee in turn. "It was quite interesting. That was, I would say, a change. I have never known her to be that gregarious," said Deanna Wood Perschbaker.

During the 1970s Perschbaker lived two blocks from Martha in Mississauga. Owen and Perschbaker's daughter took swimming lessons at the same pool, but Martha never showed much interest in passing the time of day with her former classmate when they ran into each other. On that reunion night, however, Martha was eager to gab to everyone. "Nobody else who wasn't there phoned," said Perschbaker. "But, you know, as we age, I think you start looking back to the past and you become a bit nostalgic." Each of the women at the dinner took home a few of the flowers from the bouquet. Those remembrances marked the first time any of them could recall receiving anything from Martha other than short shrift.

Martha is also taking the time to travel to more exotic destinations. "She loves to see historical sites. She's a very engaging travelling companion," said Judy Romanchuk, Martha's broker friend. In 1999 the two women visited Machu Picchu, the sacred fortress city of the Incas, a site that requires sustained climbing and physical effort to visit the terraces and ramparts high in the Peruvian Andes. Out of deference to her friend, Martha trekked far higher than she should have with her asthma, until, finally, she fell ill because of the altitude and the humidity.

At home, Martha has been equally loyal. Romanchuk was devastated when the cat she had owned for thirteen years died. Martha spent a day taking Romanchuk to half a dozen Calgary pet stores looking for a replacement kitten. They weren't successful, but she admired Martha's caring concern, given her allergic reaction to cats. "There is a great sensitivity. That's something I appreciate and people miss."

Martha has also assumed a higher-profile philanthropic role. In the past she tended to be a quiet contributor to specific fundraisers or charities that caught her eye. Her role as honorary chairman of the Canadian Tire Foundation for Families, founded in 1999, was little known. Money raised locally by dealers is matched by Tire and donated to community assistance organizations. The foundation has also responded to disasters by providing bottled water, showerheads, and tap aerators to such communities as Walkerton, Ont., after an E. coli outbreak, and Glace Bay, NS, when heavy rainstorms contaminated the water table.

In May 2001 Martha drove seven hours from Calgary to join in the foundation's efforts in North Battleford, Sask., after thousands of residents were infected by a parasite in the water supply. "When you see a neighbour in trouble, you don't walk away," she said, while helping the local Tire dealer distribute bottled water that had been trucked in by the foundation. She explained that this was the first such relief operation in which she'd been able to participate. "Crisis response happened and I just wasn't there, but I was so close this time I thought Yes! I made a few phone calls and e-mails and here I am."[1]

Whereas some wealthy Canadians seek to have their names

---

1   *National Post*, May 11, 2001.

commemorated on buildings through donations to hospitals or universities, Martha's magnanimity has so far taken a lower profile. While she has been involved in making arrangements for Tire to match the money raised by dealers for the Foundation for Families, her philanthropy as far as the foundation is concerned stops there. She has not written a personal cheque to the foundation nor donated any money from her holding companies.

IF MARTHA BILLES WERE CAST in a movie she would be Joan Crawford in *Mildred Pierce*, all high cheekbones, bright eyes, and firm practicality. The parallel goes beyond their looks to the kind of life the two women led. In that 1945 classic, Mildred Pierce is at first the hausfrau, kept slaving in the kitchen by a lout of a husband whom she finally kicks out. Pierce goes into business, running a chain of restaurants to gain her independence. Successful as she is, however, her choice for a second husband turns out to be no better than the first. All he wants is her money and the lifestyle that results from such resources. As with Mildred, Martha possesses both money and moxie, but she never knows if a man loves her for her fortune or for herself. After all, relationships are all about how another person makes you feel. If a man can make a woman feel intelligent, loved, and desired, she is fulfilled. If he cannot, she falls apart.

Martha came to every relationship haunted by her last failed relationship. Her father tried to keep her down and so did her brothers. The husbands she chose were lesser lights that she thought she could control. Once she came to see them as second-raters, she turned on them for their flaws and became angry that she had sold herself short. Again. Martha's inability to stay emotionally involved is a trait more normally associated with powerful men. The classic type-A male chief executive never gives a second thought to working one hundred hours a week and abandoning his family for days on end when a deal is in the works. For such a man, divorce, affairs, and lawsuits are normal. If Martha Billes were a man, she would go about her business life unobserved.

Judy Romanchuk recently held a dinner party in Calgary attended by a dozen successful women. At one point during the evening she realized that nine of the twelve, including Martha, were divorced. "That has to tell you something. All were very interesting people and had accomplished great things," she said. "In life, you can't have it all. There's always give-up."

For Martha, in spite of her efforts, the "give-up" was a conventional home life with a loving spouse and family. For all the changes in society that have occurred for women, from the birth control pill to equality in the workplace, women are still forced to choose. Maybe they can have it all, but they can't have it all at once. Martha realized her professional goals, but not her personal aspirations. That's why she flitted from one lover to another, from one discarded husband to another. She needed love, she craved love, but she could not accept love because she couldn't trust what it felt like after lacking for love in her youth. As a result, Martha could not know at what point her partner would withdraw his love or abandon her to her own devices, because, well, wasn't that how people acted? So, rather than wait for the inevitable, every once in a while Martha needed a roadkill to prove to herself that she had been in control all along: Roger Henry, Dennis Gardiner-Billes, Fred, David, Paul McAteer, the list is long. No one would ever get the better of her because she would beat him to the punch, even if he had no such plan — not even a plan to have a plan.

After the worm had turned and the man in her life saw he was being dumped, he rounded on her, only proving to Martha once again that she had been right all along. Then vengeance became the only possible path. At that point, Martha alone got to do what she wanted, because getting what she wanted was what her enemies had always tried to keep her from achieving.

Martha was like a lot of little girls growing up: her father was the first man she loved, yet she failed the one she most wanted to please. Her father is dead now, but even when he was alive he couldn't fathom why she acted the way she did. A.J. garnered no pleasure from her tenacity. Martha never understood that she gained nothing by fighting so hard for her father's respect. After all, A.J. didn't want her to be part of the company in the first place.

Today, Martha has enough money to buy whatever she wants. At one point she decided to build a trout pond at Shanty Bay. When the contractors didn't show up, she went to the local equipment dealer, bought a backhoe, and she and her hired man dug it themselves. "Anything material of that nature she could take care of simply by writing a cheque," said Bob Murray. "But the other things that she didn't get growing up [were] love from a father and interaction in a normal family with her brothers. She never got that with her marriages, they were always on the rocks. She just kept going from pillar to post, looking for love."

The search for affection is not helped by her complicated person-ality. "It would be hard for anyone to establish a relationship and bring the relationship to fruition with Martha because of all her complexities," said Ken Mann, the Tire dealer and trustee on Owen's estate. "There are a lot of very successful people who are not easy people to live with, and I would guess that Martha would be a difficult person to understand and live with." Added a former Tire director: "Professionally, I can see that she could rise above her inner-child syndrome. Maybe the very thing that drives her, sibling rivalry and the desire to control Canadian Tire, affects her in another way, negatively. Because she's a strong female, perhaps she ends up with weak men. When you get a woman that's driven, then there's some-thing down here [in the gut] that's vulnerable."

Anyone, male or female, risks being transformed by a single-minded search for power. "I always liked Martha, but I realized she was troubled," said Jean Pigott, who was on the Tire board in the 1980s and has stayed in touch. "That's not unusual. It happens with men and it happens with women who have power. Power is strange. You're not trained with how to cope with it. Do you know many very happy men who have a lot of power? Take a look at politics and what it does to people. I've watched it for twenty-five years."

Whether it's the leadership of a country or a company, the relentless search for power at any cost has withered many a heart. Just as A.J. was held back by his brother, Martha was kept in check by her siblings. But J.W. died and A.J. was able to thrive. Martha had to kill off her brothers, in the corporate sense, to do the same. Perhaps if Martha's youth had been more like Maureen Sabia's, Martha would have avoided some heartache. "I grew up in exactly the same time, but I had two parents who were ahead of their times," said Sabia, who is a year younger than Martha. "A lot of people know that my mother was an advocate for women, but not everybody knows that my father was equally adamant because he had three daughters before he had a son. He never wanted his daughters to be dependent, as he put it, 'on any Tom, Dick or Harry.' He always wanted his daughters to be able to look after themselves. You put those two parents together with a family of three girls and you get a different dynamic. It was unfortunate and a tragedy for Martha that she did not have those opportunities."

Martha overcame that handicap and beat them all. But why did she try so hard to gain control of Tire, if not to run it? "If you had this wonderful hen that keeps laying golden eggs for you and other people," asked Martha rhetorically, "don't you want to keep her alive and in the best possible condition?"

Martha has become like Queen Elizabeth, reigning benignly by right of place in the familial line. At Canadian Tire no major decision is made without her approval, no senior officer or director is appointed without her consent, no strategy is devised without her intimate involvement. Her power flows because she is on the throne and because those around her rely on her grace and favour to retain their own roles at court. As a result, her influence is far subtler, but no less secure, than a corporate owner who takes on a job title too. "A publisher doesn't need to print a sign and hang it on the notice board to influence what takes place one way or another in that publication," said Hugh Macaulay, who was chairman of the Tire board from 1984 to 1994 and then remained as a director until he retired in 1996. "It's the same with directors. Where there's a controlling interest which can call the shots, then the people who are charged with the responsibility of representing the shareholders are not going to challenge that, unless it's a very major issue in which their own integrity may be at stake." That situation makes for a delicate balance between the requisite deference from her courtiers and their expressions of independence. "Martha is happy to have all points of view brought out," said Macaulay. "I don't think she wants to exercise censorship. As to what the ultimate outcome is, that may be different. If she thinks she's right, then she wants that point of view to prevail. People who are there because Martha asked them to be are bound to be favourably disposed towards trying to find a common ground among points of view that are expressed around Martha's opinion."

A cause for her royal reserve may be rooted in the reason she is there at all. According to Stephen McLaughlin, the urban planner Martha dated in 1989–90, Martha saw herself as a victim of her birth as much as the guardian of a tradition. McLaughlin paraphrased a line from Theodore Sorensen, counsel to President John F. Kennedy: "Some people are burdened by power and some people thrive on it." Applying the epigram to Martha, McLaughlin said: "She had a poor relationship with her family, with her brothers, her mother, and her father. 'Look what they've done to me. They've given me this big problem, this thing called Canadian Tire, all these horrible brothers, now I've gotta solve this — and I'll do it.' It was a burden as opposed to a joy."

Martha described her role in a similar way during that 1997 speech to the Canadian Club. "Many, those who do not know me well, have asked me why I decided to take on the awesome responsibility I have. Those who know me had no need to ask." After that sentence in her speech notes, the word "pause" appeared as a reminder to herself to let the impact of what she had just said sink into the psyches of the audience. "The answer is quite simple," she continued. "Above all else I have cared deeply about the great enterprise that is Canadian Tire and about the people who have helped to make it great." Then Martha made a most revealing admission. "I have always invested all my emotional capital in Canadian Tire. In buying the shares from my brothers, I have simply matched that emotional capital with more financial capital."

All my emotional capital. No wonder personal relationships were difficult to build. People in her life wanted more from her than she could give. For Martha, her desire to control Tire was all-consuming. She characterized her decision to buy out her brothers as the equivalent of going into the desert to fast before taking a life-altering step. "During the weeks leading up to my purchase of both my brothers' common shares, I spent many hours locked in reflection. Many memories of times past resurfaced. Many conversations with my father, A.J., came back to me and I thought more vividly than ever before of all that I had learned from him. Once asked the secret of his success, my father replied: 'Striving always to make things better.' For me that will always be a guiding principle. Because to me that means winning . . . and winning is what it's all about."

Of all the interpretations of "striving to make things better," surely winning is only one among many possibilities, but for Martha it is the only meaning that matters. An individual could strive to make things better for any number of other reasons, even selfless ones. By contrast, Carly Fiorina of Hewlett-Packard likes to quote Socrates, who said: "We cannot live better than in seeking to become better."

If winning is all that Martha's life is about, then self-esteem and ego are at the wheel. "The larger you get, the bigger the strokes you need," said Macaulay. "There is a mix of stuff there that has to do with all of the points of influence that she can bring to bear in the company's affairs. She'll listen to other people, she'll take their recommendations, and may well act on them. But she may well act on her own and there's nobody else that can do that. You'd be less than human if you didn't have some sense of self-fulfillment or satisfaction out of being able to do those things. That's just what moves the movers and shakers. It isn't the money. Martha's not a big spender, she's not building big castles to her memory."

Gaining power at Tire was the ultimate aphrodisiac. "Some people in control may get satisfaction, may get reward, may get comfort, may get perquisites, may get benefits of all kinds, but that basic feeling of being in control is its reward itself," said Macaulay. "Sometimes it's just enough to know that you're the controlling shareholder. Just the mere sense of being the mistress of all she surveys."

Power has been defined as the ability to influence people and events. But such influence isn't always positive. Like the moon, Martha has a dark side. "I don't approve of her personal life," said Arch Brown, who retired in 1996 after thirty-three years as a dealer in Barrie, Ont., and who owns lakefront property a mile from Martha's cottage at Shanty Bay. "She was very naive in the early stages of the problems she had in Calgary. I'm not saying it hurt the company, but it certainly didn't help the company. It's not the type of advertising or promotion that you want with a family organization." Canadian Tire mirrors that constant personal interplay between good and bad, right and wrong. "Power is very important to Martha," said Brown. "There have been periods when it's been very negative. The fact that she's maintained the status quo as far as the ownership of the company is concerned, the dealers take that positively. I think there's a real weakness in Canadian Tire. We have a few very influential and very wealthy dealers who may not be on the floor of their stores much of the time. I think that's bad."

The question then becomes: Can Tire survive under Martha's thumb? "I think she should sell the company," said Bill McFarland, an electrician who has worked twenty-seven years at Canadian Tire and is the sole elected employee representative on the deferred profit-sharing plan. McFarland says that employee morale is low, the close-knit nature of the family business is gone, and many employees are anticipating cutbacks in the workforce. "Our biggest fear is having a job in five years. The big bright light of Canadian Tire used to shine. Now we feel they've come to the end of the road. They're followers, not leaders."

Fred has predicted Tire's imminent demise ever since 1980, when Martha joined the board. He blamed his own share sale and departure on her, so his harsh views must be seen in that bleak light. "If she would quit, and walk away and leave the thing alone, that would be interesting, but I will not go back in there whether she quits or not," said Fred. "There are a number of people who would not go back in there with Martha, and may not go back in there without her. Have you followed the stock value? Now, she may mend her ways and it may go back up again. And she may not."

Canadian Tire has not been a good place for Martha's money these last ten years. Dividends flowing into her hands amount to about $1.1 million annually and receive more favourable tax treatment than other types of income, but she would have been better off had she cashed out a decade ago and put her money in a stock-market index fund. The price of a common share in July 2001 was $38 and the non-voting share, $25. Although those prices have fluctuated over the years, they have changed little since 1989. (Her 2,101,150 voting shares were worth $80 million and her 725,460 non-voting shares $18 million, for a total of $98 million.) "This isn't a rational investment; it's her life. She has a deep commitment to the company," said Alan Goddard, vice-president, corporate affairs. "She likes the cachet. Without Canadian Tire she'd have nothing — she'd just be another wealthy woman."

Such fealty might be fine for her, but shareholders want steady appreciation for the investment, not simply a feeling of pride. The number of non-voting shareholders, the little people who have never had a say in how the company was run, has fallen from a peak of 15,891 in 1985 to 6,495 today. A lot of Martha's former subjects have given up and abandoned the kingdom, never to return.

Part of the reason may be due to the fact that Canadians don't praise their own, said Wayne Sales, yet they all too readily embrace American retailers who come to Canada. "We've gained market share in the face of entry of everything that the U.S. had to throw at us," he said of Wal-Mart, Home Depot, and the others. "They're good companies, they do a lot of things well. But we're a great company and we're very unique in the marketplace. We don't get the same positive view that they get. It really bothers me that Canadians won't give it the same due."

As an American who worked in retail for twenty-five years before coming to Canada in 1992, Sales said that the perspective Americans have towards themselves and their business success stories is far different. "Americans don't hesitate to give credit. I use the word 'patriotism' in terms of how proud they are. People [in Canada] want to drag Canadian Tire through the mud in comparing it to people south of the border. I really can't figure it out," he said. Since 1990 Wal-Mart, Home Depot, and fifty other U.S. banners ranging from The Gap to Talbot's, Price Club/Costco to Starbucks, have expanded to Canada. Yet they were hardly the first cross-border invaders. Woolworth's successfully expanded to Canada before the First World

War and Sears-Roebuck arrived in 1953. The plain fact is that Americans are good at retailing. Canadians are not alone in welcoming American concepts. That's why there's a McDonald's in Moscow and why Nike shoes can be found on so many foreign feet.

In separate interviews, both Sales and Martha referred to a phrase used by a retail consultant in 1994 shortly after Wal-Mart arrived in Canada, when Tire was described as "a deer in the headlights." Those words still niggle seven years later, long after everyone else has forgotten them. "I certainly don't like the media," said Martha. "I don't like certain representatives in the media. I don't like certain aspects of the media, and I think that the media has been very, very cruel to the success of their own Canadian people. We, as Canada, have a glorious history, I think, a far, far, more interesting and colourful history in many respects than the Americans do, and much more upstanding as far as some of the goals are concerned. I think the Canadian psyche as demonstrated by the media tends to look elsewhere for praise. The Canadian media simply magnifies that weakness in our society. They play it up for all it's worth. We have an excellent reputation. Somehow we've forgotten how good we are and we don't want to talk about it — too shy, too retiring, we go out and we do a helluva lot in the world, but no one broadcasts it. [We] let the Americans take over."

In fact, much praise has been heaped upon Tire. Even the "deer in the headlights" description didn't survive. In a lengthy and positive feature article on Steve Bachand published in *Canadian Business* in 1995, the phrase was recalled, then dismissed. "Canadian Tire, to almost everyone's surprise, is proving to be more of a Mack truck than a deer. With neither Wal-Mart nor Home Depot Inc. faring as well as expected, the chain is behaving like a company unwilling to yield the road to a band of US retail predators who came roaring into Canada expecting easy pickings."[2]

In the last half of the 1990s, no retailer and its boss received more accolades from his peers or praise in the press than Canadian Tire and Steve Bachand. In January 2000 the *Report on Business Magazine* put Canadian Tire at the top of the thirty-five best companies to work for in Canada. Even the usually acerbic Terry Mosher, the Montreal cartoonist who calls himself Aislin, took a positive, if puckish, view of Canadian Tire. A two-panel drawing showed a television news reader saying: "In the latest dramatic move towards sovereignty, Jacques Parizeau's Parti Québécois government has nationalized all Quebec outlets of a large Canadian hardware chain . . . the Premier denied that Quebec did this to get the Canadian Tire money."[3]

No other shopper loyalty program has attained a profile anywhere near as positive as Canadian Tire money. A scene in *Playoff*, a television series about a hockey team in Hamilton, Ont., recently showed Gordon Pinsent wooing an American player. Pinsent held up an open briefcase stuffed with currency, but as the camera moved in for a close-up, it became evident that the notes were Canadian Tire money. Said Pinsent, "Don't whine, it's more stable than the looney." At any given moment, Canadians have $100 million worth of coupons in their wallets, kitchen drawers, and glove boxes.

As for the argument by Martha that Canadians praise foreigners to the exclusion of home-grown talent, Canadians readily give local retailers their due when it's deserved — and even when it's not. The Eatons were revered as a family and their department stores were respected long after either should have been kept in such high regard. When Eaton's closed its catalogue in 1976 there was an outpouring of sadness across the land, a bereavement for an old friend that had passed away and would be sorely missed.

No, Canadian Tire does not inspire anywhere near the praise that Eaton's did in its prime, nor do the members of the Billes family come close to being worshipped as the Eatons were. Life is about connec-

---

2   *Canadian Business*, October 1995, 28.
3   *Montreal Gazette*, May 16, 1995.

tions and affinities. Part of the problem may be the self-effacing view that Canadian Tire has towards itself. In 2001 Tire lost in an attempt to stop a London, Ont., construction worker from using www.crappytire.com as a website address. Canadians might call the company Crappy Tire, but they really didn't mean anything derogatory by that phrase, claimed the company's complaint to the World Intellectual Property Organization, the Geneva-based body that ruled against Tire. "Canadian Tire is also colloquially referred to or known as Crappy Tire," said the company's filing. "The term Crappy Tire is a slang expression derived from the Canadian Tire trade marks [and is] frequently used by younger Canadian Tire customers. In the vast majority of cases, the usage does not have a negative connotation but is an impertinent reference to a mass merchandiser."[4] The company said that it had found four hundred and seventy-eight websites using the words "crappy Canadian Tire." That's a lot of impertinence.

NOW THAT WAYNE SALES has been appointed CEO and a corporate strategy has been devised, Martha's key challenge is succession — how to ensure that what she has created continues after her death. If Martha were hit by a bus tomorrow, neither Tire's management nor her board of directors knows what would happen to her control position.

One possible answer is Owen. With Martha as Queen, Owen is the Prince of Wales, next in line to the throne. Since 1992 he has worked in various areas at Tire, including such head office departments as automotive marketing and dealer changeover, where a team goes into a store to audit inventory and make certain that the transfer to a new dealer is smooth and fair.

For the last two years Owen has worked at the A.J. Billes Distribution Centre in Brampton, Ont., overseeing truckloads of goods being

---

4   *National Post*, April 17, 2001, C9.

shipped to the dealers. His shift starts at 4:30 a.m., so he rises early for the forty-five-minute drive from the downtown Toronto condo owned by Martha that he shares with his mother when she's in town.

Owen is well aware that his colleagues watch him closely and wonder what to make of this third-generation Billes working among them. "You're going to be a curiosity," he said. "All the stuff in the paper all the time." Many employees at the distribution centre know who he is, but he doesn't lord his name over them. "I don't march in and say, 'I'm Owen Billes, everyone stand back.' I'm quiet; I slink in. When I meet people around the company who don't know me, I never use my last name. I'm not stupid enough to think they don't already know. It's just a name that happens to be attached to a company. I don't think it makes a person any different. I have more fun hanging out at the distribution centre with all the guys than hobnobbing or anything like that. Maybe that's the outsider thing; I don't know. I'd rather be among the real people."

Owen does not take himself too seriously, preferring to make light of past problems. Once when he dined with Diana, daughter of David and Donna, they joked about family feuds. "Look out," Owen said, "we're in the same room together, we might start a fight, there might be blood." He knows the Billeses are not a family like the others. "Money is like a big microscope. As soon as there's money involved, it's just that much more exciting. It's in the paper. I read it and say, 'Wow, these people are nuts. Oops, nope, that's us.'"

Owen has no expectation that he will become a member of senior management. He'd like to work next at Canadian Tire Acceptance Corp., located in Welland, Ont., on the assumption that the more he understands about the inner workings of Tire, the better off he is. "If I stay with it, and it continues to be part of my life, then there's a 99 per cent chance that I will end up with some chunk of her holdings, if not all," said Owen. "She hasn't come right out and said it, but I'm obviously the next in line. I just have to go along in good faith. Her main concern is Canadian Tire and keeping it together. If I was off doing something else, or sitting on a mountain in Peru, or had taken a different path, I don't know that I would have a chance of getting any of it. And that would probably be the right choice for the business. The person who has been around and understands the business might make a better go at it."

Martha could, if she chose, anoint someone else from Owen's generation to carry on as the controlling shareholder. In fact, Martha has said she has not ruled out, as a fallback, ownership by some combination of her eight nieces and nephews, unlikely though such an outcome may be. Why work so hard to win Tire away from her brothers, only to turn it over to their children?

No member of the third generation is being groomed to take over from Martha. None of Fred and Barbara's five children, who range in age from forty-two to thirty-one, work at Tire. Alfred, the eldest, was a store manager for his father, but now operates a children's clothing store in Toronto. Heather's husband was a Tire dealer, but they are divorced. Deirdre lives on Grand Cayman and works for her father. Maeve and Garth live in Ontario and have interests other than Tire.

David and Donna's three children are all in their thirties. Only Diana, the eldest, is employed by Tire, at head office in market research. Alen followed his father into engineering and automotive racing. Karen, a graduate in kinesiology, works with horses. Cousin Dick's daughter, Elizabeth Ann, runs her own interior design business. Dick's son, Rob, is an independent computer software engineer who writes programs for cash registers. Tire is his only client.

Because there is no obvious succession, dealers are worried about what comes next after having a Billes as owner of Canadian Tire for almost eighty years. "I have concerns and so do dealers," said Steve Groch, the Calgary dealer and president of CTC Dealer Holdings Ltd., owners of 20.5 per cent of Tire's voting shares. "We do not know what would happen if Martha was not able to continue on in her present responsibility, for whatever reason," said Groch. "The dealers have an investment of over $1 billion in equipment and inventory. What if Martha decided she didn't want to be involved with Canadian Tire and decided to sell off her control shares? The dealers are not in a position to be able to purchase control. I'm not sure whether she, in her own mind, even knows today how she sees the future for Canadian Tire if she were to not be part of it."

Groch, who is halfway through his three-year term as president of dealer holdings, wrote to Martha in March 2001 asking that she actively consider succession. The previous president, Brian Domelle, made the same request after she bought out her brothers. "I think she's still trying to put all that into the context of what it all means and how she should be moving in the future," said Groch. "She hasn't been too quick to respond to our concerns."

Groch made a little more progress than Domelle. That first letter went unanswered. Martha has told Groch she will discuss succession with unnamed advisers. Said Groch: "Martha feels that the status quo is satisfactory and I guess maybe we're all human and we don't think we're going to die tomorrow or get hit with a truck tomorrow. There's a feeling of 'Yes, I'll get to it, there's time.'"

Martha has consistently kept her plans secret. "I've read the letters. My advisers have read the letters and are continually working on what my plans are," she said. "The world keeps changing around us. Everything's continually under review. I go to bed every night thinking about it. The plan is ever-evolving." Perhaps such secretive behaviour should not be surprising. She has always played her cards close to her chest.

One likely strategy would be a family foundation to hold Martha's controlling interest. In such an arrangement, Martha might not necessarily designate Owen as her sole successor, although he could sit on the board of such a foundation along with professional trustees and managers. The income flowing from dividends might benefit specific individuals or Tire's Foundation for Families. Martha Billes has spent her life struggling to get what she thought she wanted, what she believed was her due. With that goal accomplished, she now seems ready to adjust her sights. When asked recently what she wanted to do next, she replied: "Grow old gracefully. Do a few things on the way. Whenever you've reached a goal you have to find the next goal, don't you? You know, a lot of my life has been put before me. There were things that happened. There was a progression because of where I grew up, who I was, people around me, what happened to them. [I have to] create the next goal for myself. It's a bit of a challenge."

They say money can't buy happiness. In the case of Martha Billes, personal wealth seemed only to hinder her search for love even as it helped her reach her professional goal of owning Canadian Tire.

Martha has said that she wants the words on her tombstone to read: "Nothing ventured, nothing gained." As a summation of her life, no phrase could be more fitting. "It's mine," said five-year-old Freddy when he visited the store. No, said Martha at sixty-one, it's mine.

INDEX

Abella, Irving, 29
Ablett, Brian, 249
A.J. Billes Distribution Centre, 266
Albikin Management Inc., 67, 165, 173, 185
Aldamar agreement
  1983 agreement, 84, 133
  new accord signed (1989), 137–38
Aldamar Corp., 53–54, 85
Allard, Dr. Charles, 156
Anderson, Walker, 11
associate dealers. *See* dealers
ATCO Ltd., 3
"Aunt Mae" (nickname for Martha), 21
Australia, attempted expansion into, 75–76
Auto Source, 140
  chain closed, 199

Bachand, Stephen, 207, 247
  as CEO, 242
  praise for, 263–64
  relationship with Martha, 221–22, 223–24
  replaced, 241
  retirement from Tire, 222–24, 225
  successes as new president, 196–201

Bagelworks, 234–35
Bargain Harold's Discount Ltd., 106–7
Barron, Alex, 56, 70, 79, 80
  backing of Dick in J.W. shares bid, 84
  favourable to "coat-tail" plan, 88
  fired, 89–90
  on shareholder protection, 123–24
B.C. Bearings Group, 3
Beck, Stanley, 124
Bennett, Gil, 240, 241
  on Martha, 240, 247
  on Martha and Bachand, 221, 222
  new chairman (1996), 205, 207
  offer to resign, 216
  on Wayne Sales, 246
Billes, Alfred Jackson (A.J., Martha's father), 2, 7, 21, 30, 75, 125
  abilities, 54–55, 202–3
  adjusts corporate history, 59–60
  belief in conflict, 46
  blocked from control by J.W.'s will, 44
  chooses Martha as board replacement, 73–74, 214–15
  as creator of Tire money, 51–52, 202–3
  death, 202

disagreements with Muncaster, 96–97
establishes Aldamar Corp., 53–54
family business view, 113–17, 122–23
family problems, 59
on firing of Muncaster, 106
Hall of Fame induction, 150–53
involvement with business, 43
management views of, 25
opens gas stations, 50–51
personality of, 12, 22–23, 43, 46, 96, 110
power struggle with Dick, 47–48
profit-sharing ideas, 24–25, 97–98, 203
quotes on business, 10, 12, 13
relationship with family, 23–24, 203–4
remarriage to Marjorie, 116
retirement as president, 54–55
urges rejection of Imasco offer, 83
will, 203–4
Billes, Barbara (Fred's wife), 31, 62, 214, 229
Billes, Betty (John's wife), 44
Billes, David (Martha's brother), 2, 42, 267
on A.J., 74–75
childhood, 14, 15, 18, 21, 52, 53
and Dennis, 69–70, 115
director, part owner, 53–54, 78, 103, 139
engineering interests, 34, 112–13
on J.W.'s voting shares, 84
low interest in Tire, 47, 55, 74, 112–13, 202, 203
on Martha, 22, 38, 63, 70, 110, 138–39, 212, 234

proposed sale to dealers, 112–13, 117–18, 123
sells shares to Martha, 207–13
on share split to purchase control, 89
sued by Martha, 130–31, 132–33
Billes, Dick (Martha's cousin), 16, 43, 211, 267
bids for J.W.'s voting shares, 81, 84, 85, 86
as director and dealer, 55–56
on family conflict, 52, 66, 78
on his brother John, 44–45
on his father (J.W.), 27, 151
loses power to A.J., 47–48
removed from board, 91
Billes, Fred (Martha's brother), 2, 34, 42
and A.J., 203
on Bachand's resignation, 224
and Bachand's strategy, 201
childhood, 14, 15, 18–22
children, 267
continued antagonism toward Martha, 62
countersuit against Martha, 133
decides not to go for CEO, 110
at family meeting, 114, 115
on father, mother, and business, 52, 53
on Groussman, 112, 142
interest in selling, 112–13, 117–18, 138
on J.W.'s voting shares, 84
marries Barbara, 31
on Martha, 53, 115, 210
and Martha's marriage to Dennis, 69, 70
opposes Martha's directorship, 74, 78

on Owen, 95–96

as part owner, director, dealer,
53–54, 76

personality of, 46–47, 55

public image of, 109

on sellout, 212, 213

sells shares to Martha, 207–13

studies, 31

and Whites stores, 100, 108–9

Billes, Gladys (Martha's aunt), 17, 27,
43, 44, 81, 85

Billes, Gwen (Martha's cousin), 16,
43, 85

Billes, Henry (Martha's grandfather), 7

Billes, John (Martha's cousin), 16, 43,
44, 45, 85

Billes, John William (J.W., Martha's
uncle), 2

on dealers, 11

early business success, 7–8

fondness for boating, 16

illness and death, 27

opens tire store with A.J., 9–10

personality of, 12, 50, 110

renames business Canadian Tire, 10

sale of voting shares from estate,
81–86

will, 43–44

Billes, Marjorie (A.J.'s second wife),
116, 203

Billes, Martha Gertrude

allergies from first job, 57, 68

appearance of, 1

attachment to McAteer, 159–68,
171–77, 183

and Bachand, 199, 221–22, 223–24

business relations with father, 74–75

buys out brothers for control,
210–12

on the Canadian media, 263

childhood antagonism with Fred,
19–22

and classmates, 6, 29–30, 31–32, 34,
39, 40–42

considers selling shares, 113,
118–19, 121

corporate memories, 205–7

and Dennis, 63–65, 69–70, 131–32

and Devoncroft, 157–61, 167–68,
170–73, 175, 187

differences with Groussman,
111–12, 142–43

dogs, 206, 249, 250–51

early fascination with cars, 14–15

early years on board, 76, 77–79

emotions for business, not people,
259

expectations of directors, 139–40

on family, 52, 82–83, 152–53,
206–7, 214–15

fiftieth birthday party, 159–60

fights with brothers, 2, 4, 135–36,
213

first marriage, 42, 62–63

friendship with Maureen Sabia,
218–20

future, 269

goal of Tire directorship, 70–71, 73

interest in business, 17, 24, 38, 92,
206

investments, 66–69, 155–56,
234–39

joins brothers to buy J.W.'s voting
shares, 81–86

lawsuits (McAteer, Dennis), 4,
145–47, 196, 227–34

named A.J.'s replacement on board,
73–74

as new head of business, 213–18

opposition from board members, 91–92

outcast from family business, 53–54, 60–61

and Owen, 93–94, 95–96, 148–49, 170

personality of, 2, 21, 29–34, 38–40, 65, 70, 210–12, 215, 220, 248–54, 256, 259–61

philanthropy, 253–54

power at Tire today, 256–61

problems with her eyes, 238

relationship with brothers, 15, 19–22, 257

relationship with family, 58–59, 61–62

relationship with father, 22–23, 34, 37–38, 66, 116–17, 153, 203–4, 234

relationship with mother, 18–19, 58–59

relationships with grandmothers, 23

relationships with men, 148, 206, 234, 239, 254–55, 256

relationships with others in business, 112

as research assistant, teacher, 57, 61

at school and college, 18, 28–42

stock values (2001), 261–62

strategy for ownership, 113, 116–17, 121–22, 127–28, 132, 137–39, 149–50, 212

succession, 265–69

sues brothers, 130–33, 138, 212

summers as a child, 23–24, 32, 37–38

on women in business, 219–20

Billes, Muriel (Martha's mother), 8, 15, 24, 44, 52, 58, 60, 94

death and will, 72

ideas for family property, 61–62

illness, 18–19

interest in business, 17–18, 153

quarrels with A.J., 22

Billes, Owen George, 62–63, 68, 69, 79

college, 178

inheritance from grandmother, 72

Martha's complaints about, 148–49

and McAteer, 163, 190

present and possible future, 265–67, 268

relationship with Dennis, 94–95, 132

relationship with parents, 93–96, 170

schooling skills, 92–93

trust fund and Devoncroft, 160, 168, 171, 172, 179, 181, 193

work in Winnipeg, 178, 184

Bliss, Michael, 14

Boublil, Alain, 239

British Columbia, 75, 90–91, 97

Brown, Arch, 17, 52, 55, 60, 93, 248

on Martha, 260–61

Brown, Ian, 126

Bucci, Adam, 197

Burgin, Aileen Selves, 36, 39–40

"butterfly," 53

Cameron, Joan, 107

Canadian Business, 263–64

Canadian Business Hall of Fame, induction of J.W. and A.J., 150–53

Canadian Club of Toronto, 214, 219, 259

Canadian Officers Training Corps, 37
Canadian Tire Acceptance Corp., 57,
   266
Canadian Tire Corporation
   attitude toward women (1960s), 59
   basic facts, 3
   catalogue covers, 49–50
   changes under Muncaster, 55–56,
      57–58, 71
   community involvement, 26
   company history, 59–60
   competition, 214, 243, 262–64
   computer systems, 58
   credit cards (see Canadian Tire
      Acceptance Corp.)
   distribution, 58, 91
   divided nature of board (early
      1980s), 79
   employees (see employees)
   expansion to Australia, 75–76, 243
   expansion to U.S. (see Auto Source;
      White Stores Inc.)
   future, 242–47
   gas stations, 50–51
   growth (to 1952), 10–11, 12, 13–14
   image, 264, 265
   inefficiencies (1989), 144–45
   new format stores, 199
   non-voting shares (see non-voting
      shareholders)
   Oshawa store, 58
   owner-managers (see dealers)
   ownership transfer by A.J. to
      Aldamar, 53–54
   pride in Canadian identity, 12–13
   product mix, 90
   profitability decline (1977–80),
      71–72
   profit-sharing arrangement, 24–25

   promotion, 57, 129–30
   as public company, 14
   roller skates worn by clerks, 13, 52
   sale of J.W.'s voting shares, 81–86
   sales increase under Groussman,
      144
   share prices (2000), 225–26
   store at Yonge and Davenport, 54,
      109
   store in Winnipeg, 56
   success under Bachand, 196–201
   Tire money (see Canadian Tire
      money)
Canadian Tire Dealers Association,
   142
Canadian Tire money
   comments on, 202–3
   introduced in western Canada, 199
   start and growth of idea, 51–52, 153
   success of program, 264
Carling O'Keefe, 112, 113, 117
cars in Canada, growth (to 1930), 10
Chapnick, Sandy Goodman, 29
charities, and J.W.'s voting shares, 81,
   82, 85
Cheesbrough, Gordon, 216
Chile, 246–47
Class A Shareholders Action
   Committee, 134–35
Clemente, Lilia, 220
"coat-tail," 88, 113, 124, 126, 137,
   208, 211
Code, Bill, 228
competition, 243, 262–64
   Martha's views on, 214
computers, 58
Cook, Linda, 4
Copeland, Deanna, 42
Coté, Pierre, 104

Cristall, Jeffrey, 158
Crooks, A.H.D., 79
Crow, Rita, 35–36, 40, 41
CTC Dealer Holdings Ltd., 118

Davis, Fred, 151
Davison, Brian, 228, 230–31
Dawson, Bill, 56, 59, 72
dealers, 25–26, 268
  accumulate wealth, 71, 120
  attitude to Muncaster after firing,
    106
  disagreements with Groussman,
    140–44
  and fifty-fifty split idea, 97–98
  liking for Bachand, 197–98
  Martha's speech to at 1996 meeting,
    205–7
  for new outlets in 1930s, 11
  relationship under Muncaster, 90–91
  remuneration, 245
  response to Wayne Sales, 245–46
  takeover bid, 118–27
  tension with management, 242
  upper limit on holdings, 138
Dennis, Marjorie O'Neill, 36
Devoncroft Developments Ltd.
  appraisal, 157–58
  effects of recession, 159, 178
  elements of project, 154–55
  financial problems, 167, 171, 172,
    179–80, 185, 187, 189, 194–96
  Martha's investments, 157–61,
    167–68, 170, 175
  receiver's report, 194–96
  shareholders' meeting (1992),
    190–92
Dey, Peter, 118
distribution centre in Brampton, 58

dogs, 206
Dolphin, Ric, 232–34
Domco Site Service Ltd., 234
Domelle, Brian, 268
Dominion Bond Rating Service Ltd.,
  197
"double dip," 105–6
dual share structures, 87
Dutton, Robert, 200

Eaton's, 265
e-commerce sales, 242
Elite Bureau of Investigation, 145
employee profit-sharing plan
  bids for J.W.'s voting shares, 85
  as shareholders in Tire, 82, 83
employees
  chances for wealth, 25
  information in 1937 catalogue, 12–13
Etrog, Sorel, 227

factoring, 155–56
family foundation (future possibility),
  268–69
Financial Post, 82–83
Financial Post Moneywise Magazine,
  127
Fiorina, Carly, 4, 260
Fisher, James, 216
Forest Hill Collegiate, 28–34
Frank (magazine), 229–30
Free Trade Agreement, Canada–U.S.,
  144
Freewheeling (Brown), 126
Froese, Murray, 193
Fung, Robert, 118–19

Gardiner-Billes, Dennis, 229
  divorce from Martha, 129, 131–32

early relationship with Martha,
63–65, 68
at family meeting, 114, 115
marriage to Martha, 69–70, 79
relationship with Owen, 94–95,
132
sued by Martha, 145–47
Gardiner, Casey, 64
Gardiner, Dennis. *see* Gardiner-Billes,
Dennis
Garrison, Stephen, 102
gas stations, 50–51
Gaunt, Bobbie, 4
Gerstein, Irving, 144
Giancamilli, Andy, 241
Globe and Mail, 125
Goddard, Alan, 262
Godin, Marty, 155, 160, 169, 183–84,
234
Golden, Anne Richmond, 29
Gooderham, Elsie (Martha's aunt),
17
Gordon Capital, 118
Grady, Wayne, 202–3
Gram, Marie, 1
Graydon, Cathie, 42
Groch, Steve, 79–80, 141, 245–46,
267–68
Groia, Joseph, 123, 124
Groussman, Dean, 189
as CEO of White Stores, 110–11
conflicts with dealers, 140–44
departs from Tire, 144
on family, 113
on Martha, 108
named CEO of Tire, 111
on proposed family-dealer sale, 122
relationship with Martha, 111–12
Guillevin, Jeannine, 3

Haan, Ralph, 136
Hall, Lynne, 80
Hamilton Tire and Garage, 8, 9
Hamilton Tire and Rubber Co., 9–10
Harms, George, 178, 179, 186,
189–90, 229
Hartman, George, 71, 221, 224–25,
226
Hasenfratz, Frank, 4
Hasenfratz, Linda, 3–4
Henry, Roger Pearson, 95, 96, 153
marriage collapses, 49, 62–63
marries Martha, 42
as Martha's beau, 36–37
Henry, Sharon, 95
Hiscott, Judy, 145, 146, 147
historical revisionism by A.J., 59–60
Hobbs, Richard, 43, 72, 73
appointed a vice-president, 56
on Dick's bid for J.W.'s voting shares,
85
on Groussman, 141
opposition to Martha, 70–71
Holland, Mr. Justice John, 82
Home Depot, 200, 214, 262, 263

Imasco Ltd., offer for Tire shares,
82–84

James, Bill, 107
James Bay project, 155–56
James Richardson & Sons Ltd., 3
Jarislowsky, Stephen, 121, 128
Joudrie, Dorothy, 205
Joudrie, Earl, 156, 205
just-in-time shipping, 91

Kagan, Joan, 29
Kaufman, Martin, 99

Kerr, Nancy, 35, 37, 41–42, 63
Kierans, Tom, 124
Kishner, Gerald, 225
Kitchen, Barbara. *see* Billes, Barbara
Knelman, Martin, 238
Kron, John, 56, 78, 79, 80, 90
  fired, 105–6
  on shareholder protection, 123–24
  as White Stores president, 98, 99,
    101, 102, 103

Labarge, Suzanne, 2
Lafleur, Martin, 145–46
Lannan, Patrick, 228, 231, 232
Lavery, Michael, 154–58, 175, 184,
  187
Law, Robin, 79, 96, 103
  removed from board, 91
  on shareholder protection, 123–24
Lever Brothers, 57
limited partnerships, 67
Linamar Corp., 4

Macaulay, Hugh
  on Bachand, 198–99
  on family and company, 89–90, 91
  on firing of Muncaster, 100, 104, 105
  on Groussman and dealers, 142
  on hiring of Groussman, 110
  on Martha's power, 258, 260
  named chairman of Tire, 90
  on negative publicity, 134
  on recovery of profit (1986), 127
MacDonald, Sandy, 25, 26
Macdonald Institute in Guelph,
  34–35, 252
Mackay, Gillian, 71
MacLaren, Roy, 217
MacLeod-Stedman Inc., 72

Magna International Inc., 3
Mann, Ken, 58, 136, 230, 256
  on Groussman, 143–44
  warns Martha about Devoncroft, 180
Marcoux, Rémi, 216
Marlore Enterprises Ltd., 67, 68–69,
  165
Marowe Investment Corp., 74
Martha Billes Family Trust, 165
Mason, Pamela, 154, 158, 161–62,
  163–64, 165, 170–71, 179, 230
  at Devoncroft meeting, 189, 190,
    191, 192, 193
  partner with McAteer in suit, 196
McArthur, Jack, 120
McAteer, Paul, 156–57, 158, 170, 178,
  186, 201
  breakdown of business relationship
    with Martha, 184–94
  comments by receiver, 195
  financial problems, 167–68, 179–80,
    196
  lawsuit against Martha, 4, 227–34
  relationship with his children, 170,
    171
  romance with Martha, 159–68,
    170–77, 181–83
McCaffrey, D'Arcy, 188
McCarthy & McCarthy, 113
McCready, Dr. Margaret, 42
McDonald, Wendy, 3
McEwan's Ltd., 75–76
McFarland, Bill, 261
McLaren, Sherril, 38–39
McLaughlin, Stephen, 148, 150, 159,
  258–59
McTear, Ron, 99
media, Martha's low opinion of, 263
Medland, Ted, 139, 140

Merrill Lynch Canada Ltd., 113, 117

Mofina, Rick, 205

Moore, Bertha (Martha's maternal grandmother), 8, 23

Moore, Delford (Martha's maternal grandfather), 8

Mouthpiece (company newsletter), 25

Muncaster, Brenda, 107

Muncaster, Dean, 7, 80, 88, 112, 123, 198, 243

A.J. and, 45–46

appointment as director, 47

backs Dick's bid for J.W.'s voting shares, 84

and Bargain Harold's, 106–7

changes at Tire, 55–56, 57–58, 71, 90–91

disputes with family, 96–98, 101, 102–3, 104

fired, 100, 101–5, 107

on Martha, 76, 77, 78–79, 121

problems, 71–72, 98–101

reaction to family control, 88, 89

responds to criticisms, 75, 76

and Whites, 76–77

Muncaster, Vic, 25

Muncaster, Walter, 45, 47

Murray, Bob, 256

comments on Martha, 149–50

friend to Martha, 159, 160

on McAteer, 158, 171–72

Napoleon, 235–39

National Post, 2, 228–29

National Trust, 81

Newmat Drilling, 67, 175, 176, 193–94

non-voting shareholders, 87–88, 134–35, 262

considered by Imasco, 83–84

proposed family share sale, 120–21, 123–25

represented on board, 128

Oberlander, Ron, 128

oil and gas investments, 67, 68–69

Olansky, Russell, 169

Olijnyk, Zena, 213

Ontario Securities Commission, 2, 85

blocks dealer takeover, 123–25

owner-managers. *see* dealers

Paré, Paul, 83

PartSource, 243

Performance Engineering, 112

Perkins, Roger, 28, 29, 30, 31–32, 236

Perschbaker, Deanna Wood, 252

Phillips, Frances, 109

Pigott, Jean, 80, 87, 91–92, 95, 256–57

Plowman, Mayne, 17, 21, 47, 61, 69

recollects J.W. and A.J., 11–12

Potter, Frank, 217

power, 256–61

Premier Pipelines Ltd., 34

profit-sharing programs, 24–25

planned fifty-fifty dealer-employee split, 97–98

Quebec Hydro, 155–56

Quebec, Tire stores in, 13

Rankin, John, 223, 245

recession (early 1980s), 96

recession (early 1990s), 159, 178, 196

Reid, Justice Robert, 125–26

Reid, Tom, 135

Reid, Tony, 58

Reimer, Ruth, 169, 176–77

Report on Business Magazine, 264
Richardson, Muriel, 3
Robertson, Heather, 10
Robinette, J.J., 81
roller skates, 13, 52
Romanchuk, Judy, 228–29, 252–53, 255
Rona Inc., 200
Rooke, Justice John, 227, 230
Rubenstein, Ernie, 235–36

Sabia, Laura, 80, 215, 219
Sabia, Maureen, 80–81, 127–28, 139, 200, 222, 257
  friendship with Martha, 218–20
  on Martha, 211–12, 215
Sabia, Michael, 80
Sabiston, Andrew, 235–36, 237
Sable, Martin, 28, 29
Sable, Myra Miller, 29
Sales, Wayne, 265
  chosen CEO, 241–42
  plans for future, 243–45
  relationship with Martha, 246, 247
  response from dealers, 245–46
  on U.S. retailers in Canada, 262, 263
Sali, Len, 188, 189, 190–93
Sanderson, Mark, 229, 233, 251
Sasaki, Fred, 46, 47, 51, 73, 77
  on the A.J. family, 114, 115–16, 203–4
Saturday Night, 232–33
Saxon Petroleum Inc., 67
Schulte-Nordholt, Astrid, 41
Setnor, Barry, 106
Shanty Bay property, 61–62, 93, 171, 248–49
share split, 87

Shelter Hydrocarbons Ltd., 67
Sill Streuber Fiske Inc., 194
Simon, William, 111
Sinclair, Selby, 101
Slater, James, 155–56, 234–35
Smith, Geoff, 237, 238
Smith, Marlene, 227, 235, 239, 251
Smith, Mike, 203
Sorensen, Theodore, 258
Southern, Nancy, 3
Southern, Ron, 3
Stephenson, William, 60
Stone, Marion, on A.J. and Martha, 73–74
Stransman, John, 118, 131, 216
Stronach, Belinda, 3
Stronach, Frank, 3
Stymiest, Barbara, 2
succession, 265–69
Sunfire Energy Corp., 69
Sutherland, Sylvia, 30

Tedesco, Theresa, 122
Thompson, Lahni, 147–48
Tire money. *see* Canadian Tire money
Toronto Humane Society, 81
Trott, Ralph, 245
Tuckman, Mae, "Aunt Mae" (Martha's aunt), 32
TV commercial, 129–30

Universal Explorations Ltd., 69
U.S. retailers in Canada, 262–64

Van Norman, Ian, 106
van Straubenzee, Mary, 248
van Straubenzee, Tony, 248–49
Vertulia, Sally, 64
Villeneuve, Jacques, 107

Wal-Mart Stores Inc., 200, 262, 263
Webber, Andrew Lloyd, 239
Weber, Paul, 126–27
Wenzel, Ed, 168–69, 170
Wesray Capital Corp., 111
Western Auto, 111
White Stores Inc., 76–77
  and "double dip," 105–6
  Fred and, 100, 108–9
  problems, 98–101, 110
Williams, Timothy, 236
women
  attitude of Tire toward (1960s), 59

double standard for men and, 230
in management at Tire today, 220
at Martha's birth, 6–7
personal problems for successful
  women, 255
secondary role of, 24, 32, 34, 35,
  37–38, 66
Wood, Kimba, 229

Yonge and Davenport store, 54, 109

Zale Corp., 144
Zambello, Francesco, 238

THE GROWING YEARS 🦋